MY NAME IS IRAN

MY NAME IS IRAN

a memoir

DAVAR ARDALAN

HENRY HOLT AND COMPANY · NEW YORK

Henry Holt and Company, LLC
Publishers since 1866
175 Fifth Avenue
New York, New York 10010
www.henryholt.com

Henry Holt® and 🄷® are registered trademarks of
Henry Holt and Company, LLC.

Distributed in Canada by H. B. Fenn and Company Ltd.

Library of Congress Cataloging-in-Publication Data
Ardalan, Davar, date.
    My name is Iran : a memoir / Davar Ardalan.
        p.   cm.
    ISBN-13: 978-0-8050-7920-3
    ISBN-10: 0-8050-7920-3
    1. Ardalan, Davar. 2. Iranian American women—Biography.
3. Iranian Americans—Biography. 4. Radio producers and directors—
United States—Biography. 5. Women radio producers and directors—
United States—Biography. I. Title.
    E184.15A734 2007
    973'.0491550092—dc22   2006049520
    [B]

Henry Holt books are available for special promotions and
premiums. For details contact: Director, Special Markets.

First Edition 2007

Designed by Kelly S. Too

Printed in the United States of America
1   3   5   7   9   10   8   6   4   2

To my children,
Saied, Samira, Aman, and Amir:
May you always honor and cherish your
Iranian and American ancestry.

To my mother, Mary Laleh Bakhtiar,
I owe a great debt of gratitude. Our family historian
and a noted scholar, she shared research, experience,
and inspiration without which the writing
of this book would have been impossible.

· contents ·

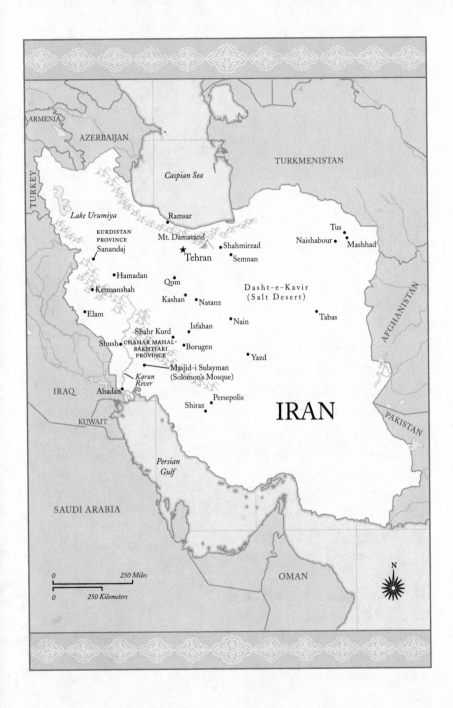

From America to Iran,

1964–66

I took my first steps amid the ancient ruins and oil fields of Solomon's Mosque in Iran. It was the fall of 1964 when my family left the urban bustle of San Francisco and touched down in a tiny airport. The short runway was surrounded by barren hills dotted with towering flare stacks. I was barely six months old, and my mother, Laleh, remembers holding me close while my father and sister walked ahead of us to the terminal, a stone hut with two small windows and a corrugated metal roof. The offensive smell of sulfur from burning gas was everywhere. As the sun beat down mercilessly, my father, Nader, remembers an overpowering feeling gripping his gut: "What the hell am I doing here?"

My parents, raised in America, were proud of their Iranian heritage even though they barely spoke a word of Persian. So when the opportunity came for my father to work in Iran, they jumped

Solomon's Mosque (*Masjid-i Sulayman*), September 1966. (Photograph Jay
R. Crook, September 1966)

at it. Being hippie intellectuals, their souls were ready for adventure. The design director of my father's architectural firm in
America remarked to him upon his departure: "Nader, don't pull
the cave in after you!"[1]

First impressions of Solomon's Mosque went downhill from
there—the taxi drove my parents past poorly cast curbs painted
alternately black then white along a narrow asphalt road winding among the hills. An occasional donkey crossed the scene and
a lone, leathery-faced nomad from the ancient Bakhtiari tribe
watched as we passed. He wore traditional dress: a domical black
felt hat, black-striped vest, and hand-woven shoes called *givehs*.[2]
Welcome to the neighborhood! Arriving at our first home, we
found a scantily furnished apartment with no curtains for privacy: My parents hung bedsheets as drapes until our furnishings
came from America.

A Harvard-educated architect, my father had accepted a job with the National Iranian Oil Company to design housing for its workers in the oil fields of southwestern Iran. This barren land would be where our family made its first attempt at integrating modernity, in the form of architecture, into a place steeped in tradition. My father's mentor—the great American architect Louis I. Kahn—had observed that traditions are "great mounds of golden dust free of circumstance. If you grasp of this golden dust, you will gain the powers of anticipation of the future."[3] Determined to learn the valuable truths held by the architectural traditions that surrounded him, my father wanted to incorporate the essence of lasting tradition into his own modern work, thereby rendering a new, similarly timeless tradition.

Solomon's Mosque, known as Masjid-i Sulayman in Persian, is some hundred miles from the mouth of the Persian Gulf, where the Tigris, Euphrates, and Karun rivers join in the province of Khuzistan.[4] It was in this place that the first modern oil wells were drilled in the Middle East. On May 26, 1908, British adventurer and financier William Knox D'Arcy struck oil. In 1914, on the eve of World War I, Winston Churchill managed to convince the British parliament to buy 51 percent of D'Arcy's company. The oil from Solomon's Mosque fueled the Royal Navy's creation of APOC—the Anglo-Persian Oil Company.[5]

Solomon's Mosque later became the center of British and American military operations during World War II. The Allies used Iran as a staging ground to ship supplies to the Soviet Union. American soldiers stationed there shortened the name of the town to MIS. During that time, my maternal grandfather,

Abol Ghassem, lived there for several years. An American-trained physician, he was head of the department of surgery at the oil company.

The town was, not unexpectedly, even more desolate back in 1943. Every afternoon, on the hills behind Abol's home, the servants fetched the herd of cattle, milked the cows, and served the family pure cream with dates for a delightful afternoon snack. The afternoon entertainment consisted of my uncle Jamshid, then a young boy, wrestling a wide-eyed calf while his awestruck siblings stood by. Jamshid would charge, grab the calf, and bring it to the ground, to the laughter and cheering of family and servants who had gathered to watch. When the children were fast asleep under the night sky, protected from merciless insects in great big mosquito nets, the night watchman warded off the bandits who were known to roam about. In the nearby country club, British oil workers and engineers dined and drank.[6]

By the time we arrived in Solomon's Mosque some twenty years later, none of my mother's family still lived there. My parents thought that they would be going to a traditional Iranian town, but what they found instead was a planned company town like one you would find in the West, conceived by non-Iranians who had neither lived in nor visited the region. Solomon's Mosque and nearby towns like Abadan became essentially "frontier migrant towns" arranged to meet the needs of the oil industry rather than the social and environmental needs of the people.[7]

Still, my parents were pleased to find neighbors who were British-trained Iranians also employed by the oil company. A well-dressed couple who had come by to welcome us had a brand new Chevrolet parked outside their home; my father could not help thinking to himself: "Have they made the same mistake?"

We soon moved into a residential area reserved for management. My parents had been led to believe that there would be a company store "just like an American supermarket." In reality, a hand-cut stone room with great big air-conditioning units shoved into all the windows passed as a meager general store. Inside were nearly bare shelves with just a few items for sale, such as canned foods from England. For anything fresh we had to go to the local bazaar, where camel caravans had come with goods from along the ancient silk route for centuries.

Our new home shared the supermarket's aesthetic. The stone walls had been cut from the surrounding hills. They were three feet thick, and small windows were set into them amid large rooms with fourteen-foot-high ceilings.

After some time our car and household belongings arrived by ship from America. Unfortunately, the huge crates had been stored in the open so that rain and then mildew had ruined just about everything my parents had shipped. We did receive our car—a beat-up secondhand VW Beetle. Bewildered, the man at customs asked: "When you were entitled to import free of charge any fancy car that you could resell for a fortune, why did you bring this?" But a big sigh of relief came when my parents discovered that their Eames chair—made by the architectural team of Charles and Ray Eames from bent rosewood and black leather upholstery—had arrived in perfect condition. It became our source of pride in our stone house under Solomon's Temple.

According to Shia tradition, King Solomon was a legendary architect and builder as well as a judge who was known for his wisdom and justice. "Solomon" means "peaceful" and there are ancient sites throughout Iran named after him. Said to have had a magic carpet and to have spoken the language of the birds, he gave generously and in exchange asked only that those to whom he gave be obligated to act with compassion. Local tribespeople described an eternal flame of the Zoroastrian faith that had burned at Solomon's Temple.[8] It was perhaps an important sign that oil was first discovered in Iran in a place named after him.

The site was built around the time that all of the Fertile Crescent came under the rule of Cyrus the Great in the sixth century BC, at which time he issued the famous Seal of Cyrus. Inscribed on a clay cylinder, it is the first human rights decree, as Cyrus proclaims: "I am Cyrus, King of the World. When I entered Babylon I did not allow anyone to terrorize the land. I kept in view the needs of the people and all its sanctuaries to promote their well-being. I put an end to their misfortune. The Great God has delivered all the lands into my hand; the lands that I have made to dwell in a peaceful habitation."[9]

SOLOMON'S MOSQUE WAS THE PRECURSOR OF THE GREAT COMplex built by Cyrus in Pasargadae, where he was buried, and which would ultimately culminate in the creation of the ritual city complex of Persepolis. Magnificent cyclopean stone blocks were built against a hilltop; they were cut out of solid rock and extended into a terrace, on which had most likely stood a square stone tower, inside which burned the Holy Fire, symbolizing truth and purity.

It is unclear when the temple was named Solomon's Mosque (Masjid-i-Sulayman or MIS). My parents believed that it probably came after the Islamic conquest of Persia in the seventh century AD, when a sacred place in the eyes of the new rulers had to be a place of prayer. By the time we lived there, it was only a historic monument and no one related to it in a sacred way except for my parents, who perceived it as an important milestone in the development of the ancient architecture of Iran. It was for this reason that a year after we arrived, my father found himself in a fight to save the temple from being destroyed to make way for a housing development. Quickly he helped organize public awareness and also sought the help of government authorities, taking his fight all the way to the governor general of that province. The governor general, who had been a protégé of my paternal grandfather (he had once served in the Finance Ministry), took the case to heart and stopped the housing development. My father's persistence awakened the authorities to the value of preserving the past. He then donated his design for a museum to display the archaeological finds at the temple site. His decision to fight to preserve this temple instilled in my older sister, Mani, and me the importance of tradition in the way we live our lives in the present day.[10]

MY PARENTS REMEMBER ME AS A RESTLESS CHILD, LOVABLE BUT also temperamental. "I remember your curly hair, your little nose, and penetrating Bakhtiari eyes," my father says, "but you would become moody and sullenly aloof, silent. We understood in time that it was something that you just went through, like an inner storm, and once it had passed, you were our jovial, lovable little girl again."

Mani and I spent many early mornings running in the fields among the red poppies, called *laleh* in Persian. Friends from the company gave us a collie, and we naturally named her Lassie. We fell in love with Lassie and were heartbroken after tragedy struck in the form of a snakebite. Soon enough we found out that there were not only snakes here but also scorpions. Heeding the elements, my parents turned one of the rooms in our house into a playground with swings hanging from the exposed pipes in the ceiling, a sandbox, and monkey bars. Our indoor playground became an absolute necessity when the temperature would reach 140 degrees—in the shade.

In the evenings there would be the occasional trip to the open air theater. One of the feature films at the time was the 1962 Hollywood hit *Brothers Grimm*. I was not even two years old, but my mother remembers me being captivated by the fairies and princesses as I watched the movie under the moonlit sky.[11]

In her attempt to learn more about her Persian culture, my mother would recount bedtime stories to me and my sister from the *Shahnameh*, the Arthurian–like chronicle of the mythical and historical early kings of Iran. The 60,000-rhymed-couplet poem took thirty-five years for the poet Abol Ghassem Ferdowsi to compose. My mother would take special care to find stories about women in this famous *Epic of Kings*.[12]

One of her favorites was the story of the female heroine who acted independently, ignoring the "what will people say?" admonition. This "lioness" broke free of the biological role that had been cast upon her as a woman and became a warrior. She had been inspired by fate to be fearless and bring wholeness to herself. In another story a woman crowned "king" was not afraid to mete out justice; "She ruled the land with gentleness so great that even the wind of heaven did not leap from the dust."[13]

IT MUST HAVE TAKEN A LEAP OF GREAT FAITH FOR MY PARENTS to leave San Francisco for Solomon's Mosque. They had lived in an artists' community on Wisconsin Street in Potrero Hill near my American grandmother, Helen, whom we called Mama Helen. My father had been hired at the prestigious architectural firm of Skidmore, Owings & Merrill, where he collaborated on the John Hancock Building, and designed his first building on the UC Berkeley campus. My mother would walk to the local market and had a close circle of friends with whom she traded babysitting duties. My parents participated in many of the San Francisco peace marches against the Vietnam War. My mother loved playing the guitar, favoring songs by Joan Baez and James Taylor. One of her older sisters, Paree, who had changed her name to Love, had moved to the Bay Area and opened up a hamburger shop that served hundreds of Love-burgers and Love-dogs a day. It was the early 1960s, a time of soul-searching for American people.

My sister, Mani Helene, was born in 1962 in this cultural wave. She was named after my paternal grandmother's nickname (Mani) and my grandmother Helen. A year and a half later, anticipating my birth, on April 1, 1964, my mother walked into

Just one year old, Iran Davar inside
the family home in Solomon's
Mosque with the Eames chair.
(Author's personal collection)

the delivery room at San Francisco's French Hospital, and after a
relatively painless delivery gave birth to me and walked out of the
delivery room that same day. My father called his maternal aunt,
Afsar, the only immediate family he had in America, to tell her
the good news. Being an Iranian, she was hoping for news of a
son. When he told her that my mother had just delivered a second daughter, she said: "Nader, is this an April Fool's joke?"

They named me Iran, after the ancestral homeland they
longed for. For a middle name, they chose Davar, after my paternal great-grandfather, Ali Akbar Davar, an important historical
figure in Iranian politics. After I was born, my family's life would
take a course different from the one they'd expected.

The word *Iran* means "Land of the Aryans" and comes from
the invasion of Indo-European tribes from Central Asia into the
region sometime after the Ice Age. They moved onto the Iranian

plateau in large numbers around 1000 BC. They spoke a language called Aryan, a word meaning "aristocrat." The birth and infancy of the region are described in the mythical part of Ferdowsi's *Shahnameh,* based on the oral history passed from generation to generation among the *dehqan,* or landed gentry.[14]

Ferdowsi asked: "Who was the first who invented kingship and placed a crown on his head?" The *dehqan* answered: "That time goes back in the memory of human beings. A son was taught it from his father who related every detail as he had received it from his father."[15]

IN THE SUMMER OF 1964, MY MOTHER'S SISTER SHIREEN AND her husband wrote to my parents from Abadan, in southern Iran. Both my aunt and uncle worked for the oil company and suggested that my father consider a job designing housing for its workers.

Having been part of the folk, peace, and civil rights movements in America, my parents now longed to renew their Eastern roots, to awaken to its possibilities. In San Francisco my father worked in a large, hierarchically structured firm where he was considered a young designer, one of many, who brought in a modest income. However, in Iran, the cost of living was lower, the respect he could earn was exponentially greater, and he had the opportunity to become a great architect.

For my parents the possibility of going to Iran meant that they could finally learn what it was to be an Iranian instead of just having the nationality. Having been raised in America from a young age, they did not really know what it meant to live as an Iranian or a Muslim. They were drawn to the land of their ancestors because they wanted to experience their heritage.

Being Iranian meant knowing the poetry of Ferdowsi's *Shahnameh* as well as the moral voice of the poet Saadi, and, of course, the mystical poetry of Hafez.[16] It meant practicing hospitality, friendliness, and joy while knowing a bit of the history of each Iranian city and the country's rich culture of both the arts and the sciences. It meant experiencing the architecture, touching the handicrafts, relishing family and religious ties, and finding out what it meant to be a "pure Iranian." Having been influenced by their American upbringing, they realized they could never be "pure Iranians," but the rest was in their reach, waiting in the stillness of time.

By the 1960s the Iranian oil company was actively recruiting American-trained Iranian professionals to replace British Petroleum staff after the oil industry had been nationalized, making the housing of employees the responsibility of the Iranians. My father's cousin was a board member at the oil company and was instrumental in recruiting my father.

A year after we arrived in MIS, my mother wrote to one of her sisters that it seemed as if her life in San Francisco had never existed. She wondered why she and my father had not come to Iran sooner. The words of her brother Cyrus must have had an impact on her: "Too many Iranians have lost faith in their own culture, have forgotten their great history, have abandoned their arts . . . for what? For this materialistic civilization of the Western world!"[17]

It did not take long for my father to realize that he too was glad they had come to Iran. While working as head of the oil company's architecture department, he began to get involved in archaeological digs in the area. A French archaeologist, Roman Ghirshman, who was working on the Achaemenid and Sassanian sites, asked my father to spend weekends with him documenting his findings in the south of Iran.

There, my father first noticed the care with which an archaeologist took a half-inch-wide sable paintbrush to the centuries of dust that covered the stone threshold of a temple, the seventh-century Bardi-i Neshandeh, under which lay gold coins that could date the site. It was here that it was made apparent to him the real value that history places on his chosen profession; he realized that architecture had very deep meanings, particularly in an ancient land such as Iran.

Whenever possible we traveled as a family throughout the south of Iran. We went on special tours to the town of Shush, where Shia tradition says Daniel of the Bible is buried, and Shushtar, where an underground city of flour mills from Sassanian times leads to cavernous openings into the river. We also saw the ancient Elamite site of Choga Zanbil and the Dez Dam.[18]

WE HAD ARRIVED AT SOLOMON'S MOSQUE IN THE FALL, WHEN the Bakhtiari tribe migrates to Solomon's Mosque and the surrounding areas for the winter. Twice a year one million Bakhtiari tribal people cross the Zagros Mountains with all they possess in search of grass for their flocks of sheep and goats. They cross rivers on inflated goatskins that they lash together, before pitching their black tents at sundown to prepare the fires for dinner. Alongside the hills and mountains we would see tribal Bakhtiari women dressed in emerald-and-crimson-colored clothes and wearing elegant, long, bright orange-and-yellow headscarves with gold trim, which didn't completely veil their hair. Some carried brightly colored thick wool rugs with the classic Bakhtiari medallion design. The women looked like fearless princesses, their gold anklets clinking and clanking.

My mother told us that my grandmother Helen had made this same migration many years before; as the wife of a Bakhtiari, she'd joined a tribal group. Along the journey thieves as well as wild animals—including a leopard—had accosted her. She had passed through narrow gorges, unpacked and made fires in front of the tent to bake bread, then packed up again—only to repeat the routine the next day. As we looked toward the distant hills and watched the tribes descending the mountain, we would dream of my grandmother Helen on horseback riding on the plains of red poppies.

JUST BEFORE SPRING THAT FIRST YEAR IN MIS, MY MOTHER began the spring cleaning of our home. This spring would bring not only the Persian New Year, but also my paternal grandparents, Abbas and Mani joone, who were due to arrive from Tehran to celebrate. My father was anxious, hoping his parents' first visit to our home would go well. My mother was concerned about formally meeting her in-laws for the first time. I was only a year old that first Persian New Year, but my family began a tra-

Noruz with paternal grandfather Abbas in 1966.
(Author's personal collection)

dition that I have continued to this day: to celebrate not only the New Year, but also my birthday, which falls within the same period.

Iranians have for centuries celebrated the first day of spring, the day of the vernal equinox that typically occurs on March 20 or 21. Ferdowsi writes in the *Shahnameh* that the founder of the day was Shah Jamshid, the mythic builder of Persepolis. As Ferdowsi describes it, Shah Jamshid made a marvelous throne, which was lifted into the air with the help of genies, where he then sat as the sun sits in the heavens. To celebrate that day, he called it "a New Day," and so began the festival of Noruz, the first day of the New Year.[19]

The celebrations for Noruz last for thirteen days, but the preparations begin weeks ahead of time. Two weeks before the first day of spring, my mother planted wheat or lentils by first putting the seeds in water to germinate. Then she would spread the seeds on a plate to allow them to sprout before placing them on the New Year's table. By then they had grown several inches high. This was referred to as *sabzeh*, from the word *sabz*, meaning "green."[20]

My grandparents arrived a few days before the first day of the celebration. My parents need not have been worried about this visit; my grandparents were happy to be with us all in Iran. They had always hoped my parents would return to Iran so that they could spend the last years of their lives near all their grandchildren.

At dusk on the night of the last Wednesday before Noruz, my father prepared for the traditional event preceding New Year. He gathered piles of brush, arranged them in a circle, and set them on fire. All of us jumped over the fire, saying: "My yellowness and pallor to you, your redness and fiery health to me."

The moment of the vernal equinox is marked when the sun crosses the equator and moves from Pisces to Aries, a time calculated exactly by astronomers every year. In anticipation of the moment, we placed a candy in our mouth and a coin in one hand as harbingers of goodness and prosperity for the year to come. The local radio station began a countdown. That year the sun crossed the equator at 5:49 a.m. and at that precise moment, we exclaimed, *"Eideh shoma mobarak!"* or "Happy New Year." We kissed and hugged one another as we sat around the table, on which my mother had placed a hand-woven tapestry tablecloth, called *termeh*. On the table was the *haft seen* or "seven s's"—seven items that begin with the letter *s* in Persian: apple (*seeb*), hyacinth (*sonbol*), vinegar (*serkeh*), sumac (*somagh*), coins (*sekkeh*), garlic (*seer*), and *samanou,* or cooked wheat germ. Each of these items represented a virtue, such as patience, wealth, health, guarding against the evil eye, or beauty. There was also a mirror, a bowl full of water with goldfish, rose water, painted eggs, and all kinds of sweets and fruits. Iranians from all religious faiths celebrate Noruz. Many place their sacred book on their table of seven *s*'s. We had the Koran on ours not as a religious gesture, as my parents were secular, but to follow the tradition of their Muslim ancestors.[21]

On the thirteenth day of the New Year, the celebrations finally ended. Since the thirteenth is traditionally considered to be an unlucky day, our family went on a picnic and took along the *sabzeh,* which we threw into flowing water to banish any misfortune in the coming year and to refertilize the earth.

Spring in MIS was a very short season. Soon after my grandparents returned to Tehran, the Bakhtiari began their migration back to the Chahar Mahal area for the summer, as weather in MIS began to get too hot to enjoy the outdoors during the daytime. For the next six months, we would stay indoors trying to avoid the terrible heat.

IN 1966, JUST TWO YEARS AFTER ARRIVING IN IRAN, MY FATHER was offered an associate partnership in a leading architectural firm in the capital city of Tehran. This was a dramatic change as it meant that we would now be exposed to everything an Iranian metropolitan city had to offer to a privileged upper-middle-class family. There were so many shops to choose from, filled with

Western products as well as traditional handicrafts and rugs. Tehran also had many beautiful parks, and the climate there was wonderful, with four separate seasons.

My sister and I were enrolled at the Hekmat School. Each year, the school had an elaborate ceremony to mark the end of the year. Our first year in Tehran, I led the school procession, holding the flag of Iran and leading the entire school singing *"Parcham-i man"* (My Flag). My parents claim that I stole the show. My mother said the teachers adored my "fiery" personality in comparison to my sister's calm nature. "What did you expect?" my mother said. "Iran is an Aries and Mani is a Libra."

A couple of years after our arrival in Tehran, much to my father's delight, my mother delivered a son. They named my brother Karim, meaning "generous," which is one of the ninety-nine attributes of God, according to Islamic belief. By this time, my father and mother had purchased a home near Tehran University, just a few blocks away from my father's office. After my brother was born, we moved into the house, our *kolange,* or forty-year-old house in Tehran. *Kolange* is a word used to refer to old homes that are about to be demolished to make way for modern buildings. Always the architect/designer, my father felt strongly that he wanted to save the building, so he updated it while retaining its traditional features.

Repairs had not been completed the first winter we were in our *kolange.* Three Coleman kerosene stoves heated the entire house. My bedroom was like a sauna while the living and dining rooms were too cold. My sister, mother, and I had to wear every warm piece of clothing we had while my father looked like old man winter himself, ready to do battle with ten-foot-high snowdrifts. The lack of heating made my mother frantic. When pressed, my father would respond, "It's healthy this way!" It wasn't long before our family *korsi*, a low square table covered with thick comforters under which a charcoal brazier or electric heater was placed, gave way to central heat.[22]

My parents hired an Iranian nanny who was quite different from a Western one. In our case, she was called "the master's maid servant," hired to be totally devoted to the son of the family, seeing to his every need. It is common in Iran for young boys to have their own nanny. My brother's nanny was named Shamsi and she also cooked for the family and generally ran the household.

With my father making all the decisions about how to renovate and decorate the house and Shamsi cooking and babysitting, my mother found herself with free time. Although motherhood was definitely her top priority, she heard about classes that were held once a week, in English, on Iranian and Islamic culture. She was particularly attracted to the classes offered on Sufism, the mystical dimension of Islam that is as old as Islam itself. These classes were being taught at Tehran University by the Islamic philosopher Seyyed Hossein Nasr.[23]

My mother was mesmerized by Nasr's lectures on Sufism, much as her mother, Helen, had once been enthralled with Iranian culture when listening to the *Shahnameh* being read aloud by Abol in New York in 1927. At one point, Dr. Nasr asked my mother what faith she practiced. My mother said she had been brought up as a Christian. He said that now that she was living in Iran and had an Iranian father, everyone would expect her to be a Muslim. She said she knew nothing about Islam. He said: "Well, learn!" These words opened the door to Sufism for her.

Still, Thanksgiving and Christmas were American holidays that my mother continued to observe in Tehran. It became a tradition for my grandmother Mani joone and her family to celebrate with us, because she had lived in America for many years and loved these celebrations as well.

ONCE WE WERE SETTLED, MAMA HELEN LEFT AMERICA FOR THE last time to live near us in Tehran. She moved into an apartment just a few doors down from our house.

I always felt close to her. The hallway leading up to her second-floor apartment was often filled with the aroma of homemade fudge. Inside her apartment were Bakhtiari handicrafts, beautiful carpets, carved ivory boxes, delicate porcelain vases, and antique chests filled with treasures from her many travels. Each item had a history that would evoke a story from a distant land from her journeys to Shalamzar, Baku, Kashmir and Bombay in India, Samarqand and Bokhara in Uzbekistan, and Kabul, Afghanistan.

For me, her bedroom was the greatest room. In each of her mahogany dresser drawers were perfumed lingerie, cashmere scarves from Kashmir, and embroidered blouses from Samarqand that I would wear to play dress up.

I remember one particular event that we shared with her soon after she had moved to Tehran. On October 26, 1967, Mama Helen, my mother, my sister, and I stood on the sidewalk alongside millions of other Iranians, waving the Iranian flag, watching the coronation procession of the Shah of Iran.[24] It was at this ceremony that Mohammad Reza Pahlavi crowned himself King of Kings, or *Shahanshah,* and his queen, Farah Diba, became Empress Farah. My mother said the regal and serene look on Empress Farah's face reminded her of the story from the *Shah-nameh* of the woman who ruled with such gentleness that even the wind from heaven was stilled.

For Helen, it was as though she was living a page from the *Shahnameh* as she witnessed a Persian king crown himself. She described the procession in a letter: "We were able to get a marvelous view of the Golden Coach with white horses carrying the King of Kings and Queen and then the handsome Crown Prince Reza in another coach, alone. He looked out of the window at the crowds lining the street with great interest and curiosity. Tehran was made as beautiful as possible with millions of colored lights, arches, and decorations. It was a glorious, festive occasion."

Helen had also attended the celebrations in Tehran of the first wedding of this same Mohammad Reza Shah Pahlavi in 1939 to the Egyptian princess Fawzia. Their wedding had been held in Cairo, but celebrations were held in Tehran upon their return. Fawzia, daughter of King Faud I of Egypt and sister of the last Egyptian king, Farouk I, was known as one of the world's most beautiful women. Tragically she was divorced from the king in 1948 after failing to produce a male heir to the throne. Helen and my grandfather Abol Ghassem had attended the Tehran celebrations. Helen described to us all her trips to the dressmaker to make sure that the dress and hat she wore to the celebration were the latest fashion. My grandfather had looked so handsome too in his top hat. Mama Helen thought to herself:

Here I am, Helen of Idaho, attending the marriage celebration of Iran's future king.

Helen would often reminisce about her romance with my grandfather, a man whom I knew best through stories of his adventures, whose fiery spirit and creative endeavors in medicine continued to fascinate Helen long after their lives together ended.

West Meets East,

1927

M y grandmother Helen got off an east-bound train at New York's Grand Central Station in the fall of 1927 all alone. When she asked a policeman for directions to Harlem Hospital, he replied, "Put 5 cents in the slot and get off at 125th Street."

"I came upstairs at three in the afternoon and everyone was Black," she remembers.[1] Helen had traveled three thousand miles by train from Los Angeles to begin to teach nursing. Standing in the heart of Harlem, she walked to 135th Street and found Harlem Hospital. A fellow nurse welcomed her and showed her around the hospital. As they were talking, Helen asked about the doctors. She was told that there were some Italians, some Jews, some Blacks, and one Persian. "Persian," my grandmother thought. "I have never met a Persian."

The residents had gathered in the courtyard through which my grandmother and the nurse had to pass. My grandmother asked

Davar's maternal grandmother,
Helen Jeffreys, in her official
portrait as a nurse, 1926.
(From the Laleh Bakhtiar Collection
of Family Photographs)

the nurse which one was the Persian. The nurse said, "Dr. Bakhtiar, the one with the bald head," before introducing my grandmother to the whole group of doctors: "This is Miss Jeffreys from California. She will be teaching anatomy to the nurses."

An Italian was the first to ask her for a date. He took her along the East River where he became too friendly. When she began to cry, he took her home. The next day she saw my grandfather at work. He had heard about her date and how it had gone. He asked her not to accept any more dates without first consulting him. Not long after, she was in Central Park on a date with him!

It was there, among the burnished orange and reds of the fall foliage, that my grandfather courted my grandmother through the *Shahnameh*. Feeling insecure about their age difference—he was thirty-three years older—he wanted to impress her with a story from Iran's national epic. He chose the love story between Zal and Rudabeh, the parents of the famous mythical hero Rostam. Once Helen heard the story of Zal, she asked Abol his age. He told her that he was fifty-five. He certainly did not look his age and his sincerity and caring protection of her won her over.[2]

My grandfather recounted the story, sometimes reciting it in Persian. He explained to Helen that Zal was born with white hair and was therefore considered old at birth. His father, the hero/warrior (*pahlavan*) Sam, was afraid that his enemies would claim that Zal was a child of a genie, so Sam ordered that he be taken away. Zal was taken to the base of the Alborz Mountains, where he was left to die. But as fate would have it, a mythical bird called the Simorgh saw him and took pity on him, carrying him to her nest and raising Zal with her own young. When Zal grew to maturity, his distinguished white hair set him apart. Capturing the attention of some travelers, they reported back to Zal's father. Having repented for abandoning his child, Sam set out to search for him. They were happily reunited and the Simorgh gave Zal one of her feathers when he left. He was to place the feather on an open fire whenever he wanted the help of the Simorgh.

Zal, now recognized as the son of the warrior Sam, became yet another hero of Iran. He began to travel to distant lands. He first went to Kabul, Afghanistan, where he fell in love with Rudabeh, the daughter of King Mehrab. King Mehrab was an enemy of Iran. Both Sam and his son, Zal, had given their allegiance to the Shah of Iran, therefore King Mehrab was considered their enemy. Not only was Mehrab an enemy, but his daughter,

Rudabeh, was non-Iranian—an unacceptable match for Zal. After Rudabeh's mother, Sindokht, intervened and pleaded on their behalf, Zal and Rudabeh were united.

Rudabeh became pregnant. At the time of delivery she was having great difficulty. Zal put the Simorgh's feather on the fire and called for her help in the birth of his child. A son was delivered by Caesarian section. As the child was born, Rudabeh cried out, "Rostam!" And so her son, the most famous Persian hero of all time, was named.[3]

As my grandmother heard Abol recite the myth in Persian she became mesmerized. She had never heard this language before and the rhythmic beauty of the *Shahnameh*'s verses nearly put her in a trance. In less than a week, my grandfather proposed marriage. The first time she responded by laughing. Though she knew how she felt, she was embarrassed to admit it even to herself. He persisted, telling her of all the pioneer work she could accomplish in the field of nursing in Iran. With a fascination for faraway lands, having listened to her father's stories and imbued with the pioneering spirit of her ancestors, Helen heard the words of Abol resonating deep within her.

MY GRANDFATHER HAD ENDURED MANY HARDSHIPS GROWING up in a remote village in the Bakhtiari tribal area of Iran. His mother died when he was born in 1872. He and his stepmother struggled to meet their basic needs as my great-grandfather, Haji Hasan, was often away, leading caravan journeys to Mecca in Saudi Arabia. Hasan's work was to make the pilgrimage to Mecca and carry objects to Mecca on behalf of people who were

Davar's maternal grandfather, Abol Ghassem, wearing the traditional Bakhtiari hat in Borugen, Chahar Mahal, Iran. (From the Laleh Bakhtiar Collection of Family Photographs)

unable to do so themselves. There, he would see that the objects were blessed and returned to the owners as a sacred memento.[4]

During his childhood my grandfather had overcome both smallpox and typhus. It was his stepmother who insisted he go to the local one-room schoolhouse in the early 1880s, where he experienced strict discipline and harsh punishment from his teacher. At the age of ten, having finished third grade, my grandfather's teacher told him that he had completed his schooling, and, at the insistence of his stepmother, he had to find a job. For the next fifteen years, he undertook multiple odd jobs doing what he could for him and his stepmother to survive. He mended shoes, sold groceries, and finally chose to assist a traveling peddler.

Their journeys were long and treacherous through Iran's

valleys and mountains following the migratory Bakhtiari tribes while carrying big bundles of merchandise on their shoulders. In several instances, his feet were frostbitten after crossing snow-covered mountain ranges by foot—they were too poor to have a horse or a mule—on his way back home.

In order to enter his home in the small town of Borugen in Chahar Mahal near Isfahan in central Iran, he went through a *takiya*, or Hosseiniyyeh. Similar to ancient Greek theaters, a *takiya* is the place where passion plays are performed in memory of the third Shia Imam, imam Hossein.[5]

In addition to having to enter his home through the *takiya*, the local mosque was across the street. His extended family had often heard him reciting from the *Shahnameh*, which was not uncommon in rural Iran, and commented to neighbors about his powerful voice. Soon after that the leader of the prayers at the local mosque asked him to give the call to the five daily prayers from the minaret of the mosque in the days before the microphone to let the people in that area of town know it was time to pray.

When my grandfather was twenty-five, his stepmother and rarely seen father took ill and died. His father, being of meager means, bequeathed him two things—the Sufi cloak of a master and a dervish "begging bowl." Never having thought of his father as a Sufi or a mystic, he began to be curious about what his inheritance meant. He thought perhaps his fate was to be a wandering dervish. Family members of a deceased person would pay dervishes to recite prayers or fast on behalf of their dead relatives for all the prayers they'd missed during their lifetime. To test this theory, he decided to go to Karbala, in Iraq, the place where Imam Hossein is buried and an important Shia site of pilgrimage.

Just as he was about to leave home, he received a letter from a cousin. Knowing my grandfather's love for learning, the cousin mentioned that the wife of one of his tribal leaders was looking for a tutor for her two young nephews, who lived in the village of Shalamzar in the Bakhtiari region of Chahar Mahal. Whereas Karbala was my grandfather's ultimate destination, Shalamzar was on the way, so he decided that he should at least go and inquire about the position.

He walked the two-day trek to Shalamzar, and there he met the legendary Bakhtiari tribal leader, Morteza Qoli Khan Samsam, and his wife, Bibi Mah Begum. Much to his joy, he was hired as a tutor for their nephews. Finally, he felt, he could make use of his early education, rather than earning a living through odd jobs alone. At the same time, he collected the letters that the Khan received and copied them over and over again in an effort to improve his penmanship. Eventually, he was asked to write letters for the Bibi—the Bakhtiari title for a wife or daughter of a tribal leader—in addition to tutoring her nephews. All the while he continued to memorize the *Shahnameh*.

After five years, in 1911, the Khan family decided to move to Tehran. Bibi Mah Begum wanted to put her nephews in a boarding school in the capital city and she had two choices: the French school or the American Mission School. She chose the American Mission School (later called Alborz) and decided that my grandfather could continue to take care of the young boys by accompanying them to school. His hopes for his own education were revived.

He would not be disappointed. For three months he sat in the hall outside the classroom of one of his pupils, listened, and began to learn English. He then approached the school's director, Dr. Samuel Jordan, and told him that he wanted to enroll as a scholarship student who would help with the younger boys. My grandfather was forty years old by this time, the same age as the principal. Dr. Jordan said he would consider it if my grandfather stopped smoking opium and drinking alcohol. It was only my grandfather's strong will and deep desire for an education that enabled him to quit his addictions on the spot, only then to endure what Iranian society considered to be a disgrace—sitting as a pupil alongside seven- and eight-year-olds.

Each day he would wake up at four in the morning to study under a kerosene lamp until seven. He would then run about three miles to a local pool for a quick swim in summer and winter before running back to get the little boys dressed for school. By the end of the year, my grandfather entered the sixth grade, having just begun to read and write English.

In 1914, he helped plan one of the school's greatest adventures—climbing the 18,602-foot Mount Damavand, the highest volcanic mountain in the Middle East. The mountain, immortalized in many Persian miniatures, has a patriotic hold on Iranians. It is the scene of many battles where the great heroes of the *Shahnameh* won victory. The group of twenty-five students walked four days to get to the base of the mountain and spent three days climbing to the top. My grandfather, the leader, was the first to summit Mount Damavand, four hours ahead of either the teachers or other students.

In 1918, when he graduated from the American Mission School, Tehran was gripped by famine. The Qajar Dynasty was still in power when America sent food and supplies through the Near East Relief Organization. Dr. Jordan recommended my grandfather, who was comfortable with English, to the head of the Near East Relief Organization as someone who could be of invaluable help in distributing food. Through this work, my grandfather became friends with the head of the Near East Relief Organization in Iran, Leland Rex Robinson, who was impressed with my grandfather's enthusiasm. In a letter back home, he described Abol: "There are five or six Persians who want to come to America with me. They dream of America as the Land of Promise, of 'sages' as one of the seriously minded among them said. In some ways they will surely not be disappointed; but there will come days of heartsickness, of longing for the huge, empty, gray valleys of their impoverished, yet not unhappy, country. One is a young Bakhtiari tribesman, but a thoroughly urbane and cultured one." Fulfilling my grandfather's dreams of an education, Mr. Robinson offered him a scholarship to study in America.[6]

My grandfather arrived at Ellis Island, in New York harbor, on October 29, 1919, and that winter was accepted at Columbia University in New York City. After three years as an undergraduate he moved to South Dakota to take part in a special accelerated premed program. On the way out West, he joined a carnival in order to earn some money for his education and was introduced as the "Persian Lion." Win or lose, it cost a dollar a minute to wrestle the Persian Lion. It was not surprising that he was drawn to wrestling as so many of the heroes of the *Shahnameh* had been. At the end of the summer, Abol was a thousand dollars richer but also in considerable physical pain due to the cauliflower ears and back strain that resulted from his carnival work. It took years before his ears returned to their normal size.

After finishing the premed program in South Dakota, he was accepted at Syracuse University Medical School, from which he graduated in 1926 at the age of fifty-four. His dream was realized only because he kept himself in the best physical, spiritual, psychological, and moral condition. He would wake up at four a.m. every day to exercise. He believed in being chivalrous toward others, and especially felt protective of women. He moved back to New York City in the fall of 1926 and began his internship and residency in surgery at Harlem Hospital.

Davar's grandfather, Abol Ghassem, graduates from Syracuse Medical School in 1926.
(From the Laleh Bakhtiar Collection of Family Photographs)

HELEN HAD BEEN BROUGHT UP IN A STRICT CHRISTIAN HOME IN the small town of Weiser, Idaho. She could trace her lineage back to 1751, when her ancestor John Mackey emigrated to America from Ireland with his wife, Ann Alexander. They settled in North Carolina, where they had nine children. Their oldest son, James Mackey, was born on May 24, 1759, and fought in the Revolutionary War. He was wounded in the Battle of Bunker Hill on June 17, 1775, when he was sixteen years old, but lived to witness American independence.[7]

John Mackey was Helen's great-grandfather on her mother's side. Her grandmother, Ruth Sophronia Mackey, married John McRoberts on July 27, 1865. McRoberts had fought in the Civil War in a Union Army regiment from Des Moines, Iowa. After the war ended, he and his wife and daughters crossed the plains along with five hundred wagons moving westward from Bigelow, Missouri, in 1875. Pulled by a team of white mules, the wagons carried cheese, flour, dried fruit, bacon, clothing, and bedding.[8]

At Salt Lake City, thirteen people, including John and Ruth, broke off from the others to head to Idaho, where they settled in Midvale, originally called Middle Valley. John McRoberts first ran the post office and the ferry service across the Weiser River during high water at Midvale. He later took up a 160-acre homestead, where he raised cattle, pigs, and horses. The family befriended Chief Joseph, the leader of the Nez Perce Indians, who sometimes came to their home for dinner. Whenever John had to travel, Chief Joseph would send some of his friends to watch over my great-grandmother and her six daughters and protect them from harm.

Once they were married, Helen's parents moved to Weiser,

twenty miles southwest of Midvale, where Helen, her brother, James, and twin sisters, Mary and Mildred, grew up with her father's family under the watchful eye of his Baptist mother, Sarah Elizabeth Anderson Jeffreys. Sarah's crusade was to convert the Nez Perce Indians to Christianity. Helen's mother, Nell, a tall woman, was said to have had a great Irish sense of humor and raised her children as Baptists, strictly observing the tenets of the Bible. Smoking, drinking, and profanity were forbidden in the family. Ruth Sophronia Mackey, Nell's mother, like other mothers in the early West, carefully watched over her daughters. Even the slightest sign of "foolish" behavior among the girls would cause their mother to faint.

My great-grandfather, James Woodson Jeffreys, also grew up in Weiser, where in 1898, at the age of nineteen, he was recruited for service in the Spanish-American War. He wrote that he took part in the capture of Manila, serving under General Arthur MacArthur in the Philippine Insurrection.[9]

Later, during World War I, my great-grandfather served for fourteen months as a captain in the U.S. Army commanding a machine gun company stationed in Paris. After the war, he returned to Weiser and was elected mayor. Unwilling to deal with a life in politics, he later resigned and moved his family to Los Angeles.

My grandmother always regretted leaving Idaho and with it the closeness of her extended family. Even memories of the winter snow and ice did not lessen her nostalgia for the state. Her heart was like a mirror—bright and clear. Hearing her father's stories of the strange and distant lands he had visited during his military career awoke in her a desire to travel. A seeker of adventure and romance, she was not like her older twin sisters—also nurses—who were satisfied with the status quo. Accepting a scholarship to teach nursing in New York City, she left her sheltered home and family in Los Angeles to travel three thousand miles by train to see for herself what the Big Apple had to offer.[10]

EVEN AFTER TWELVE YEARS IN AMERICA, MY GRANDFATHER never entertained the idea of staying, because of the deep need for Western-educated physicians in Iran. My grandmother, for her part, was intrigued by the thought of going to a foreign country and helping to heal people with her new medical training. They shared the same dream. Her decision to accept my grandfather's hand in marriage and to move with him back to Iran would be her crusade to do God's work on earth in a faraway land that could benefit from her knowledge and experience.

Once my grandmother accepted his proposal, she realized that her parents back in Los Angeles would never agree to her marrying a foreigner, especially one who practiced a different faith, spoke a language they had never heard, and was older than James, her father. Helen decided it would be best for them to marry in a civil ceremony, after which she would send a telegram to her parents explaining that a church wedding back home would come later.

The local justice of the peace had to be convinced that my grandmother, given her youth, had not been rushed into making her decision. He asked her how long she had known my grandfather. She answered, "A couple of months." He asked if she had her parents' permission. She said she was going to tell them, but as they lived in California and she was in New York and the distance and expense made it difficult for them to meet him in time, she would do so after the ceremony. He then asked her for a copy of her birth certificate to ensure that she was twenty-two.

She had not included the document among the belongings she brought to the East so she wrote to the Idaho County Courthouse for a copy. They responded that the courthouse had burned down and with it, birth, death, and other records had been destroyed. They enclosed a blank, stamped birth certificate and told her to fill it out for herself. Once the justice of the peace saw it, he could no longer legally refuse to marry Abol and Helen.[11]

They had both agreed to keep the marriage a secret from the people at work because it would affect my grandmother's job. My grandfather's excitement, however, could not be contained; elated, he called a mutual friend of theirs, an Iranian, and told him the news. The friend asked why he was crying and he told him that he was crying because he was so happy.

Once he had broken the news to his friend, it was even more difficult not to share it with the hospital staff. He called my grandmother in her classroom at the hospital and told her to come downstairs to join in the congratulations. Soon afterward a reporter called her—the word was out.

The hospital's chief nurse was the first one to speak to my grandmother privately. She was appalled that one of her staff nurses had married a foreigner from a country where women

Helen and Abol are married in New York City on October 27, 1927. (From the Laleh Bakhtiar Collection of Family Photographs)

had no rights. Just eight years prior, the American women's suffrage movement worked toward the ratification of the Nineteenth Amendment to the Constitution, which gave American women the right to vote. My grandmother's decision was deemed a step backward. Helen underwent interrogation during which she was asked if she was planning to move to a country where women were veiled. Undaunted, she explained that she had considered these points before and, yes, she would move so that she could be among the first to train nurses there. The chief nurse then told her to leave the dormitory facilities as they were not meant to house married women.

Disappointed as she was by the head nurse's response, she thought about the reporter who had called and realized she had better let her parents know before they read about her marriage in the newspapers. She finally sent an overnight telegram to her mother, Nell. When the telegram was delivered to her by telephone, Nell fainted. Her parents felt that they had lost their daughter to a man they had never met.

My grandmother had not only found the love of her life but also a man who would help her achieve her unspoken longings for adventure and dreams of service to others in need. Helen had moved beyond the world of her parents, recapturing the vision of her early ancestors, who had uprooted themselves from Ireland and moved westward to the new land. My grandmother was, however, geographically and spiritually, reversing the process in an eastward movement. Her love of knowledge and her American dream would journey with her to the ancient land of Persia.

· 3 ·

The Bakhtiars and the Ardalans

Three years after my grandparents' marriage, Iran's minister of education wrote to my grandfather asking him to return to Iran to serve the people. By then, he and my grandmother had two young daughters, and she was pregnant with her third child. When they left America in 1931, Helen became one of the first Americans to have married an Iranian in America and then to have moved to Iran. Helen knew that when she arrived she would be confronted with great difficulties. She, nevertheless, was eager to penetrate beyond the limits of what she knew. And Abol had assured her that once in Iran, she would be able to practice nursing because, like all upper-middle-class Iranians, they would be able to afford to hire servants to look after the children.[1]

Aware of the hazards in the south of Iran where life was similar to that of the lawless West, they took a ship to Baghdad, Iraq, and then they went overland to Tehran, driving the Buick that they had brought with them. My grandfather's friends and relatives flocked to Tehran to greet the new bride and their two small daughters. When they saw that my grandmother was pregnant, they told her now that she was on Iranian soil, she would definitely bear a son.

Among those who had come to Tehran from the Bakhtiari country to greet my grandfather were the tribal leaders (Khans) and their sons, some of whom had played a prominent role in saving the 1906 Constitution from being withdrawn by the Qajar kings.

While Iran had been ruled by Shahs for 1,400 years, in 1905 a movement began for reform of the ruling Qajar Shahs. A nationalist movement headed by tribal leaders and intellectuals alike led to the writing of a constitution and the formation of a national assembly. The first national assembly consisted of 136 elected members who established a constitutional monarchy. But soon, the Shah, who had agreed to follow the new constitution, died, and his son and successor wanted to have nothing to do with it. The new Shah ordered the Cossacks—Iranian troops who were under the command of Russian officers—to mobilize in Tehran to keep order and dismiss the assembly, which they did.[2]

It became clear that the Shah would not agree to constitutional reform. He proceeded to arrest the leaders of the nationalist movement and suppressed the press. In 1909, the Bakhtiari Khans marched with their army on Tehran to ensure that the Shah would accept the constitution. The Shah's forces opposed the Bakhtiari army but were defeated. The Shah was formally deposed and his son, a twelve-year-old boy, was made the next Qajar Shah.

Once the national assembly was able to meet again in 1911, they appointed the father of Morteza Qoli Khan Samsam, the man who had hired my grandfather to tutor his nephews, as the prime minister and his brother as the minister of the interior. All of Iran rejoiced, as the Bakhtiari had played a major role in saving the constitution.

In 1931 when Abol and Helen went to Iran, the Bakhtiari Khans invited my grandfather to dinner. When he walked into the room, they all stood up to honor him for his persistence in getting an education and proclaimed him an honorary Khan.[3]

My grandparents rented a large house in Tehran, which would double as their private hospital, one of the first of its kind in Iran. As grandmother Helen would later tell her children, it never felt to her like a home, but rather like living in a hospital. As soon as she would decorate a room, my grandfather would move in a patient or a cadaver. Anatomy was still not being taught to Iranian student physicians because of opposition from the clerics. My grandfather, realizing how essential anatomy was to learning medicine, began to teach it. He would go to the public coroner's office and retrieve unidentified corpses, housing them overnight before transporting them to the newly formed Tehran University School of Anatomy, which he eventually headed.

By having a home in their place of work, my grandparents were able to keep close watch over their children. Following the birth of my twin aunts—proving wrong the family member who had predicted a son—Helen and Abol had two sons, Jamshid and Cyrus, and then finally my mother, a total of seven children.

When my mother was born in Tehran, she was given the name Mary Nell—not a Persian name like all her siblings had.

This had been at the explicit request of Helen's parents in letters written frequently to her from her father, as her mother had never learned to read and write: "Can you please choose a name we can pronounce!" The children were named Lailee, Shireen, Paree, Parveen, Jamshid, and Cyrus. Having asked that at least one grandchild be given a familiar Christian name, my great-grandparents' wish came true with the birth of my mother, named Mary, after Helen's sister, and Nell, after Helen's mother.[4]

In those days Iranian homes had no furniture. Instead, the living and sleeping areas were covered with beautifully designed hand-woven Persian carpets, with cushions lining the walls. It proved to be a very flexible arrangement that could be converted into two living rooms or two dining rooms as necessary. When the family ate meals, they would place a tablecloth on the floor and remove it once the meal was over.

Abol preferred having a dining-room table and chairs. But it had to accommodate himself, Helen, the seven children, as well as each child's nurse. Often there were guests as well, and my grandmother once described a dinner-table scene of twenty-four chairs surrounding a very long table.

My grandfather continued to be very health-conscious, paying particular attention to his children's need for fresh air. He had the servants set up nine beds on the roof so that summer and winter, the entire family could sleep under the stars. In winter, each child had a hot water bottle in their bed and heavy quilts on top of them to protect them from the snow. In summer, each bed was surrounded by mosquito netting. Each child had a milk bottle filled with pasteurized milk, an important health innovation that my grandparents helped introduce in Iran.

Helen struggled with kerosene lamps and stoves for her first four years in Iran before there was electricity. She oversaw the work of the hospital as well as the home, often carrying a baby on one hip while another child was tugging at her to be held. Their days began early in the morning, when Abol would rise at four a.m., shave his face and head, and listen to the BBC news on a shortwave radio. He would then do laps around the balcony for twenty minutes. As he ran, he recited the *Shahnameh* to himself. Then, summer or winter, he would wake the children and line them up under the shower as he continued to chant to them from the *Shahnameh*.

Word reached the monarch, Reza Shah Pahlavi, that Dr. Bakhtiar had returned from America as an American-trained physician. Reza Shah had been a colonel in the army who rose to power in the early 1920s, just after my grandfather arrived in New York City. In October 1925, he succeeded in deposing the last Qajar Shah and proclaimed the founding of the Pahlavi Dynasty, thereby limiting the role of the national assembly. Once Reza Shah met my grandfather, he would summon him to the palace in Tehran to treat him or some member of his family. My aunt Lailee and my uncle Jamshid would often accompany him to the palace.[5]

By 1936, Reza Shah had changed the name of the country from Persia to Iran, and instituted dramatic modernization measures. He outlawed the traditional Iranian dress for men and women. Only clerics were allowed to wear their religious garb; all other men were to adopt Western attire. The chador or veil was outlawed for women. My grandmother Helen thought about the chief nurse, who had chided her for moving backward, and wished she could let her know how things in Iran were changing for women.[6]

In 1937, six years after their arrival in Tehran, Helen's sister Mary came to visit them from Los Angeles. This was the first time anyone in Helen's family had met my grandfather, much less journeyed all the way to Iran. Despite Reza Shah's attempts to modernize Iran, it was still a third world country and there were many things about Iran that were not up to American stan-

Davar's great-aunt Mary Jeffreys visiting Iran (*left to right:* Aunt Lailee, Uncle Jamshid, Helen holding Uncle Cyrus, great-aunt Mary, Abol Ghassem, Aunt Paree, Aunt Shireen, and Aunt Parveen), Tehran, 1938. (From the Laleh Bakhtiar Collection of Family Photographs)

dards. In most of the country at that time, there were no indoor toilets. Located some distance from the house, the toilet consisted of a hole in the earth where one had to squat, somewhat similar to an outhouse. On Mary's way to Tehran to see her sister, she'd arrived in Kermanshah in southeastern Iran and had fallen into one of these toilets, which only added to her quickly growing disgust with Iran and with what she found to be the people's backward way of life. On her way to Tehran through rural Iran there were few cars or even paved roads. Many areas still did not have electricity or running water. Without realizing at the time that her own mother had grown up in much the same type of life in rural Idaho, it was hard for Mary to believe that her American sister was willing to put up with all the difficulties and inconveniences of life in Tehran, at the same time that she had seven small children and was in charge of the private hospital. Mary blamed Abol for her sister's difficult lifestyle. Upon her return to the States, she wrote negatively to Helen about how she saw her life in Iran, hoping that she would listen and return to America.[7] My grandmother was exhausted and probably became more aware of how tired she really was from her sister Mary's visit, feeling overwhelmed with raising seven children, all under the age of ten, and she began to think: What if they had more? Even with all the children, she continued to make the rounds in the hospital. Her various excursions resulted in a dislocated hip and great pain. In need of rest, she decided to visit her parents in America. She had not seen them in twelve years, and they had not met any of her children. Helen and Abol decided that she would make the trip first and he would follow.

Helen left Iran in 1939 on the eve of World War II. As she

was preparing to depart she heard from the American missionaries that all Americans had been advised to leave Iran because Reza Shah was beginning to side with the Germans. This only reinforced my grandparents' decision that Helen should leave with at least two of her children, the American-born Lailee and Shireen, and my mother, Mary Nell, whom Helen was still nursing.

They set off on the long journey from Tehran to Los Angeles, overland to Beirut, by ship to Trieste, Italy, and then by train to Paris. From there, they traveled to the French port of Le Havre from which they boarded the SS *Vollendam*, a Dutch steamer, for the long ride to New York. From New York they took a train to Los Angeles, where they arrived, three months later, in late August. Two days after their arrival, Hitler invaded Poland and World War II commenced in Europe, restricting travel between America and Iran as all available overseas passage was being used by the Allied forces. As a doctor, my grandfather was not permitted to leave Iran.

While my grandmother remained in Los Angeles with three of their children, my grandfather was left to care for the other four. Unable to run the private hospital without her, he accepted a job with the Anglo-Iranian Oil Company in southwestern Iran in Solomon's Mosque and moved there with the children.

My grandmother began to petition the State Department to speed up her return to Iran, but she was told it was not safe. As she found it impossible to reunite with the rest of her family, she decided to further her education by obtaining a B.S. in Public Health Nursing from UCLA. After all, she had to support herself and her three children while she waited for the war to end.

My grandmother, aunts, and mother lived with Helen's parents, Papa and Grandma Nell, for three years at 821 South Holt Avenue in Los Angeles, one block south of Beverly Hills. My mother's name, which set her apart from her siblings, also had the effect of making her grandparents feel a special bond with her. As she was their youngest grandchild, they doted on her and enjoyed teaching her Christian values, which included learning their favorite Christian songs, "Onward Christian Soldiers" and "Amazing Grace." Their new home was quite different from the one my mother and her sisters had left behind. Papa's military photos from his service in the Spanish-American War as well as World War I decorated the living room along with his gun collection. When Papa answered the home phone he would say, "Captain Jeffreys speaking."[8]

Once my grandmother graduated in 1944 and found a job, she was able to buy her own home. Now a single parent, Helen worked nights at the UCLA student infirmary, where the university had just set up a women's student health center. By then Aunt Lailee was fourteen and Aunt Shireen was thirteen so they took care of my mother, then four years old, at night while Helen was at work. Being on her own, earning her own living, completing her associate degree in nursing with a B.S. in Public Health Nursing, she now felt independent from both her parents in Los Angeles and her husband in Iran.[9] Abol could not support his family from so far away, so she had to provide for herself and her three daughters. Helen became a pioneering woman in her own right at a time when most wives were in the home, supported by their husbands.

Once World War II ended, my grandmother and her three

children were able to secure passage back to Iran for a few months in 1945. They traveled from New York on a Portuguese steamer to Portugal, from there on a British Royal Navy ship to Gibraltar, and from Gibraltar on a British troopship to Alexandria, Egypt. From Egypt they went by train to Basra, Iraq, and from there they took a boat to Khorammshahr, Iran, in Khuzistan province.[10] By the time they arrived in MIS, the family had been apart for six years. There is a memorable photograph of my grandparents and their seven children, taken on the day of their reunion. Although my parents were overjoyed at having the family unit back together, this was a difficult time in their marriage.

While my grandmother had been willing to struggle in Iran during the early years of her marriage, she was not willing now to live in a company town like MIS. She missed Tehran and her friends, including those she made among the royalty and other well-to-do families. In MIS there was no room for Helen's independent spirit. Everything was provided by the oil company; you could not even change a lightbulb by yourself. Instead, a call had to be placed to the company's maintenance department. The British lived in their own upper-class area and the Iranian physicians in the middle-class area. The poorer Iranian workers, who might have benefited from what Helen knew about public health, had been placed in yet another neighborhood of their own. The mixing of classes was frowned upon. None of this sat well with my grandmother's American spirit.

In addition, my grandfather, who was by then seventy years old, insisted that he wanted to have more children. Confronted by perhaps the most blatant difference in attitudes between East and West that Helen was to encounter in her marriage, she must have thought: I have given him "the seven wonders of the world"—why does he want more? The many years of separation and financial hardships had taken a toll on their relationship. My grandmother did not want more children. As it was, she had missed many of the formative years of four of her seven children. The siblings, who had lost touch in those years, needed time to reacquaint themselves with one another and with their absent parents. This was no time to add more children to the mix.

ABOL AND HELEN DID, HOWEVER, AGREE THAT IT WAS BEST TO raise the children in America. They decided that the seven children should accompany Helen to America, where they could finish their education until my grandfather could join them. My grandmother chose not to return to Los Angeles but rather to relocate to Washington, D.C., as the Iranian Embassy was there and she hoped that it might help her because her children had four different citizenship and visa statuses. It must have been tragic for her to return to America without Abol, her prince, the man she had fallen in love with in Central Park.

At the same time, she could never have foreseen the terrible financial struggle she was about to undergo. On her first journey to Iran, the longings and dreams that she brought with her became a reality during her ten years in Tehran. Now, at age forty, she was embarking on yet another adventure, but this time one she had never imagined she would have to face.

For five years she struggled with the stress of having little or no money. Four of her children did not speak English. Five of them were now teenagers. My grandfather was not often able to obtain dollars on the open market, so he began sending beautiful Persian carpets instead, which my grandmother sold to support herself and the children. Finding buyers always took time, though, and the landlord and food markets weren't willing to wait for payment, so she took a job as a real estate agent, which offered flexible hours so she could better meet her children's needs.[11]

Even after living full time in the United States for three years, Helen had not lost her love for Persian culture. Being with Iranians felt like the only light in her dark, desperate tunnel. Shortly after moving to Washington, Helen met Mohammad Nemazee, a wealthy Iranian businessman, who held an open house every Sunday at his home in Bethesda, Maryland. What seemed like all the Iranians in the area gathered for a Persian feast. My mother loved the flavors of Persian food, the saffron rice, the pomegranates and walnut sauce. One of her twin daughters, Parveen, would sing in her beautiful voice Armenian songs she had learned in MIS. Everyone at the open house spoke Persian. Just a child, my mother could walk around without anyone paying any attention to her. Little did she know then that her future husband, my father, was among the Sunday guests.[12]

My grandfather Abol was still forbidden to leave Iran as physicians were needed in the country even after World War II. Once it was clear that he would not be joining them, my grandparents decided to get a divorce. As tragic as it was for their seven children, the divorce was a mutual decision. Helen wanted to focus on raising her children in America and Abol married a Bakhtiari woman named Turan, who bore him ten more children over the next sixteen years.[13]

My mother survived her parents' divorce relatively unscathed by immersing herself in two passions: books and religion. From the age of eight until twelve, she would walk several miles by herself every Sunday morning from Harrison Street at the district line, to get to church. Having awoken early to make the trip, she would also fast in order to receive communion.

During those years, she had a friend named Martha Mitchell, whose father, Howard Mitchell, was the conductor of the National Symphony Orchestra. They were classmates at St. Anne's Catholic School. Beside Martha's house was a garage with a loft area. The two set up an altar there, where they placed religious icons of Jesus, the Virgin Mary, and many of the saints. My mother's favorite saint was Saint Teresa; when she was baptized, my mother took her name.[14]

Every chance they had, Mary and Martha would pray at the altar they had built. They would also put on long dresses and walk through the neighborhood praying. Religion, faith in God, belief in an afterlife, and wanting to develop her full potential as an individual chosen by God to inhabit this earth always preoccupied my mother's mind.

She was twelve before my mother realized she did not really know her father. By this time, my grandmother had bought a house on O Street in Georgetown, just a few doors down from the Catholic church Mary had traveled so far to reach every Sunday. Suddenly it was too easy to go to church. The challenge was gone. My mother learned that her father had remarried, and she was also aware that he and his wife were having more and more children. She thought to herself: He does not even know who we are and there he is having more children! As only a child might, she connected this central fact about her father's life to the Catholic church and its decree forbidding birth control. From the day of that realization, Mary grew distant from her faith.

By 1950, five of my grandmother's seven children had either married or left for college. Though it was a struggle for my grandmother, my grandparents firmly believed that the education of the children in America would lead to a brighter future for them. After all, my grandfather had come to the United States to be educated, and he wanted the same—the best—for his offspring. My mother and her siblings—half-Iranian, half-American—were now fully entrenched in living the American life.

Helen kept herself informed about the unfolding political events in Iran. The news in America often made reference to Russia threatening to interfere in Iran's internal affairs. At one point she wrote to Abol that she feared that Iran might be taken over by communists and that he should send all his money out of the country. Despite their divorce, my grandparents wrote to each other to discuss the children and what each of them was doing. As the children grew older, each of them developed a long-distance letter-writing relationship with their father. These letters accumulated into a detailed account of their respective lives.[15] It was in 1950 that my grandmother heard about an opportunity to work for the United States Public Health Service on a mission to Iran. Her love for helping the Iranian people was still with her. Taking just my uncle Cyrus and my mother along, she accepted the job.

MY GRANDMOTHER HAD AGREED TO WORK IN PART OF PRESI-
dent Truman's Point Four Program. She would serve as a public health nurse in Iran with the rank of a lieutenant commander in the United States Navy. The governments of Iran and the United States began cooperating in the Rural Development Program in Iran in October 1950.[16] Once Helen arrived in Tehran, Dr. Emil Palmquist, medical director for Point Four in Iran, gathered the assembled team of nurses and said: "I will make it very brief. You are to learn Persian. You are to drive a jeep and you are to start your program." And with those orders Helen was off. Having by this time mastered Persian, she had a head start on her mission.

The Point Four Program's dual objective was to help Iran develop in the areas of agriculture, public health, and sanitation while preventing the spread of communism within its borders. Communists tended to direct their efforts toward people in rural areas, so if Americans could reach these people before the communists did they could delay or even hold the spread of communism. In his book, *Mission for Peace,* William E. Warne, the head of Point Four in Iran from 1951 to 1955, wrote of an exchange between himself and Iran's prime minister Mohammad Mossadegh. Dr. Mossadegh had just made the point that if it was not for the neighboring Soviet Union, the Americans would not be in Iran and that the Point Four Program had political motivations, to which Warne replied:

Grandmother Helen meeting with a group of village children when she was serving in Iran under President Truman's Point Four Program, circa 1952. (From the Laleh Bakhtiar Collection of Family Photographs)

I don't wake up each morning, Mr. Prime Minister, wondering what I can do this day to fight Communism. No, I wake up wondering how I can better help the Iranian people fight ignorance, disease and starvation. If carrying the fight against these ancient enemies of mankind attacks the roots of Communism, then it must be a despicable plant indeed to grow only in such soils. If by cleaning out these backyards of the world we eliminate a noxious weed it will still be but one incident in the work of improving the lot of mankind.[17]

Warne wrote extensively about Point Four's ambitious programs. In coordination with Iran's Ministry of Health, Point Four helped rescue Iran's malaria control project. A new health division called the Public Health Cooperative was created and

Point Four grants allowed Iranian experts to travel to the United States for further study, which all led to the eradication of malaria in most parts of Iran by 1955. Furthermore, sanitary engineers helped create a modern water supply system in Tehran as well as designing smaller water systems for village baths. American technicians also taught villagers how to protect food from getting contaminated, how to construct sanitary toilets, and lectured on the importance of using boiled water. The idea was to decentralize Iran's health activities and create rural health units to serve Iranians from all walks of life.[18]

Helen was one of the members of the mobile health unit that traveled to distant villages inoculating schoolchildren against typhoid and other diseases. She also trained local health workers, focusing on the importance of creating community health programs especially for expectant mothers.

Warne writes of some of the challenges that health specialists such as Helen had to overcome:

Mrs. Helen Bakhtiar started a school for village girls near Ali-Shah-Avaz in the Shahriyar area (near Tehran). She had to beat the bushes for recruits. Finally one day her problem was solved. A particularly timid girl of about thirteen slid through the door and took a seat in the back of the room. She was the daughter of an influential mullah in a near-by village. Once it was clear that the mullah's daughter had actually entered the class, other volunteers came. Helen, being a wise woman, arranged to call at the mullah's village to thank him for sending his daughter. She had met the mullah before and had found him somewhat less than cooperative.

But when she thanked him, now the mullah said that he had been thinking over what Mrs. Bakhtiar had said about the importance of improving the health of the villagers. He had decided, he added, that if such work were to be carried forward among the village women, men could not appropriately do it. So he had sent his daughter to be trained. Thus, walls are broken down and light filters through.[19]

But during this same period in the early 1950s, the political situation for Americans became precarious and they were told to send their dependents out of the country. Mohammad Reza Shah went to Rome in exile, as nationalist prime minister Mossadegh called for the nationalization of Iranian oil. Two years after his rise to power, through a CIA–backed coup d'état, Mohammad Reza Shah Pahlavi was returned to power and Mossadegh was imprisoned.[20]

During this political turmoil, my grandmother Helen ended her work with Point Four and moved to the city of Isfahan. Helen, like my grandfather Abol Ghassem, disdained politics. Furthermore, the American government recommended that dependents of Americans working in Iran be sent back to America. Helen sent my mother, fifteen, and my Uncle Cyrus, seventeen, back to the D.C. area to attend boarding schools to prepare them for college.

In Isfahan, my grandmother grew close to the Bakhtiari people and was even able to renew her friendship with the noted Bakhtiari leader Yahya Khan, whose home in Isfahan she rented. She also visited his summer villa in Dastana. In her diary she wrote: "A perfectly beautiful place, so many trees with a large stream running through the village. The Bakhtiari Mountains are within walking distance, and we were able to see snow on the mountains. There is a project being contemplated, which would assist primarily the tribal people, and I am delighted to be in on the planning of the program."[21]

The villagers of Iran loved my grandmother, a blond, blue-eyed, selfless woman who spoke Persian with an American accent. When she fell ill in the city of Isfahan in 1954, Yahya Khan held a prayer vigil for her in his home, where those who attended said twelve thousand prayers in hopes of her recovery. They also sent her flowers and burned incense to ward off the evil eye.

It was there in the heart of the Bakhtiari Mountains and their quiet solitude, that Helen finally found peace of mind. She would from then on often speak of the sheer beauty of "the daisies, bluebells and yellow buttercups, the wild roses and blossoms" of Bakhtiari country. For hours on end she watched the tribal women weaving their legendary Bakhtiari carpets. She would talk about how they used walnut juice for the buff color as well as pomegranate juice and other dyes obtained from flowers for their creations. Of the pastures, she wrote: "The clamor and the clangor of the bells rhyming and chiming—jingling, tinkle, tinkle bells of goats and sheep—harmony of cowbells tinkling, jingling, and jangling in the balmy air of the night."

MY MOTHER ATTENDED A PRIVATE GIRLS' BOARDING SCHOOL, Holton-Arms, in Washington, D.C. Her high school year-book quote was: "My plume on high, my flag unfurled, I rode away to save the world." She excelled there not only in academics but also in athletics. She became head of the athletic association playing field hockey, basketball and softball, and swimming.

Her brother Jamshid was attending the University of Virginia, where he played football. As Charlottesville was within driving distance of Washington, D.C., my mother and her sister Paree would go to see as many of his games as possible during football season.

Jamshid's football success made my mother one of the more

Uncle Jamshid is voted All-American in 1957, University of Virginia. (From the Laleh Bakhtiar Collection of Family Photographs)

popular girls at her school, particularly among the junior college students, because they all wanted to date the "Persian Lion," a title Abol Ghassem had used when he was wrestling in the carnival. In Persian tradition, lions are a symbol of power and majesty; in fact, a statue of a Persian lion adorned the ancient Persepolis. In 1957 my uncle Jamshid became the first Iranian American All-American football player.

Following her freshman year in college in 1956, my mother traveled to Iran for the summer, where Mama Helen took her to meet Yahya Khan. My grandmother told him that my mother was searching for a Persian name. Yahya Khan looked at her and said: "Laleh,"[22] a popular girl's name that is the name of the wild opium. But my mother continued to use the name Mary Nell as she prepared to return to college in Pittsburgh, Pennsylvania, the same city where my father attended college.

MY FATHER, NADER ARDALAN, IS A DESCENDANT OF THE KURDS from the feudal aristocracy of the Ardalan Dynasty. For some seven hundred years up to the mid-nineteenth century, the Ardalans ruled an area in northwest Iran, currently encompassing the province of Kurdistan. The Ardalans were known for cultivating literature and music. Our ancestor Mastoureh Ardalan (1805–48) was a Kurdish writer and poet who wrote in the Kurdish Gorani dialect as well as in Persian. She wrote numerous books of poetry and was recognized as a historian for her other writings, including her book on the history of the Ardalan Dynasty.[23]

Our immediate Kurdish lineage can be traced back to my great-great-grandfather, Reza Qoli Khan, the governor general of Kurdistan. The Kurds of Iran were fearless in seeking their independence from the Qajar king of Iran, Nasser-ed Din Shah (reigned 1848–96). The king decided to send his aunt, Tuba Khanom, the daughter of Crown Prince Abbas Mirza, a legendary Qajar warrior, to my great-great-grandfather as a peace bride. The Qajar monarch felt that this might be a way for the rebellious Kurds to conform to his ways. Instead, Princess Tuba Khanom fell in love with Reza Qoli Khan and the courage and patriotism of the Kurds, and, as it turned out, the Kurds in no way desisted from their rebellion.

Given the continued unrest in Kurdistan, the Qajar king devised a plan to do away with Reza Qoli Khan. Knowing that he had an eye problem, the king invited him to go to Tehran to be treated by his personal physician. There, according to family accounts, "He was given the final medication in a cup of Turkish coffee." Meanwhile, the intentions of the king had reached Kurdistan, and my great-great-grandmother Princess Tuba Khanom immediately left the province. Determined to intervene to save her husband from death, "She rode on horseback through the night with her son, a few attendants, and a chest full of jewelry to persuade the king to save her beloved husband. She arrived too late and the damage was done." Princess Tuba Khanom and my great-grandfather, Abol Hassan, who was just seven years old, were received at the palace and would live under the king's protection for life.[24]

Abol Hassan Ardalan, therefore, grew up in the Qajar Court

and also married a Qajar princess. Later appointed commerce minister, he would often take his entire family, including the babies and their nursemaids, along with him on his travels. The family rode in covered wagons, while Abol Hassan rode his horse so as to better hunt for the wild game that he would provide to his entourage.

Among Abol Hassan's eight children was my paternal grandfather, Abbas. Once grandfather Abbas was appointed economic attaché at the Iranian Embassy in Washington, D.C., he and his family moved to America. They arrived in 1947 first by way of Iraq, then England, and finally on the USS *Aquitania* to Montreal, Canada. Abbas's primary role was to negotiate the U.S. Marshall Plan loans to Iran and to promote commercial exports and imports, strengthening the economic ties between the two countries.

Davar's father's paternal grandfather, Abol Hassan Ardalan, son of the Qajar princess Tuba Khanom, circa the 1910s. (Photograph Pari Ardalan Malek)

Abbas, his wife, Mani joone, their daughter, Pari, and my father lived on Livingston Street near Chevy Chase Circle. My father loved baseball and spent hours listening to adventure serials such as *The Lone Ranger* and *The Shadow* on the radio. He was also an avid Eagle Scout at the St. Albans School, with a collection of merit badges. But his true love was art. Several Ardalan uncles had studied painting under the great Iranian master Kamal-ol-Molk. From an early age, my father was an award-winning student at the Corcoran College of Art and Design. Traveling back and forth to class in Washington, D.C., he dreamed of one day being an artist.

Another favored aspect of my father's early life was a weekly open house at Mohammad Nemazee's home. Whereas my father was quite young, his sister especially remembers meeting my grandmother Helen and her seven children there for the first time. The gathering that took place there every Noruz was always special. Not only did Mr. Nemazee lay out the most beautiful spread for the Persian New Year, but each woman in attendance received gifts—very expensive, latest-style purses or scarves.

In 1952, my grandfather Abbas moved his family to New Rochelle, New York, because of his new job at the United Nations. As head of Iran's Narcotics Commission to the United Nations, his duties included discouraging the planting of poppy seeds in the countries that produced opium for uses other than medicinal and replacing them with other products.

After graduating from New Rochelle High School, my father was awarded a scholarship to attend Carnegie-Mellon in Pittsburgh, where he studied architecture. Quite talented, he was a natural and enthusiastic about his chosen field. Once his father's tour of duty at the United Nations had concluded and my father was enrolled in college, my paternal grandparents moved back to Tehran, leaving my father on his own. His sister, Pari, was already married by this time and living in Tehran. My father filled his time in college with his passion for architecture and the social calendar of his fraternity. He took any opportunity to flex his creativity, expressing his talent in designs for the college homecoming and spring carnival displays and decorations for his fraternity's house parties.

A FRENCHMAN BY THE NAME OF SAM KISS ARRANGED A BLIND date between my parents in the winter of 1957. Sam Kiss knew my father at Carnegie-Melon, and early in the fall Kiss had checked out the girls at Chatham College where he met my mother. He knew they were both Middle Eastern and thought they would find each other interesting, which they did, hitting it off instantly. As they recalled their childhoods to each other, they each realized that they must have seen the other at Mr. Nemazee's Sunday open houses. It seemed impossible that those same two young children had now fallen in love.

There were other things, too, that they had in common— their Western upbringing combined with their Iranian heritage, their passion for learning, writing, and history. "This is a secret between you and me," my mother wrote my grandmother Helen. "I think I have found the boy I am going to marry."[25] The two were just nineteen years old when they went on their blind date to a dance at Chatham College.

Nader, an extrovert, loved my mother's passionate, emotional, expressive family. The Ardalans were more reserved. They were also a smaller immediate family. My mother was an introvert—the only one in her family of seven siblings and ten half-siblings from her father's second marriage. The Ardalans with their royal lineage and European-influenced upbringing were more formal. Laleh's family was casual by comparison—the tribal ancestry of the Bakhtiaris and the American influence created what was, especially for the time, a unique hybrid. The contrast between Nader's and Laleh's upbringings complemented each of them and brought them closer together.

Longing for the precious treasure of Iran—a longing for the country, itself, which they had each developed in childhood and which extended to include their parents, who were living there—they agreed that once they were done with their education they would give up the comforts of America and return to Iran. Discovering that they shared the same dream may have cemented their love.

My mother would write in her diary: "Dear Diary, as of today, March 19, I love everyone in the world and the world itself. There are so many beauties, if only I could fully appreciate one, I would be happy. I picture myself as some sort of a giver to the race of mankind and particularly IRAN."[26]

My mother was taken aback by her worldly ambitions at age nineteen, thinking herself idealistic and even pompous to have such thoughts. At that moment the love of her life, Nader (or Ned as she called him, and he called her Nell), was on a trip to visit family in Iran in the summer of 1959. Without him, she was beginning to feel helpless. As she listened to Tchaikovsky's

Violin Concerto in her college dorm room, the music drowning out all other thoughts, she felt pain in listening to it instead of feeling the uplifting spirit of the music. She wrote in her diary: "The days pass so quickly. If only one minute of every day could last one minute longer, I could live two lifetimes!" Then quickly recognizing her own state of sorrow and emotional pain, she wrote: "I wonder if I would enjoy it?"

That summer, my father wrote to my mother about his impressions of life in Tehran. For the first time since he was a child, he was in the country, but now as a young man in love. He was captivated by its beauty, which triggered his imagination. The custom at that time, as in Abol Ghassem's home, was to sleep on the roof to avoid the heat that accumulated indoors during hot summer days. Located on a five-thousand-foot plateau, Tehran greets you with a dry climate that turns cool by morning. Summer nights there can be pleasant if you stay outside. Nell had told Nader to expect this and to anticipate the welcoming breezes of the morning air. Nader wrote that it was "cool and starry" just as she had described it. Atop the house where he was staying he could hear the faraway sound of a dogfight, a baby crying, and someone playing an old, scratchy record of a tender Persian love song.

Nader had difficulty sleeping the first night because of his excitement at being back home and seeing his parents. One of the drawbacks of sleeping on the roof is that you must rise early in order to avoid the heat of the sun. By six a.m. it seemed like everyone in Tehran was on the move.

For me, this letter served as a fascinating window into my

father's early impressions of Iranian culture. Among the most memorable sights and sounds that he wrote about to my mother were "the roosters crowing, the rise of the sun, the multitudes of roofs, walls and gardens that could suddenly be seen from the rooftops as the sun lighted the areas; and the most memorable of all, the cry of the fresh fruit peddler peddling his wares in his distinct and inimitable style of song."[27]

He was soon introduced to his extended family, who called early in the morning to see if the *farangi* (foreigner) had arrived. They did not stand on ceremony by calling ahead but rather dropped by to see my father. There were few Iranians abroad in those days, particularly Iranians who had gone to the faraway land of America and then returned for a visit.

My grandfather Abbas and his brothers hunted regularly each week. A favorite Ardalan sport for centuries, it was a great honor for my father when his father and uncles invited him to join them in the special summer hunt for royal partridge, which can only be found high in the mountaintops. He wrote my mother describing what had become almost a rite of passage for him.

The hunting party drove to a little village that rests in the foothills of the Alborz Mountains, north of Tehran. As my father described it in his letter: "Eight would-be hunters, a servant and several mule drivers started off to reach the heights of the very distant mountaintops. These 14,000-foot Alborz mountains can be seen from all parts of Tehran." The humor of the scene got to him as he contrasted this experience, including the initial preparations, with the reactions he had had to the

Davar's paternal grandparents, Farangis ("Mani joone") and Abbas, Tehran. (Photograph Pari Ardalan Malek)

African safari movies he had seen where the *Bawana Koumbah* (or "white man") is packing his equipment "while hundreds of little children are running in and out of the scene. At the time, the whole village is in a general excitement over the white *bawanas* with their long guns, their flashy camping equipment and the numerous boxes of supplies."

Evoking a scene from *Don Quixote* he wrote this description: "The spirit of a forthcoming 'big hunt' seemed to even spread, or I should say, affect the hunters themselves who atop their sad-eyed 'chargers' waved one hand in the air and made the hills resound with their throaty cries. Then off toward the awaiting enemy we rode, as cheering peasants waved us luck and the local dogs leaped and barked at the totally unimpressed 'chargers' who had experienced these petty goings on for, oh, so many times."[28]

Leaving behind the village and its trees, they ascended to barren hills graced with only occasional greenery. On the journey they were accompanied by "the constant jingling, jangling and clanging of the animals' bells" following them for the entire six-hour journey. "It was a constant symphony of bells (R. Kipling would have loved it!). The peaceful concert was maliciously interrupted occasionally by the *bawanas* who took every opportunity possible to yell profanity and loving curses at the ones who seemed most deserving. When the 'roads' (hah!) permitted, super-sonic races were had and it really seemed like the fifth at Churchill Downs when the old boys got going.[29]

"My uncles had undergone this ritual of the hunt for most of their adult lives and, now, sometimes having difficulty just getting out of bed, they would somehow have a surge of energy when it came time for the 'hunt.' There was great rivalry among them as to who would actually see a royal partridge, much less be able to hunt it." He continued: "As usual, or at least I think it to be so, some one always got stuck with a lemon mule who wouldn't go any faster than it felt necessary. This poor soul happened to be my Uncle Nasser Qoli (a member of parliament), who made a picture to remember as he and his mule driver pushed, pulled and coaxed the ever obstinate animal up the hills."

Nader wrote of a donkey path that led to a religious shrine high up in the mountain. Pilgrims traveled on foot, some with bare feet, carrying large plates of food to offer to the people at the shrine. He added: "One thing that really impressed me was the attitude of these people to each other and to us. A friendly hello and a wish for a safe journey greeted us as we passed these people and I know damn well that they really meant it."

What drew his attention to these simple peasant people, traveling this long way up the mountain on foot to seek intercession from the saint buried there, were the women pilgrims, who all wore the chador. It was only in outlying village areas like this that one would see chadored women during the Shah's rule and it surprised my father. "Even if these women were in danger of falling off the cliff, they would cover themselves with their chadors as we passed. Even the smallest female child had one and would be quick to hide her pretty face."[30]

When they were finally able to pick up their shotguns and begin the work they had come to do, they each went to a separate area to await the appearance of the royal partridges, which are rare, large, turkey-sized birds that migrate long distances. As the day dawned and progressed, they were forced to seek shelter because of the burning ultraviolet rays, more powerful at that altitude. My father felt lucky to find a good shelter, but he never saw a royal partridge. His eldest uncle, Amanollah, then seventy, was the only lucky one: "Strong as an ox and who through some strange luck ran into four of these 'prizes' and managed to shoot two."

The rejoicing of the younger uncles at Amanollah's success was spread from one mountaintop to another. The trip back was uneventful as they all looked forward to the feast he would have cooked for them featuring the two royal partridges.

Once back in Tehran, like a dutiful future son-in-law, Nader arranged a meeting with Nell's father, whom he referred to as "the chief." Abol Ghassem's house was halfway between the heart of the city of Tehran and the summer retreat at the base of the Alborz Mountains known as Shemran, where Tehranis flock in the summertime to take in the cool mountain air after the heat of the Tehran summer day. As my father and his father, Abbas, were guided up the stairs to Abol's living room, my father wrote that a huge bundle of living, youthful flesh spied on them and cried out in a ringing voice, "The guests have arrived." It was as if the entire house had suddenly been turned upside down by a troop of ten children, my mother's half-siblings, each of whom emerged from a different nook and cranny. Nader and Abbas stood surrounded, targeted by twenty deep-gazing Bakhtiari eyes. Nader appeased the natives with a box of chewy Bazooka Bubble Gum. "The measly gift," he wrote, "was enough to permit an audience with their chief and what a wonderful chief he was and is."

Abol Ghassem was dressed in white cotton trousers, a short-sleeved white shirt, and an ear-to-ear smile. My father wrote that he immediately felt at home in his company and was greeted with unexpected and warm welcoming hugs and kisses. Abol and Abbas had actually known each other in secondary school. Abbas had also attended Dr. Jordan's American Mission School at the same time as Abol. The two had not seen each other for some forty years. As they spent the evening talking about themselves, there was no chance for Nader to ask for Nell's hand. Abol Ghassem left the next day for Abadan, so my father wrote him a letter asking for his permission to marry my mother.

Both my grandfathers felt that it would be best if my parents waited until they had finished college to get married. In that first meeting, Abol Ghassem had emphasized to Nader the importance of knowledge. In his letter to him, my father did the same, adding that for both my parents, gaining knowledge that led to wisdom was life itself. My father said that both he and my mother felt that the very essence of a "good" life is the total of one's acquired and applied wisdom—wisdom or knowledge not just from books, but also from dialogue with others, human observation, and discovery. He wrote: "Knowledge not only of the atom, but of Adam or man himself, in order to find the Why, the What, and most important of all, the Who behind man's existence on earth."

My father explained that he was aware of a purpose in life and that the key to its attainment lay in the as yet only partially opened book of knowledge. He went on to explain that more than anything else in life he wanted to seek that proverbial truth. "It is because I earnestly believe that only with Laleh by my side that my dreams will materialize that I have asked for our present engagement and future marriage." He ended his letter saying: "I am proud of the prospect of becoming a member of your most wonderful family."[31]

At the end of the summer, my father returned to America and to college in Pittsburgh. He and my mother decided to arrange an engagement party at the Iranian Embassy in Washington,

D.C., where his uncle Dr. Ali Qoli Ardalan served as ambassador to the United States from Iran. My father asked my grandmother Helen if she would make the arrangements since she was visiting Washington at the time.

After the successful event, my father wrote a letter to my grandmother thanking her for her efforts. He added: "I already feel that I am one of your sons—if you will have me—and so I am concerned with your welfare. I want you to know that my home is forever yours, my love with you wherever you go and my thoughts will be of you. You are alongside my very own parents, whom I love and respect. May the Lord be with you."[32] Due to the success of the engagement party, my parents asked grandmother Helen to make their arrangements for a June wedding in Washington, D.C. My grandmother asked her old friend, Mr. Nemazee, if they could hold the wedding at his new home in Potomac, Maryland. He agreed and asked my grandmother to be sure and invite her good friend Supreme Court Justice William O. Douglas to the wedding.

Grandmother Helen, a close friend of Yahya Khan and now partner with him in a rug-weaving business, had met the Douglases in Iran when Yahya Khan had invited them to his village in the Bakhtiari region of Chahar Mahal known as Dastana. They spent one night sleeping in a tent in the mountains with the tribal people. That had been the third visit to this region by Justice Douglas.

Grandmother Helen asked Justice Douglas about his previous visit to the Bakhtiari tribal area in the fertile valley of Shalamzar, the same town where my grandfather Abol Ghassem had found employment as a tutor in 1907 for the nephews of Bibi Mah Begum and Bakhtiari tribal leader Morteza Qoli Khan Samsam. In 1949, Justice Douglas had met with Morteza Qoli Khan, still the Bakhtiari tribal leader, who had remained in Shalamzar living among the tribesmen.[33]

Morteza Qoli Khan Samsam had also been one of the cavalry leaders of the Bakhtiari who in 1909 had helped depose the then ruling Qajar monarch and restore the 1906 Constitution. The Bakhtiaris were able to finance their assault to save the constitution because of the revenues they had received from the recently discovered oil fields on their land in Solomon's Mosque. This, in turn, allowed the 1906 Constitution, which had limited the power of the monarchy, to thrive. It had also given rise to a legislative body that represented many of Iran's provinces.

When they met, Morteza Qoli Khan Samsam described to Justice Douglas how he and his father and uncles marched into Tehran. "As Morteza Qoli Khan finished he raised a clenched fist and said, 'That was a proud day for Persia. That day we saved liberty and independence for our people. Now our people have a forum where they can complain even against their rulers, where they can pass laws that will improve their conditions.'"[34]

Sitting in the mountains, the justice talked to my grandmother about his early years growing up in Yakima, Washington. It turned out that one of his teachers, Frances Galloway, was a good friend of my American great-grandparents and was born in Weiser, Idaho, of a pioneer family.

When my grandmother invited Justice Douglas to be a witness at my parents' wedding, he agreed joyfully to bear witness to

Davar's parents, Laleh (Mary Nell) and Nader (*at right*), at their wedding in Mr. Nemazee's home in Potomac, Maryland, June 6, 1960, with Helen and Mr. Nemazee. (From the Laleh Bakhtiar Collection of Family Photographs)

the union of my mother, a Bakhtiari raised in America, and my father, a Kurd who spent the bulk of his life in America.

My parents were married on June 6, 1960, in a Persian wedding ceremony. Mr. Nemazee's new home had a beautiful garden and a swimming pool edged with flowers. The food was a delicious, traditional Persian feast and the guests—Americans and Iranians—could not pull themselves away from the buffet table. All seven of grandmother Helen's children, their spouses, and grandchildren were present along with my father's cousins. In the midst was Supreme Court Justice William O. Douglas, who signed my parents' wedding certificate as a witness.

My grandfather Abol Ghassem could not attend, even if it was the first time since 1945 that all of his and Helen's children were able to be together. My father's parents, Abbas and Mani joone, were also unable to make the long journey to the wedding. The sheer numbers of the Bakhtiar family made up for whatever lack there was in Ardalans. My father was officially embraced into the family.

After their honeymoon in upstate New York, they returned to Pittsburgh for my father to finish his last year at Carnegie. In the summer of 1962, Laleh and Nader moved to San Francisco where my grandmother Helen lived and where my father planned to pursue his career in architecture.

· 4 ·

My Childhood

When my father was renovating our Tehran home, he added a series of barrel vaults to the ceiling, similar to what he had seen in his grandmother Khanoom Maman's home. Also inspired at the time by the great international architect Louis I. Kahn, who had placed dramatic barrel vaults at the Kimbell Art Museum in Fort Worth, my father used Kahn–style oak paneled doors in each room, merging them with the *kolange*'s traditional stucco arches. This integration of modern innovations and traditional design would later become a trademark of his work.

In our newly renovated home, my parents had finally set down roots completing their family of five. On the first floor was the social hub, with the living rooms that opened onto each other through arched entryways, a double-sided fireplace in the dining room, and a kitchen and a large patio porch area that extended along the width of the house. Overlooking the back-

The author's family: father, Nader; sister, Mani; Iran Davar; brother, Karim; and mother, Laleh, in the courtyard outside their house, Tehran, 1971. (From the Laleh Bakhtiar Collection of Family Photographs)

yard was a walled garden, as in many Iranian homes, with a pool, fruit trees, and dramatic lighting. My father went a step further, paving the whole yard in white marble tile. For us children he built a custom-made stucco playhouse, which on one side featured ascending stairs that ended at the top of a slide. Below the slide and stairs was an arched space to play in, with its own niche just like the ones inside the house. We spent hours playing there as well as swimming in the pool.

On the second floor were four bedrooms and one bathroom for the children and guests. The bathroom had white marble tile on the floor and walls. From the bedroom there was a balcony that overlooked the yard. The third floor was our parents' domain. It contained a bedroom, a library, a prayer room, dressing room, bathroom, and a small outdoor patio. The stair landing between the second and third floors was our favorite indoor place to hang out; the view from it, framed by a huge picture window, was of the entire street below, including the neighbors' homes.

As a young child in Tehran, my father made many visits to his grandmother's home. She lived in a similar *kolange* to ours but in the older section of Tehran. The approach to her house was through a series of winding, narrow alleyways, which had open streams of wastewater or *jubes* running down the middle. Khanoom Maman had several rooms in a traditional home with a basement, where it was cooler. As a little boy, my father would step down into the yard and step down again into the cellar. The cellar was just a small room made of crude brick and mortar, perfect for maintaining a cool temperature.[1]

When he returned to Tehran in the summer of 1957, my father visited his grandmother's house again. The whole space was so absolutely of another lifetime or generation that he immediately fell in love with it. On the floor was a large Kerman rug and various smaller ones scattered on top. Huge cushions and pillows were neatly arranged in a very hospitable way—it was almost as if they were grouped in good conversation with one another. There was an old, ornate water pipe (*ghaylun*) and next to it was a beautiful silver samovar with a set of Iranian teacups and holders, also of silver. The room smelled of sweet cantaloupes and melons. As he entered the room he remembers hearing the "hush" of the bamboo curtains behind him that kept out the flies.

In later life when my father visited his grandmother, he remembers her smile through the miles of her troubled life and wrinkles. Her table was full of fruit and sherbet and choice mouthwatering tidbits and her heart and soul yearned to please her loved ones. She worshiped God, made offerings to the needy, and epitomized the hard, rock core of the Iranian people.

Years later, my father would take us to see Khanoom Maman during one of our Noruz family visits. She was old, frail, and weary but looked like an angel with her white hair, big eyeglasses, and expressive smile.

MY PARENTS LOVED THE TRADITION OF HOSTING THE ARDALAN *doreh*, or family gathering. Iranian hospitality is legendary; in fact, the *Shahnameh* refers to the feet of guests being washed with musk and rose water. Although they did not go to that extreme, my parents knew that the first family gathering they hosted would be a test to see if they could in fact extend Iranian–style hospitality. My father had just redesigned our home with built-in brick furniture, lots of colorful cushions, Kashmiri wall hangings, Persian pottery, Bakhtiari carpets, our precious Eames chair, and Pier One Japanese lanterns he and my mother had brought with them from San Francisco.

The Ardalan family gathering took place in the summertime when the evening was just cool enough and guests could sit in the courtyard next to the pool and fountains. My father had designed the pool's fountains to resemble the ones at Alhambra in Spain. Small tables with white tablecloths and chairs were set up in the backyard so that family members could play cards and socialize. As children, we were not allowed to participate in the party, though we did look down from the balcony to survey the fantastic scene.

My mother made six deboned turkeys with stuffing and the remainder of the dinner table was laden with eggplant, tomato, onion-and-bread-crumb casserole, and delicious *tahchin,* or rice cooked with chicken, yogurt, and saffron. There was also *Albaloo Polo,* rice cooked with chicken and sour cherries; *khoresh gormeh sabzi,* a lamb stew cooked with seven kinds of greens; two huge platters of fresh fruit; angel food cake with white icing and crushed pineapple; mixed nuts, raisins, and other delights both American and Persian. This was exactly the kind of dinner party Mama Helen thrived on. She loved to socialize and find out the latest family news. For her part, Helen contributed an American dish—her favorite Harvard beets with sweet-and-sour sauce.

Most of the women attending the *doreh* were very fashion-conscious. My mother remembers many conversations about Charles Jourdan shoes and whether or not to wear a mini or maxi dress. Among the most fashionable guests was my paternal grandmother, Mani joone, whose sense of style and elegance was truly one of a kind.

These were our family's happiest times as our parents settled into their lives and work in Tehran and we learned to appreciate the hospitality of Iranians. Our lives in Iran were marked by modern, Western notions of women's equality and importance, an insistence that we develop a strong command of the English language, and a directive from our parents that we must focus on our education. The experiment was working.

WHEN THEIR MUTUAL FRIEND, THE ISLAMIC SCHOLAR SEYYED Hossein Nasr, told my mother and father that the University of Chicago Press was looking for an Iranian architect to write a book about Persian architecture, it was as if destiny had taken both their hands. Dr. Nasr approached my father first and he joyously accepted. My father would later ask my mother to cowrite it with him. Each winter, spring, and summer vacation for several years in the late 1960s and early 1970s we would travel to a different part of Iran as they researched their book.

By completing *The Sense of Unity: The Sufi Tradition in Persian Architecture*, my parents combined their two passions: architectural philosophy (my father) and Sufism (my mother). The book was intended as a gift to the Shah of Iran, who planned to visit the University of Chicago to inaugurate its new Middle East Center, erected in part thanks to contributions by the Shah.[2]

Traveling with my parents to visit Iran's architectural wonders, I will never forget the sense of awe and appreciation they brought to the ancient Zoroastrian fire temple at Takht-e Sulayman (Solomon's Throne). Dating from 500 BC, it was situated in northwestern Iran, part of a volcanic mountain region, at the top of an eight-thousand-foot mountain near Lake Urumiyah. Solomon's Throne is one of the sacred places of Iran that was home

Iran Davar waving to her family atop the mounds of a bazaar on their journey through Iran's Salt Desert, 1972. (Photograph by Nader Ardalan)

to a community of magi or Zoroastrian priests. Part of the throne area was the fire temple, devoted to warriors and Shahs during the Zoroastrian pre-Islamic era, and the fire is believed to have been lit from oil in the region.

In front of the fire temple is a great, seemingly fathomless lake—two hundred feet deep—filled with the overflowing limestone-calcinated water of a warm spring. At first, my parents were fearful of jumping into this dark, foreboding water, but not my sister and I. We both dove in and, thanks to the water's calcium-sulfur composition, we floated weightlessly on the surface.

We also explored Solomon's Prison, a deep crater to the west of the lake. All that remained was a crater above which is a cone-shaped hill that surrounds the hollow shaft dropping down hundreds of feet. I wondered if any prisoner ever survived! Also on this site are Solomon's Stable and the Throne of Bilqis, who was known in the Bible as the queen of Sheba. Solomon's Throne is said to be the place where many Shahs were crowned. There was also a temple to the goddess Anahita there, the goddess of water and patroness of women.

While that visit had been exciting, the most memorable trip during our time in Iran was a two-week voyage around the Great Salt Desert, *Kavir Namak,* in southeastern Iran. We had a Land Rover that seated seven—our driver and my father and mother in front, our maid Shamsi, my sister, brother, and I in the backseat sitting across from one another. We all wore cowboy hats that my parents had bought in Fort Worth, Texas, where they had gone on one of their trips abroad to see the Kimbell Art Museum, designed by Louis I. Kahn.

Our first stop was the historic town of Nain, which in ancient times was surrounded by a four-thousand-foot citadel wall, now in ruins. Nain is most famous for its carpets, so my parents found a guide to take us to a weaving studio, where, in a small, dark mud-brick room filled with two large looms, my sister and I saw girls our age weaving. They would chant: "two blue knots, add two red, a blue in between, begin with a red, then switch to dark blue, and each with two pairs." From sunrise to sunset they worked in this tiny, almost airless space, chanting the pattern in rhyme. We had seen some of their hand-woven carpets in the bazaar. No matter how beautiful the carpets were, I knew they couldn't be worth the cost of human life.

We left Nain late in the afternoon, after dark, heading toward Natanz when suddenly the wind swept up a dust storm. The road was filled with sand swirling in front of us. Using our headlights to illuminate the sand-strewn road, we saw what looked like waves. It was as if each grain of sand had remembered when it had been under the sea and learned to move like water.

Once the dust storm passed, we stopped just short of Natanz to stretch our legs. As I got out of the Land Rover, I looked up to find millions and billions of stars. As a matter of fact, stars stretched from horizon to horizon, a road map to ancient times. Each of these little towns and villages in central Iran was an oasis in the desert, created from a small body of water and trees. After miles of sand, palm trees would just appear and with them adobe-style low-rise buildings would loom in the distance. Each small town had a mosque, which could be spotted even from far away by its dome and minaret. Each town had a little inn called a *caravanserai*, where we would stay; though very modest, they were also authentic. The inns were part of a system of guest houses that had been built years earlier along the Silk Road, within a day's travel of each other. They were recently upgraded by the Ministry of Tourism, which changed their name to *Jalbeh Sayyahan,* translated as "Enticing the Tourist." In each town, we would wake up to the sound of roosters and hear the call to prayer from the minaret.

We moved on to Isfahan where our parents thought it would be exciting to stroll through the town and visit the bazaar together. My grandmother Helen had lived in Isfahan for several years when she had worked for Point Four, traveling through the same outlying villages we were passing on our journey through Iran. We began at the Friday Mosque, which had been built over

The Isfahan Friday Mosque showing the "brick on brick" architecture. (Photograph Jay R. Crook, August 1967)

many generations. I had seen mosques before, but never one as stark as this. In my father's eyes, it was the most beautiful and truthful building in Iran, because it was an elegant construction of only one material—brick. Without anything to hide the perfect geometry of the structure, my father deemed it "pure architecture," going on to note the way the columns and domes caught the light and refracted it onto the building.

As my parents went off to measure the mosque, my sister, brother, and I listened to the guide, who told us that the mosque—the word means "place of prostration"—plays a central role in the life of the community. Mosques, he said, belong to the people and the person the people choose to run them. They are open to everyone in the town, the poor or the rich, the farmer or the merchant. He told us that in Iranian history, the mosque was not only a religious center, but the community's education center as well.

We walked through the bazaar, taking in its myriad sights and sounds. Each section was devoted to a particular craft or product, such as carpets, jewelry, pottery, copper work, leather, spices, and cloth. The vendors' stalls were aligned in rows across from each other, traversed by a hallway with high vaulted domes, at the top of which were openings where the sun filtered through. Each section was divided by a grand dome. Later my father explained that the bazaar was the model upon which Western malls were based.

When we reached the coppersmiths' bazaar, we heard hammers pounding on copper trays, etching out designs. My mother told me that the poet Jalal al-Din Rumi was once walking in the bazaar in Konya, Turkey, and heard these rhythms and beats. Overtaken by an inspiration or intoxication, he was driven to a state of ecstasy.

We felt the tempo and the musical character of the bazaar. It went something like coppersmith shop, coppersmith shop, repeated many times as a serial rhythm, then a shrine with a tank of water and a cup beside it as an interval. Then, once again, coppersmith shop, coppersmith shop, and, then, huge wooden doors opening up into a *caravanserai*, where rugs were piled fifteen high as another interval. It had a rhythm, much as the bazaar was itself like an open composition.

I had asked my mother why the shrine with the tank of water and cup had bits of cloth or locks fastened around its metal grilles. She said that water, the essence of life, plays an important role in Iranian history. The shrine is called a *saqqa khaneh* or "place of the water-bearer." Often shaped like a mosque in miniature form and carved out of brass, a *saqqa khaneh* has a cup attached to it so passersby can drink from its clean water. It is endowed by a generous patron and maintained by the leader of the nearby nosque as a religious obligation so no one will go thirsty. Along a bazaar route or at the side of any street, you could find clean drinking water provided in memory of the third Shi'ite imam, Imam Hossein, who had been denied access to water. She quoted a line from the famous Shiraz poet Hafez, who said: "What the souls of thy lovers suffer at the hands of separation, / None has experienced in the world save the thirsty ones of Karbala."

She added that the fountains are often beautifully carved out of metal or stone in circular forms with domes and minarets on top, which are symbolic of the tomb of Imam Hossein in Karbala. The carved hands above the place of water symbolize the hands of Imam Hossein's uncle, Abbas, whose arms were cut off as he tried to reach the Euphrates to bring water to Imam Hossein. It also symbolizes the five fingers, known as the five people or the Five Holy Ones of Shias: the Prophet, his daughter, Fatima, his son-in-law and cousin, Ali, and their first two children, Hasan and Hossein.

The bits of cloth or locks tied around the shrine's metal grilles or even around branches of a tree outside the shrine show evidence of a pilgrimage as well as an outward sign of the pilgrim's prayer. People often travel great distances to ask for favors from Imam Hossein or any other saint in whose name the *saqqa khaneh* is endowed.

The last steps of the Isfahan bazaar opened onto the world's largest walled public plaza, known as *Maydan-i-Naghsh e Jahan,* "the Plan of the World Square," where polo games were once held. Surrounding the grand sixteenth-century square is a palace gateway, the Ali Qapu. The small mosque of Shaykh Lotfallah is on the left, and straight ahead is the main mosque of the city, Masjid-i Shah, now called the Imam's Mosque. It was breathtaking to leave the narrow confines of the bazaar and open up onto a great square, open to the sky. After moving through the stalls of the bazaar, we followed a meandering dark path that culminated in an open plaza in front of the mosques, where mirrorlike pools of water greeted us—and, in earlier times, the weary traveler, who could reflect on the image of the domes above him. These pools provided a place for ablution prior to prayer. My father explained that the pedestrian's transition from dark to light was deliberately planned to create awe in the beholder, to strengthen his spiritual ties.

Yet it was not only the open space that caught our attention, but also the beautiful coffee-colored tiles visible on the Shaykh Lotfallah and the blue glazed *haft-rangi* faience of the Masjid-i Shah. Even at a considerable distance, both dazzled your eyes with their turquoise color, geometric pattern, stylized calligraphy, and repeating rhythm.

As we walked toward the Shaykh Lotfallah mosque, my mother told us about Bahram Gur, one of the kings of the *Shah-nameh* whose life was elaborated on in many other Persian narratives, including one called *The Seven Portraits* (*Haft Paykar*). In this long, mystical poem, the poet Nizami describes Bahram Gur building seven palaces of seven different colors for his seven wives. It was from this story that my parents developed the concept of color in *The Sense of Unity*, noting that the great painter Matisse had intimated: "The Persians are my teachers." Nizami explains how in the traditional world, everything on earth has a correspondence in the heavens, so that the seven colors correspond to the seven days of the week and the seven planets visible to the naked eye.

From Isfahan we traveled on to Kashan. On the outskirts of the city sat the Garden of Fin, where we gazed at the mountain springwater carried by subterranean aqueducts called *ganats* that flowed along in brick-lined paths. Given the climate of Iran, water plays a vital role. Cities were built near mountains, and the

Kashan's famous Garden of Fin, looking out from the pavilion down a garden waterway. (Photograph Jay R. Crook, August 1967)

life-generating force of water is considered a treasure. Built around water, the garden is the most important place in the life of Iranians. If someone does not have his or her own garden, they must at least have a garden carpet inside the home to take the place of the missing garden and a courtyard outside with a small pool or fountain of water.

One section of *The Sense of Unity* explores how a garden reflects a sense of place. A sense of place, as my parents defined it, consists of two elements: a container and what it contains. The container—meaning, what *surrounds*—was in Kashan the wall that surrounds the garden. Inside the wall is the contained—the inner space where trees and flowers are laid out in geometric compartments fed by waterways that flow along the same grid. In the middle is a pavilion, which is often open on all sides to the garden. The sense of joy and wonder of a beautiful Persian garden engulfs the senses by being first hidden then revealed, and through the use of numbers, geometry, color, and substance.[3]

The garden complement, as I learned from my parents, is the courtyard, such as the one we had in our home in Tehran. The courtyard wall protects the home's inner space and lends it privacy. When the center of the courtyard is a pool of water rather than a building, a particular sense of unity is achieved. A pool of water can be enclosed by the shape of the courtyard's walls in such a way as to reduce tension from the outside world, serving as a place of safety, serenity, and contemplation.[4]

The wall acts as the container and the garden or courtyard as that which is contained. My parents wrote that metaphorically you can see the container as the self, and the contained as the soul. Looking inward, one reflects on the inner beauty created by the Divine, looking outward, on the earthly beauty of nature.

NEXT WE TOURED THE BOROUJERDI HOUSE IN KASHAN, WHICH is famous for its wind towers. The house's roof is covered with openings to catch the wind in whatever direction it moves. Through the wind tower, air and light are carried down through the house all the way into the basement area, maintaining a cool temperature even in the hot desert climate. This architectural adaptation to Iran's climate had a strong influence on my father's work, as well as that of others who design in a manner sensitive to natural energy and sustainability.

We heard from the hotel manager that the best time to visit Kashan and its surrounding areas was in May because then, in the village of Ghamsar, five hundred tons of roses are grown, distilled, and made into rose water and rose oil. The smell of roses enchants for miles around.

The most difficult part of the trip occurred after we left Kashan destined for Mashhad, which is at the eastern edge of the Great Salt Desert. On the journey, travelers cannot count on passing any towns, nor find water or gasoline. When we finally arrived outside the first town of Tabas, we were dusty, tired, and dehydrated. We stopped the car at the top of a hill overlooking the town and got out. The earth was solid, hard, and dry. Suddenly, a few feet in front of us, we saw a desert flower—a testimony to life—pushing its way through the parched ground, a sight I have never forgotten. Tabas had a beautiful garden and I vividly remember seeing a pelican in it. It was so refreshing to come upon this oasis after our dusty and dry trip through the desert. Known as a city filled with flowers, we were not to be disappointed but instead of the trees we were used to seeing, here the garden was filled with tall date palm trees.

Next we visited three towns where great Iranian poets once lived. Neishabour held the tombs of Omar Khayyam, whose *Rubaiyat* was made famous by Edward Fitzgerald, and Farid al-Din Attar, who wrote the long mystical poem *The Conference of the Birds* (*Mantiqal-Tayr*). Then we traveled to Tus to visit the tomb of Ferdowsi, the poet of the *Shahnameh*. Each of these famous poets has a beautiful mausoleum, entered via a garden, with a covered gazebo structure and a statue. Famous lines and quotes from their poems are carved into stone walls. Tus was also the birthplace of the famous Muslim theologian Muhammad al-Ghazzali, who played much the same role in the Islamic world as Saint Thomas Aquinas had played in the Christian world. I remember it as yet another brick-on-brick building with a beautiful dome in the center.

Mashhad and the shrine of the eighth Shia imam, Imam Reza, was next on our trip.[5] The shrine is a place of Shia pilgrimage throughout the year, especially during the Noruz holidays. Pilgrims circumambulate the shrine seven times, while chanting prayers and tying wishes on the metal grilles. For those who cannot go to Mecca, Mashhad is the second highest place of religious importance in Iran. After performing the pilgrimage, we noticed another domed structure in the same complex, which we were told was the tomb of Gawhar Shad, the wife of Shah Rukh, and a great patron of architecture. Shah Rukh built the mosque complex in honor of his wife. It includes a school for theological students and a site for daily prayers in Mashhad.

We left the desert area outside of Mashhad and took the northern route back to Tehran through the great northern forest of Iran that overlooks the Caspian Sea. Here we found the northern slopes of the Alborz Mountains and the lowlands that surround them and lead to the sea. The slopes held a dense forest while the lowlands were filled with hundreds of rivers and streams. We found tall forest trees, gurgling water streams, and green hills very different from what we had just recently seen in the desert. The flourishing villages, orchards, cultivated fields, and meadows where tea and rice were grown by the local people were ample evidence of the availability of water. The weather was also different; instead of hot and dry, it was humid. The sound of crickets chirping at night could be heard for miles around.

AT THE END OF OUR TRIP, WE FINALLY REACHED THE CASPIAN Sea, the largest landlocked body of water in the world and the source of the famous Iranian caviar. The sea is surrounded by citrus orchards and rice fields until, inching closer to Tehran, you see the beautiful Mount Damavand, a cosmic mountain to the Iranian people. Seeing it as our landmark and point of direction, we knew that we were almost home. Along the route up Mount Damavand there are many streams and riverbeds. It is an Iranian tradition to place wooden platforms over the rushing waters there, spread a carpet, sit down, and enjoy a cup of tea from a samovar, while watching the water flowing by. I remember us children having a wonderful time climbing on the rocks, laughing, screaming, and trying not to get wet. We spent many family picnics along the riverbeds in this way. Many small restaurants have been created along the route to provide this classic interaction of humans and nature.

Once back in Tehran, my parents continued to research and then began to write *The Sense of Unity*. At the same time, my father's career began to take off. In a period of just a few years he helped design and supervise the construction of the Sports

Complex for the 1974 Asian Games in Tehran, the Bu Ali Sina University in Hamadan, Iran, and the Center of Creative Arts and Iranian Center for Management Studies (affiliated with the Harvard Business School) in Tehran. He was featured in *National Geographic* and *Newsweek*. It was perhaps a portent of things to come that my father was quoted in the *Newsweek* article of 1975: "The future of Iran could be something wonderful or utterly cataclysmic. It depends upon the leadership to show the way."

Mysteries of Life Unfold

F or the Noruz holidays of 1974 we traveled along with Islamic philosopher Seyyed Hossein Nasr and his family to Greece and Egypt. I was almost ten, my sister, Mani, was twelve, and my brother, Karim, was six. In Greece, Dr. Nasr wanted us to see the Delphi Oracle, a sacred place where in ancient times people came for predictions of the future. We traveled a hundred miles north of Athens to reach the temple. The Oracle of Apollo was also there, a symbol of the unity of all Greek religions. Ancient Greeks believed that this site was the center of the universe, much like the Kabah in Mecca, which is the center of the world for Muslims.

For me, it was a fantastic journey. Walking amid the ruins, listening to Dr. Nasr and my parents recount the myths and legends of the ruins, I imagined what it must have been like to have lived in ancient Greece. Was it fate or will that had taken us there? my father wondered. The temple had drawn Alexander the Great and many since and will continue to draw those on a mystical quest.

From there we traveled to Cairo, Egypt. One day we sailed down the Nile to the ancient city of Luxor in traditional dhows and sailed to the Valleys of the Kings and Queens, witnessing breathtaking architectural treasures. Here was an entire city of the dead, not just a graveyard, but tombs of ancient kings on the West bank of the Nile. In the Valley of the Queens we saw that children had been buried as well. The stories of their lives were told through beautiful paintings on the walls dating back more than three thousand years.

We returned via the Nile in the late afternoon to our hotel. Sitting on the veranda, looking across the riverbanks, we were thrilled with the day's excursion and the mint tea and cake we ate as part of my tenth birthday celebration. Leisurely looking through an English newsmagazine, we learned that Louis I. Kahn had died. I remember my father shouting "What?" and abruptly leaving the table. None of us followed him as we sensed he needed to be alone. On that day, my father came to the realization that he must continue to be inspired by the ways of this brilliant man from that point forward.

Just the year before, Lou Kahn and Kenzo Tange of Japan had been commissioned by Empress Farah—the wife of the Shah—to design a master plan for a new city center in Abbasabad, Tehran. Lou, in turn, asked my father to join them as their Iranian associate architect. It was on one of these architectural excursions to the site that Kahn told my father he should travel to the Valleys of the Kings and Queens in Luxor in order to truly understand the concept of a sense of place that he had envisioned for the Abbasabad design. Kahn had been transformed by his own trip to Egypt early in his career.

My parents were lost in grief for the rest of our trip, but for me, there were still many curiosities to unravel. As we continued our journey and wandered from one tomb and museum to the other, I continued to be awestruck by everything that surrounded me. Of particular fascination were the magical images of a cowlike goddess—Hathor, the goddess of love, music, and dance. She was often depicted shaking a rattlelike instrument known as a sistrum. My mother had told me that Hathor symbolized rebirth and happiness. She reminded me of the story of the female heroine of the *Shahnameh*.

Both my father and my mother had dreams about Kahn after his death. In my father's dream he was to defend a scheme of Lou Kahn's before the empress of Iran. It seemed like the building had a tail. In the dream my father suddenly looked and saw the shape to be a 1. He then realized that the building's form was a 1, which must be defended before Her Majesty as an example of the concept of unity.

My mother said she learned three things from her own dream, in which she was locking up her silver open-heart watch in a suitcase. (It is called an open-heart watch because all of the mechanisms of the watch are visible.). From this dream she learned first, she was telling herself to move inward; second, with the feeling of being completely lost and disoriented, she knew that she was ready to be guided; and, third, meeting a very gentle person in her dream was a reflection of her friendship with Lou Kahn.

On their next trip to America, they went to his grave site and then made a pilgrimage to as many of his buildings as they could. They visited Mrs. Kahn in Philadelphia, who told them that when Lou was three years old and living in Estonia, he walked by the living room fireplace where there were burning coals. He saw the coals were losing their red color and turning blue. Wanting to save the redness, he picked up a coal and then dropped it after being burned. The coal fell on his pinafore (it was a custom for young boys to wear them), which caught on fire. The flames consuming him, he held his hands over his eyes, palms out, so that his eyes were saved even as his face and hands burned.

Kahn had been a wrestler, like my grandfather Abol Ghassem. He loved *One Thousand and One Nights* as translated by Richard Burton, from which might have come his love of the East. He also slept very little. My parents both remarked how strange it was that someone's death can bring them nearer to you.

It was not surprising to me that my father would have found and loved such an archetype. My surprise was with how deeply my mother felt toward him. When my father told me what Lou Kahn had said to him after meeting my mother, I understood: "I remember the face of your wife well. Her name was that of a flower and her eyes were full of wonder. She is a receptacle of spiritual light. No greater reward than this could anyone wish for."[1]

SOMEONE ONCE ASKED A SUFI THE DIFFERENCE BETWEEN HER and a Muslim. The Sufi answered: You can say that a Muslim works from nine to five acknowledging the Oneness of God and prophethood of Muhammad, praying five times a day, fasting during the month of Ramadan, giving charitably, and going on the pilgrimage to Mecca at least once in her lifetime. A Sufi is a Muslim who works overtime with extra prayers, extra fasting, and concentration on the remembrance of God.[2]

Through researching and writing *The Sense of Unity: The Sufi Tradition in Persian Architecture,* my father had connected with the creative spirit of his Iranian ancestors. He found this connection in the traditional architecture of the Sufi masters. These structures were built by artisans and craftsmen who were members of guilds organized by the masters. As he was already immersed in the universal creative process and felt he had been naturally given a great gift, he was conscious of not wanting to join any group that might affect his creativity and possibly even take the gift away from him. In some ways, my father was willing to immerse himself in this world while my mother was leaning toward detaching herself from it.

On the other hand, from everything my father and mother read and heard about Sufism, they had realized that the great Sufi masters as well as their artisans not only practiced the Sufi way as part of their personal lives but that their creative acts were made possible by their transformed selves. The words of the Sufi Rumi[3] resonated with them when he said:

Twas a fair orchard, full of trees and fruit
And vines of greenery. A Sufi there
Sat with eyes closed, his head upon his knee.

Sunk deep in meditation mystical.

"Why," asked another, "Do you not behold

These Signs of God the Merciful displayed

Around you, which he bids us contemplate?"

"The Signs," he answered, "I behold within;

Without is nothing but symbols of the Signs."[4]

Another famous Sufi wrote: "The visible world was made to correspond to the world invisible and there is nothing in this world but is a symbol of something in that other world."[5]

My mother wanted to transform her inner world so that if God were to give of His grace she herself would be able to give birth to her "self." That is, her very self was her work of art. My father, on the other hand, concentrated his creative energies on transforming materials in the external world into works of art. The dichotomy was like the famous exchange in Iranian history between a philosopher and a mystic. After their first meeting, the philosopher said: "What I know, he sees," and the mystic said: "What I see, he knows." My mother began to search for what he saw while my father began to search for what she knew. She chose the way of mystical spirituality, centering on the spirit, the masculine principle, while he chose what he called sensual spirituality, stressing the soul, the feminine principle.[6] They both agreed that both ways were possible; each wanted to follow the path to where they felt they were being directed.

I was somewhere in the middle. While I did not fully understand their philosophical discussions, I could sense the family oneness was somehow in jeopardy. I emulated my father and shared many traits with him, like his passion for exploring the unknown and his creativity; at the same time, my mother was and has always been there for me, whereas my father's work often took him away. Because of her devotion and love for me, I had developed an attachment so deep it was as if we shared the same heart and soul.

AFTER THE PUBLICATION OF *THE SENSE OF UNITY* IN 1973, IT became a textbook for universities, as it was the first book to discuss the Sufi presence in Persian architecture. My mother was asked by the Thames and Hudson publishers to write about Sufism. She wrote *Sufi: Expressions of the Mystic Quest,* one of the first books in English introducing the Western world to Sufism. Somehow through the experience of researching Sufism in Iran, she had fallen in love with the meaning behind the form.[7]

On one of his travels, my father was to visit the offices of Thames and Hudson and from there he wrote my mother: "Dear Laleh Dearest: Your magic spell is everywhere. The people of Thames and Hudson have been fully captured by your profound innocence and I was moved to see the commitment that they feel to your work. More than many other works in hand, do they feel the resonance of this creative act. Love, Nader"[8]

In 1975 my father was commissioned to write another book, this time on the history of the Kabah in Mecca, to be given as a gift to the king of Saudi Arabia; he had ordered an extension to the main mosque in Mecca that surrounds the cubelike building called the Kabah where millions of Muslim pilgrims gather annually to perform the *hajj*, or pilgrimage. Originally built by Adam, according to Muslim belief, and then destroyed in the great flood at the time of Noah, it was rebuilt by Abraham and his son Ishmael. Pilgrims circumambulate the Kabah. My father first went to Mecca alone to meet the sponsors of the book, and later my mother went to complete the research.[9]

For my father, the most fascinating aspect of visiting Mecca was shedding his Western clothes and putting on the sacred dress of the Visitation. First he was given a plastic bag containing the clothes he was to wear—terry cloth material cut into two rectangles of unstitched cloth, and sandals. When he was alone in his hotel room, he also took off his watch, glasses, and throne-verse medallion (which protects against the evil eye), before putting on the sacred dress. He wrote: " I looked into the mirror and saw a man with a timeless appearance."[10]

Many Muslims—rich or poor, black or white, old or young—have said that the moment when they are asked to wear the white cloth, making it impossible to distinguish one from another, is their most humbling preparation for the Day of Judgment, when it is believed everyone will appear in this form.

MY FATHER'S CAREER CONTINUED TO EXPAND AND HIS TRIPS abroad increased, while my mother would spend the next four years enduring a series of losses that would test her inner strength. In 1971, my grandfather, in spite of his claim to live forever, became gravely ill.

My uncle Jamshid, his oldest son, who would inherit the mantle of the patriarch, wrote: "You came into a life that was full of hardships and despair. You fought insurmountable odds. You beat all of them: the environment, the money, the pride, the schools, the countless battles with poverty. Yes, you, Baba, beat all of them and became what you are. You have proven to yourself and to thousands and thousands of others that you are a man to be remembered for your devotion to love and duty. Your memory is our guiding inspiration. . . . This impulse to create, to move, to rise, to live, I am sure, has been genetically implanted in my inter-cellular realm."

Perhaps Uncle Jamshid was referring to one of the proudest times for my grandparents and indeed for all of my mother's family, when he had been selected the first Iranian All-American football player in 1957 at the University of Virginia. He appeared in *Look* magazine and on *The Perry Como Show* in New York as well as on the *To Tell the Truth* television show. He was also honored at the Washington, D.C., Touchdown Club as the outstanding area college player of the year, and was chosen for the Sportsman Award for the State of Virginia through the Bedford, Virginia, Athletic Club.

His All-American title made him a hero in Iran. The summer before his senior year, a Bakhtiari Khan arranged for Jamshid to visit several sports clubs in different Iranian cities. The Shah of Iran presented him with a beautiful silver bowl through his ambassador, Ali Amini, in Washington and also gave him a four-year scholarship to the medical school at the University of Virginia in Charlottesville, which enabled him to stop playing professional football with the Calgary Stampeders in Canada.

Jamshid's success with football attracted the Voice of America, which that began broadcasting his games to Iran. Abol

Ghassem loved sitting by the radio to hear the outcome of his son's games and his successes on the field. In a letter to Jamshid, Abol wrote: "I long to see you in one of the football games when you are in actual combat. I don't think that I could bear to sit down and watch you without running onto the field to help you carry the ball. To Jamshid Bakhtiar from this side of the ocean— Rah! Rah! Rah!"[11]

My grandmother Helen went from Tehran to visit my uncle Jamshid in Charlottesville, where she was interviewed by a local radio station. The radio announcer, Mrs. Brown, asked my grandmother: "Your son, Jim Bakhtiar, brought to us this interest in Iran. It was a happy day for the University of Virginia when he decided to come and study here and I think, Mrs. Bakhtiar, and you will appreciate this being the mother of Jim, when they began to give him the name 'The Prince,' that I felt that he is just tops. Would you tell us a little about him that he wouldn't say about himself?" Helen responded: "Well, being a mother, of course, I am very prejudiced and I could say a great deal about Jim. I happened to be in Iran when Jim was making his name in football in the States. In fact, I was in the home of some friends when I heard his voice coming over the radio, the Voice of America. Jim's games were broadcast in Iran and there were people I met later in small villages in Iran who had heard about Jim Bakhtiar."[12]

Abol Ghassem's last years were ones of loneliness. His older children were all either in America finishing up their schooling or married with many young children, with the exception of my mother, now married, and Helen, his former wife, living in Tehran. The rest of his children were too young to engage with him in the kind of deep conversations he loved about new discoveries in medicine, or what he read in his beloved *Time* magazine and *Reader's Digest*.

"Please I beg you write to me," he wrote Uncle Jamshid. "I am very lonesome. I am sure you realize how harsh it is for a man to stay in bed so many months." From his last letter on January 1, 1971, a few days before he died: "Happy New Year to you all. This is early morning of January 1971. Last night I was thinking all the time up to midnight—I was thinking of you as if you were in my bosom. No one wrote me any New Year or Christmas cards. I spent the time like a dead man."

Dreams of his older children returning to practice medicine with him had come to naught. Abol's older children, who were in America, were busy with their own careers and families and were not in touch on a regular basis.

Abol had often said he would never die—meaning, he would have a long life—because Rostam, the hero of the *Shahnameh*, lived for hundreds of years. One of his daughters, my aunt Lailee, once asked him where he wanted to be buried, to which he responded, "Tus," a city in northeastern Iran and the place where history records that the *Shahnameh*'s poet Ferdowsi was buried. "Why?" she asked him. He replied that he had had a dream that his molecules would mix with the molecules of Ferdowsi and a Rostam hero/warrior would in God's time and place then be born to save Iran.[13]

During his early years my grandfather had been a wrestler, developing great physical strength much like the heroes and champions of the *Shahnameh*. Rostam, an Iranian gladiator who embodied chivalry, loyalty, and courage, and who possessed a will of steel, was unyielding when it came to protecting his homeland. But he also had moods of darkness and indifference and was quick to take offense at anything that bruised his ego. My grandfather possessed these same commendable and not so commendable qualities.

On many occasions, Rostam stood behind and enforced the divine balance of justice for the people of Iran. During his long life, according to the poet Ferdowsi, Rostam lived through the evil, tyranny, chaos, and treachery of the various Shahs that he served. However, Rostam's loyalty to the crown never wavered because he truly believed that each Shah he served held the *farr*—the divine mandate to rule over the Iranian people and to oppose its enemies. If a Shah was unjust, God would take away his divine mandate to rule, leaving Rostam free to no longer be duty bound to serve that Shah.[14]

Abol Ghassem had redefined for himself the *Shahnameh*'s concept of *farr*. After his experience in America, he transformed it to mean: the divine mandate of giving human beings the right to rule over themselves, to make their own decisions, exercise their own free will. He had shown that it was possible for the *farr*, or divine mandate, to be given to any individual no matter what political system was in power. In fact, Abol's life in America exemplified the divine right to individual sovereignty. Abol interpreted the myth of *farr* differently, but he did not change the meaning of the myth itself—he modernized it, giving it an appropriate, living meaning. Removing the *farr* from the Shahs, Abol gave it to himself by exhibiting self-responsibility, self-sufficiency, and self-reliance. He saw his own mind as his "king" and his "hero," and as long as it listened to reason, his mind would rule over the self in a fair and just manner.[15]

By marrying a foreigner, grandfather Abol Ghassem had lived out the mythic story of Persian heroes, my grandmother Helen stepping into the role of Rudabeh. Heroes in the mythic part of the *Shahnameh* are all born from foreign mothers. The marrying of Persian heroes to foreigners symbolizes a conquest of the wife's country.

My grandfather was buried according to his wishes on January 9, 1971, in Tus, near the tomb of Ferdowsi. Helen was deeply saddened by his death. Abol's immediate family left for Mashhad, in the eastern part of Iran near the small town of Tus, early in the morning. My grandfather's casket was placed on the airplane and every able-bodied Bakhtiari Khan in Tehran was at the airport to pay their respects, to give condolences, and to honor him and his family.

When they got to Tus, my mother found her sister Maryam's husband there; since early morning, he'd been supervising the digging of the grave. It was a beautiful clear, warm day. My grandfather's face was placed toward Mecca, facing the Tus plain and the surrounding mountains.

The graveyard is situated in a very large, quiet, and peaceful expanse of land. The family felt a great sense of peace seeing the site: Abol's tomb is directly on axis with an ancient mausoleum where the famous Sufi theologian al-Ghazzali is buried. To the left is Ferdowsi's tomb and to the right is the citadel of the old castle of Tus. My parents realized that they had completed a square: Because they had chosen the grave site in the dark the night before the burial, they were not aware of this fact until morning. The men of the village were there to help and as is the custom in the province of Khorasan, of which Mashhad is the center, they all wore white turbans.[16]

As my grandfather's body was being laid to rest, a wind so strong and so powerful that one had to use great force to withstand the pressure blew by the grave totally without warning. My mother explained that she could sense the earth beginning the process of re-creating nature/man. In a sense the wind lent her a great deal of strength because she knew that one day my grandfather's dream would come true. One day his dust would mix with that of Ferdowsi's and a great poet and champion would be born to save Iran.

My mother, her sister Shireen, and Aunt Maryam's husband had all felt a great deal of loneliness when Abol's body, wrapped as is the custom only in a white material, was laid to rest. My mother ached and yearned for what she would never see again. But she sensed that her father's spirit was so strong, and so strong within his children, that they would never be apart from him.[17]

They had chosen a very simple gravestone while in Mashhad with the understanding that on the fortieth day, when a ceremony must be held at the grave site, a nice granite stone that my father had found in an old Iranian candy factory would be carved and inscribed with the poetry of Hafez and Ferdowsi.

On my grandfather's desk in Tehran my mother had found a piece of paper on which he had written two poems by Hafez and the date, twelve days before his death. These were my grandfather's last writings from Hafez. My mother recalled how Abol's father, Haji Hasan, had left two things for him; now Abol was leaving two poems for his children.

The first poem tells of the pain of loneliness, sorrow, and separation—how at every moment Hafez's desire to see the Divine Beloved increases until he finally reprimands the Divine Beloved: "You make no effort to heal me. Don't you know what ails me? You should not have left me on the earth and then fled. Pass by me again. Ask about me so that my earth dust may be delivered. The moment I am there, You will pass by and my dust will mix with Your skirt. My breath ceased from the sorrow of Your love. For how long will You deceive me? The moment I draw near to You, I vanish in Your Unity. I received the Divine Mysteries from Your lips and at that moment I gave up my heart and soul."[18]

The theme of the poem frightened me just as I had often been frightened by my grandfather's strength and powerful voice when we visited him in his home. But as my mother sat me and my siblings down to listen to both poems, she conveyed their sense of peace and calm. I realized that death is inevitable to each and every one, so how much more beautiful it was to face one's fate with love and the hope of union with the forces of nature and the rebirth of a hero than to be afraid.

What surprised me about the second poem—which gave me a sense of hope—was that there were so many elements of my grandfather's life in it that it could have been written by him instead of seven hundred years before. My grandfather had been so close to the *Shahnameh*, and now his life and his inheritance to his children was from Hafez.

Hafez had said: "For many years I followed the religion of the Sufis until through reason I was able to control my greed. I did not go to Simorgh's nest by myself. Rather, I tread the path with the bird of Solomon." Then he demands of the Divine Beloved: "Cast a shadow on my wounded heart, O You passing treasure." He tells the Beloved: "I have destroyed the temple of my body out of love for You."[19]

I could almost hear my grandfather reciting: "I long for the Garden of Paradise from whence I have come. Even though I have had a very full life, the reason why I was rewarded with the companionship of Truth in my old age was because of the patience I had in this world—the House of Sorrow. I arose early in the morning and sought good health like Hafez. Whatever I did was from the glory of the Holy Koran."

My mother arrived back in Tehran on Wednesday and that night met with the cleric who would give my grandfather a fitting eulogy. He compared him to Razi, one of the greatest physicians that Iran has produced. My mother then explained to me the similarities. Both came to medicine late in life; both had skill in prognosis and in analysis of the symptoms of a disease, its manner of treatment and cure; and both were well versed in anatomy, in the tradition of Galen.

My mother told me that we must plant a tree—a cypress, I think—near Abol's head. In fact, she said, we must ring the grave site with trees—every year planting seven, a token amount but one that she thought would help my grandfather achieve his dream of renewing the earth with trees.

IT WAS GRANDMOTHER HELEN WHO WOULD WRITE TO HER children about the funeral and burial in Tus. In fact, my grandfather had been close to death several times in his later years, and told his cousin that he was waiting for one of his "doctor children" to return. The last time my grandfather had seen Uncle Cyrus, his sixth-born, he had given him his stethoscope and blood pressure apparatus without saying a word.

Grandmother Helen in her letter to Uncle Cyrus had written how much my grandfather loved him because he excelled in wisdom and was always searching for better and higher knowledge. She then quoted from Ferdowsi:[20] "Keep well your body and your mind if you wish not to spend a dreadful time/It is strength that leads man to the right path; it is weakness that causes crookedness and abasement."

And, "In search of knowledge incline first of all to God for God is your soul's guide/It is faith and knowledge that save you. Seek through them the path to salvation."

Helen had already suffered the loss of a dear friend, Yahya Khan. After she described his tribal burial ceremony to me, I realized the differences between the way the sedentary and nomadic people are buried.

When Yahya Khan's body was taken from Shahr Kurd in Chahar Mahal Bakhtiari to the village of Dastana in central Iran, where he had lived, thousands of people lined the road—every man, woman, and child was in the streets crying. Just beyond the mountain pass that leads to Shalamzar—the town to which my grandfather had walked for two days seventy years before to find work—and Dastana in the Chahar Mahal valley, thousands more waited for the hearse.[21]

On the mountain pass from Shalamzar to Dastana, ten thousand of the Bakhtiari Sarvasvand and Osivand clans played

Bakhtiari dirges with special horns and drums while women wailed as the coffin was carried to the shrine of Haji Bibi. Seventy of Yahya Khan's horses, riderless, tense, and nervous, were led in front of the coffin as it was carried to its final resting place on a small hill overlooking the Bakhtiari mountains and beautiful Chahar Mahal valley. There he was buried beside his mother, Bibi Hamehgol, whose name means "Lady of All the Flowers."

Yahya Khan had once stated that he wanted to die in the spring. His wish had been fulfilled. Mid-May is the most beautiful time of the year in Chahar Mahal—wildflowers of all colors bloom and everywhere the grass is green almost up to snow level in the mountains.

BY CHRISTMAS OF 1972, GRANDMOTHER HELEN'S EMPHYSEMA had taken a turn for the worse. For years she had lived with the illness that she had contracted while driving on dirt roads in an open jeep during her time with Point Four. Retired as a disabled American veteran in the early 1970s, she had begun treatment at the American Military Hospital in Tehran. Not long afterward, she died on January 19, 1973, two years and eleven days after my grandfather.

The next several months were filled with mourning for this, the saddest event of my mother's life. The emptiness, sorrow, and final separation were at moments more than she could bear. "How strange!" she said: "Such a great reality appears unreal and so many illusions seem permanent. That is why we pray: O God! Let me learn to see things as they really are."[22]

She had been alone with her mother the last week that she was in the hospital. My grandmother asked my mother to read two verses from the Koran, both of which indicated death was near. My mother explained that it was as if Helen had in those moments found peace. From then on Helen's physical health became worse, though my mother had no doubt that her spiritual health increased. As my mother gratefully recounted, my grandmother had not suffered; as long as she was conscious, she had no pain.

Grandmother Helen's death devastated all of us. It was several months before my mother could write to her brothers and sisters. She told them that so many people still ask about their mother and each time it was a shock for her to say: "She has passed away." Then she added: "God love her. God remember her and take care of her until we meet again."[23]

While my grandmother had seen the burial of both a sedentary and nomadic Iranian, she chose that of the sedentary, the traditional Muslim burial. Though Grandmother Helen never officially converted to Islam, on her deathbed she asked to be buried next to the love of her life, Abol Ghassem, in Tus. My mother thought this was because she wanted to be part of grandfather Abol Ghassem's dream.

Helen's body was flown early in the morning from Tehran to Mashhad. In Mashhad, the casket was placed in Room No. 7 of the shrine of the eighth Shia imam Reza where prayers were recited for Helen all night. The next morning the casket was circumambulated seven times around the shrine, with my mother and some of her siblings following. Outside in the beautiful courtyard, before the casket was taken the sixty miles to Tus, my mother recalls prayers for the dead being recited where her grave had been readied. Bricks four fingers high were lined around the place for her body in the six-foot depth of the grave. Two villagers offered their white turbans and the body was lowered into the grave site. Her body was identified for the last time and Helen's face placed toward Mecca. Earth was thrown into the grave as prayers were recited. As was the custom, sweets, cakes, and money were given to the village people of Tus, who had come to honor the American woman.[24]

Today millions of tourists visit Tus each year. A guide told us recently that Iranians visiting from America have been known to ask about the American woman buried in Tus. We have been told that they go to Helen's grave site and say a prayer for her.

Grandmother Helen had been a writer at heart, corresponding with her seven children as they moved back and forth between Iran and America so often that it was difficult for anyone but her to know who was where when. She had always wanted to write a book about her life and Iran, a country she came to love as her own.

With both her parents gone, my mother, now contending with her loss, turned ever more to Sufism and the inner journey. While sorrow filled her heart, she contemplated the mystery of death. An unusual sense of courage settled around her as she realized that from among all her siblings she had been left with the task of arranging for the funeral and burial rites of her parents. Because Abol and Helen died in Tehran and their other children were settled in America, she was the only one to be with both of them at the end of their lives. She was able to accept the situation as part of the fate of having been given life. My mother's consolation to herself, she told all of us, was that she also wanted to be buried in Tus next to her parents so that if her father's dream ever came true, she, too, could be part of it.

THE DAYS AND MONTHS AFTER HELEN'S DEATH WERE FULL OF intricate dreams for my mother. She dreamed she was sitting next to her spiritual master who gave her a dish of pomegranate seeds, which together looked like a small desert cactus flower—multisided, geometric forms shaped like crystals and brownish in color. She took a bite of them and the juice was sweet and delicious. Then she tried to chew the seeds, but every time she bit down, they would not break. She saw that her spiritual master, Seyyed Hossein Nasr, was spitting out the seeds, and so she thought that was what she was supposed to do. She later told her spiritual master the dream and he said that the pomegranate symbolized knowledge and the sweetness meant Divine Knowledge, just as she received gnosis (*irfan*) from him.[25]

In another dream, my father had on a long, white caftan with red circles at the trim. The wind was blowing very hard. She asked my father when he would be leaving and he said at noon. She looked at her watch and it was twenty minutes to noon.[26]

She wanted to join a Sufi order and was told that she had to have her husband's permission before she could join. She asked my father if he would give his permission for her to become part of a Sufi order. He felt it was something they should do together to which my mother agreed. She thought: "Is he also ready? Is it what he really wants to do or am I forcing him into something?"

She became even more deeply entrenched in learning about

the feminine principles in Sufism, the soul, spending hours por-
ing over her translations of mystical treatises and research on the
feminine principle. She was fed up. No one was helping her on
her spiritual quest. Her professor kept her articles and translations for over a year and then handed them back with just this
for a remark: "We have to go over them." It seemed as if endless
patience would be required of my mother. Even so, she continued to have spiritual experiences she could not explain.[27]

In an attempt to understand what she was going through, my
mother expressed her frustration to my father. They had a long
conversation during which my mother described the spiritual
states she was having when she would become almost ecstatic.
As she relayed all of this, she explained that her state was
induced by relating to an internal image. She could not allow
herself to tell him what it was exactly because this image was like
a talisman; its magical property would disappear if it were
brought to the light of day.

My father told her he felt the same thing about architecture:
Why else would he stay up until three a.m. drawing trees? He
felt my mother should not wait for anyone's confirmation but
should continue with her translations of mystical treatises,
which the two of them would publish. He said that her spiritual
states should be applied to this work. Whenever she felt she
could not sleep, she should work on the translations.[28]

She then decided to confront the image in writing, to express
it to the best of her ability. It was becoming more crystallized by
the prospect of being described. She told her spiritual teacher
about her experiences and he told her he thought she was on the
verge of spiritual reintegration. My mother said: "As God is my

witness, I think about it night and day. I have completely lost my appetite and eight pounds as well. I constantly invoke the Divine. If something were to stop my progression, I am sure I would escape to some very private place. God give me strength and certitude. I am becoming the Majnun impassioned lover—as my brother Cyrus had become. I speak with the tongue of the state. Sounds and smells influence me greatly. Please God help me to continue towards annihilation and then give me strength to subsist. God please don't desert me. With Your help perhaps I can move from this station to the next, but I need Your Grace."[29]

It was just a few days later that news reached my parents that my beloved uncle Cyrus had died in a tragic boating accident on Christmas day. At the time of his death he was thirty-seven, a practicing physician at the Pentagon's civilian clinic. He and four other Iranian men had been fishing on the Potomac River. At the end of the day when they were ready to head home, they found their anchor was stuck. All five rushed to pull up the anchor, capsizing the fiberglass boat. Cyrus told his friends he would swim the fifty yards or so to shore to get help. He began to swim, but the water was not only too cold but also carried a strong current, which pulled him away. He died of a heart attack brought on by hypothermia. Three of the other men also drowned trying to swim ashore, while the one who did not know how to swim clung to the boat. Just then, a plane was coming in for a landing at Washington National Airport. The man raised his hand and the pilot saw him and radioed for help. Four days later they found Cyrus's body, which Uncle Jamshid brought back to Iran.

My mother wrote in her diary: "At the present moment I am

keeping my composure to the best I know so that I can see that Cyrus is buried in Mashhad, in Tus, next to mother and Baba joone. Cyrus joone was a Majnun. He was a dervish. His last act was the final sacrifice—the sacrifice of self. Perhaps in some way he was the Verdant One (Khidr), the fish, the intellect, which *took its way into the sea, burrowing*. May his soul rest in peace."[30]

My father, who had no brother, had been close to Cyrus and would write to my mother a few days after Uncle Cyrus's death: "A general passiveness, calm and non aggressive space pervades my very being as I travel toward Washington. I think and have thought quite a great deal about Cyrus. His passing away has left a strange and, as yet, unexplainable impact upon me."[31]

His letter to my mother continued: "I am not depressed, as much as I feel the reality of death more than I have ever before. He was a fine person, a gifted man of great insight and yet incapable of human expression in his short life. He glimpsed and tasted of the richness of the mind and the heart. You must be proud of Cyrus for having persevered unknown trials and climbed before any of us the mountain of esoteric comprehension. At least he knew, truly knew of its existence."[32]

I have thought often about the death of my uncle Cyrus, whom I also loved dearly. The last time I saw him, he had given me a marble stone on which was inscribed: "You've got a friend."

6

Struggling with Reality,
1976–79

In the summer of 1976, when I was twelve years old, my sister, brother, and I attended overnight camp for six weeks in Fairlee, Vermont, on Lake Morey. Our parents had always wanted us to continue our exposure to the Western world and the American life of green grass and barbecues that they had experienced in their childhoods. As soon as we returned to Iran in August, my mother and father sat us down and gave us the news of their divorce, explaining that my father would not be living with us anymore. We were devastated and began to cry. No one we knew at school had been divorced. It seemed to be such an American solution to their situation.

We were certain it was our fault. It was hard for us to grasp that, although they still loved each other, they had profound philosophical differences. They told us they had grown so close that their identities were intertwined, and they needed space to discover who each of them was on their own. A fine theory, but it didn't satisfy the anxieties of a twelve-year-old girl or my siblings. We had never even heard them argue other than their occasional mumbo-jumbo words that we didn't understand. Our whole world was shattered.[1]

My mother thought it was just a phase my father was going through, and that if she set him free to explore, he would come back to her. My sister and I prayed and wished that the whole thing would go away and one morning everything would be as it was again, for in spite of her rationalizations, losing her husband was more than our mother could bear. We witnessed how difficult it was for her to adjust, and at the same time recognized that our father seemed to have an easier time coping. My mother finally resolved it for herself by saying it was fate and therefore there was nothing she could do about it but live through it and experience the pain of separation.

THAT SCHOOL YEAR, WE WERE CERTAIN THAT THE WHOLE school was talking about us. We had difficulty concentrating and socializing. Our father had rented an apartment in one of the tall modern high-rises that he had designed in Tehran and it is there that we would spend weekends with him. He was driving a Jaguar, and listened to the music of Jean-Michel Jarre and the theme from *Jaws*. He traveled back and forth to America, always returning with gifts for us. Every so often my father would take one of us out to dinner, just one-on-one, to get to know us better.

On weekends when he was overseas, we would spend time

Davar and her mother, sister, and brother at an art exhibit on religious paintings her mother had helped to organize, Tehran, 1977. (From the Laleh Bakhtiar Collection of Family Photographs)

with his parents, our grandparents Abbas and Mani joone. They did not talk to us about the divorce. In fact, no one did. Our days with them were quiet days, playing cards and eating fresh fruit from their garden. With their orderly and calm demeanor, they gave us a sense of peace and security. But the change in our lives was cataclysmic, and nothing was going to mend our wounds.

The next summer my sister, brother, and I were again sent off to camp for six weeks. Just before we left Tehran for Vermont, my father told us about his fiancée, Shahla Ganji. He said he hoped we would come to love her. Too young to understand, we cried some more, clinging to one another that summer as we tried to piece together what was happening to our lives. The peaceful Lake Morey, with the backdrop of New England's Green Mountains, the sounds of children playing in the lake, the songs around the campfire, the music of birds, and the smell of fresh pine brought meaning once again into our lives.

In one of the last letters he would write to my mother, my father explained that he had been offered a visiting professorship at Harvard that would commence in the fall.[2] While he cared for her deeply as a friend and intellectual counterpart, he wrote he had fallen in love with another woman and was ready to say good-bye.[3]

> Our ways are destined to be different, yet our aim the same. I have taken the occasion of our separation and of this journey to dwell deeply into our mutual unfoldings, and with much confidence in you and myself—and yet with much sadness, but less regret, I look to being with you and of resolving that which now seems inevitable. My love to you, Laleh, whom I shall always love and care for with all my heart and to whom I shall keep my promise that with regard to our children, they shall always feel love and unity. To ourselves, we shall always know that a sense of unity exists or all would have been for naught. My deepest love to you.

And with that my father left and moved to America.

On the day my parents signed their divorce papers, my mother left for Mecca, where she would do her part of the research for the book that she had been commissioned to write with my father. She prayed that God not leave her helpless as she touched the cloth covering the Kabah, the cube-like structure in the courtyard of the large mosque in Mecca, the direction to which all Muslims pray five times a day. She asked God to help her in her endeavors, that God give her the strength to continue to do and be what she believes in. She wrote in her diary of her first experience of the Visitation to Mecca, "Oh God you have called me and I have come. Oh God you have allowed me to come to your house. Forgive me and my sins. I repent. Give me strength to continue the journey. As Hazrat Ali said: Even if I were to see God, nothing would be added to my certainty. It is mankind that I love now, not one man. I have chosen the way of God, glorified be He." As she donned the sacred clothes, she was reminded of her youth as a Catholic and the nuns she now resembled.[4]

My mother went to circumambulate the Kabah and repeated "God is Greater" continuously as she performed the seven revolutions. Overwhelmed with a sense of the sacred, she wrote in her diary of "the Presence of God in the great multitude as they pressed around the stable, permanent center, the axis of the universe, the House of God." She then described the single bird that she saw circling high in the sky, saying, "I felt so much that I wanted to be that bird. I felt like I had been living in a cage and every time the door opened, just a little way, I myself would shut it because someone needed me. I would close the cage door and put aside the idea of flying off, of riding with the wind, coasting on intuitions, exploring the non-conscious."[5]

At that time I was too young to understand the parallels between my mother's and grandmother Helen's lives. While divorce is an exercise of free will rather than fate, once the decision was cast upon them, they pulled themselves together and continued to struggle for values they had always believed in.

ONE OF THE FIRST EVENTS MY MOTHER WAS INVITED TO attend without my father was the First International Conference of Women Architects in October 1976, which was held in Ramsar, in the north of Iran near the Caspian Sea. It was a great adventure for my sister and me, who had gone along to meet some of Iran's and the world's most successful women. Famous architects such as Anne Tyng, former partner of Louis Kahn, Italian Gae Aulenti, English Alison Smithson, and many other impressive women had come from all over the world to talk about their contribution to architecture.

Being surrounded by a sea of creative workingwomen was empowering at a time when our adult male role model was missing at home. In their own way each of the women appeared to have had a realization about who they were and what they were doing, participating with their total selves to intensify the event. No one showed this more clearly than Empress Farah, who inaugurated the conference. As the empress was leaving the conference, everyone in attendance, including my mother, sister, and I, curtsied in a gesture of respect. It was the first time I had seen the empress in person since the day our family lined Pahlavi Avenue on her way to her coronation, the first woman so honored in over fourteen hundred years. Being empress meant that if anything happened to the Shah before the crown prince was eighteen, she would rule from the Peacock Throne. My sister and I were left with a sense that being Iranian and female did not mean we were second-class citizens. We stood a chance of actively contributing to the betterment of the world.

WITHOUT THE PRESENCE OF MY FATHER, IT WAS HARD FOR ME to concentrate on school. I was shocked, angry, and guilty all at the same time. I was worried about how we would be able to cope as a broken family. At the age of twelve, I felt as though I had lost my guide, as if I was rolling downhill uncontrollably in class. With a heart that was consumed by darkness, I wasn't sure how to battle the dragons and demons within me who were now standing in my way.

My mother had also grown up without a father. Among her favorite books as a young girl had been Louisa May Alcott's *Little Women*, because in it the absence of a father figure reminded her so much of her own home. She also loved *Jo's Boys*, in which Jo showed she could take charge and manage on her own. She would take the dreams and visions inspired by these heroines to her friend Martha's garage, which had a loft. There she and Martha set up an altar for the saints, displaying pictures around it, always making sure that the Virgin Mary—to whom they felt such closeness—was in the center.[6]

As I sat looking out our hall window onto the street and neighborhood below I realized life without him was not going to be easy. I thought about my absent father in a faraway land and I wondered if he would still recognize me.

Much of my sorrow would then dissipate when I reflected on my younger years. I often bathed in the bliss of memories: our family travels in the earthly landscapes of Iran, Egypt, and Greece. Those trips had taken me beyond my childhood; at times it felt I had been touched by the Throne of God. But now discouraged about life, I wondered how we would ever journey forward without my father.

My sister and I attended Iranzamin, meaning "Land of Iran," a private American missionary school in Tehran for students from kindergarten through twelfth grade. Situated in a modern *caravanserai*-style campus in the newer part of northern Tehran, its faculty consisted of some of the best graduates and thinkers of American universities. Richard Irvine, the principal, said in one of his yearbook messages: "Affection, love, joy all spring from diversity. Having spent your school years among people of diversity, you can look forward to a lifetime of lively appreciation and cheerful enjoyment of God's personal and natural gifts, which though scattered broadly across the world have been ours to enjoy at Iranzamin."

One highlight came in a class on Greek mythology when we each chose and acted out a character. I chose Artemis, the goddess of the wilderness, hunter, and the daughter of Zeus. She reminded me of the female heroines I had heard about in the *Shahnameh*, roaming mountain forests hunting for lions and panthers. To depict her, I sported a bow and arrow and a crescent moon on my forehead. I presented her gentler side as well, as she was also the goddess of fertility and protector of women and children. It must have been her fearless nature or her love of the chase that had mesmerized me.

In our school many different cultures flourished, but for the most part we were all Americanized. By 1977, the Bee Gees' hit "Night Fever" landed in Tehran and *Saturday Night Fever* was the big rage. In less than a year, murmurs of political unrest would reach our school, and even our teachers began to speak among themselves about politics. As if my parents' divorce was not enough, our entire world was turned upside down. Living as we did near Tehran University, which had become a center for demonstrations against the Shah, we could see the Shah's army from our window march down the street with rifles, looking for protesters. From our high vantage point we could see people hiding behind their gates hoping that the soldiers would not knock on their doors.

The Islamic Revolution

Life went by quickly those days, with little time for contemplation. With no adult male figure in the family, it was hard to know exactly what was going on inside Iran. My mother was amazed to hear that thousands had marched through the streets chanting: "Down with the Shah." Without any idea of the magnitude of dissatisfaction with the government, she would think, each time she heard of another demonstration, that the Shah's government would find a way to prevail. The thought that she would have to face the transformation of her homeland all by herself was more than she could bear. What would Helen and Abol Ghassem have done?

My mother had begun a small English-language publishing company—they even published our school yearbooks with a business partner—in order to make ends meet as well as to provide an outlet for writing. She had slowly started to wear bright head scarves, in the style of tribal women. She did this because she was exploring her spiritual side with more freedom.

By the fall of 1978, when I was fourteen years old, it became clear that our country was headed into chaos.

At night I could hear sounds of protesters denouncing the Shah, chanting, "God is Greater" (*Allah-o-akbar*). Then, one day, a girl came to school wearing the veil. Having been surrounded by secular upper-class Iranian families, we were stunned to have an outwardly religious girl in our school.

Beyond that, at home, we were suddenly confronted with financial difficulties. The revenue produced by the publishing house suddenly was not enough. My mother's life, as well as my own and my siblings', came to resemble what grandmother Helen had gone through. After moving to Boston to further his international career, my father was not able to send enough money to Iran. Due to the political unrest, he had not been getting paid for the Iran-based commissions that his Boston office was contractually obligated to complete.

Once my mother realized that she would have to primarily support her children, she converted our three-story house into three apartments so that she could rent the top floor. We lived on the second floor, and the first floor was used for her lithography and publishing office, which grew to include a small staff. Shamsi ventured out every day to buy fresh greens, vegetables, and meat to prepare our meals.

After her divorce, my mother felt shunned by the Ardalan family, who had previously offered an extensive family support system. She was shunned by other people she and my father had developed friendships with over the years as well because at that time in Iran some married women felt a divorced woman could be a threat to their own marriages. Also, my mother was no longer in a position to entertain or to shop in London for the latest fashions. She found herself even more alone.

Busy trying to make ends meet, she neither watched television nor read the newspapers. Aunt Shireen, still living in Abadan and working for the oil company, wrote my mother in August 1978 to say that the Cinema Rex had been burned down and hundreds of people had died because the doors had been locked from the outside. Cinema Rex was a movie house in Abadan that we all used to go to when we visited my aunt Shireen and Abadani cousins.

Just two weeks before, Uncle Jamshid had called from Isfahan to say that martial law had been declared there. He was contemplating moving to Tehran where he felt his family might be safer.

ON JANUARY 7, 1978, THE TALK IN MY MOTHER'S OFFICE WAS about an article published in the *Ettele'at* newspaper attacking Ayatollah Khomeini as a British agent and a corrupt man with homosexual tendencies. Two days later there were widespread clashes in Qom in protest to the editorial—scores were killed and wounded by the Shah's secret police. The workers in my mother's office were distraught and began talking about what was going on inside the country. "How could the government of the Shah say such things about a religious leader?" they asked. Not having read the article herself, my mother asked them who the ayatollah was. They replied that he was an important religious figure who had begun speaking against the Shah in the early 1960s and whose best-known speech was delivered on November 4, 1964, when he called for Iran not to surrender its capitulatory rights to the United States.

The law confirming their rights declared that all American military advisers, along with their families, technical and administrative officials, and servants, were to enjoy legal impunity with respect to any crime they might commit in Iran. The Ayatollah Khomeini had said: "They have reduced the people of Iran to a level lower than that of an American dog. If an Iranian runs over an American's dog, he will be prosecuted. Even if the Shah himself were to run over an American's dog, he would be prosecuted. But if an American cook runs over the Shah, the head of state, no one in Iran would have the right to interfere." My mother's employees said that after this speech, the Ayatollah Khomeini was sent into exile, first to Turkey and then to Najaf, Iraq, where he had stayed for almost fifteen years.

As an American, she thought about what she had just heard. What if someone were to make the United States agree to such a law in *their* country? What if Afghanistan had made the American Congress agree to such a law? Or France or Germany or Russia? Obviously it would mean that American laws have no teeth and that Afghan laws were more valuable.

In April 1978 a customer came to my mother's office with a book called *Fatima Is Fatima*, by Ali Shariati. My mother had never heard of the book nor the author, but she was told that he was an Islamic intellectual who had been killed by the Shah's secret police just a year earlier in London, perhaps because from 1967 to 1974 he had called for the reform of the Iranian government and Islam. A lecturer to thousands of people, Shariati regularly spoke at a center called Hosseiniyeh Irshad in Tehran. When the assembled crowds got too large, stragglers sat on the street outside the center and listened from a loudspeaker. As a Muslim sociologist, Ali Shariati yearned to empower Iranians, especially university students and graduates, to find a unified voice within Islam without importing ideas from the West. Shariati's ideas could best be described as a kind of Shia socialism as a form of liberation theology. Finally, the person who had brought Shariati's book to her suggested she translate the book *Fatima Is Fatima* into English, so that not only she but others could be made aware of his ideas. Though she had not yet completed the translation of an entire book before, her curiosity about who Shariati was and what he had said was powerful.[1]

Growing up as she had in the West and just becoming proficient in Persian, my mother only knew what she had been told about Fatima and what she symbolized for an Iranian Muslim until she translated this book. The only works available in English previous to this work on Fatima emphasized the legendary side of the daughter of the Prophet, neglecting to mention her human side and instead concentrating on miracles surrounding her birth, life, and death.

As my mother began to translate, she would tell me about Shariati's view on Fatima as a role model for the Shias. Fourteen years old now and very much under the influence of Western thought as defined by my school environment, knowing little about Islamic ideology, I learned that Shariati had written and spoken openly against widespread social views held in prerevolutionary Iran, such as the suggestion that Iranian women look to Western movie stars as models of femininity. Shariati asked why the Shia women of Iran had not taken Fatima, the daughter of the Prophet, or her outspoken daughter, Zaynab, as models for themselves. The answer and the blame, Shariati explained, lies with the clerics. While France has Joan of Arc and Catholics the Virgin Mary, Shias only have Western models. My mother had never heard anyone as outspoken as Shariati criticizing the status quo. She, too, wanted to find a role model who was an integral part of the Iranian Shi'ite culture.

Shariati concluded that there was no way to describe Fatima but to say: Fatima is Fatima. She was a cultural icon who gave birth to her own personality, a person who kept alive the spirit of those who seek justice and oppose oppression and discrimination. If anything, my mother found Shias to be obsessed with a sense of justice. While Sunnis have five basic beliefs which they adhere to and share with Shias—namely, belief in the Oneness of God; belief in all the prophets including those in the Old Testament, Jesus as well as Prophet Muhammad; belief in the sacred books such as the Bible and the Koran; belief in angels; and belief in the Resurrection—the Shias add belief in justice and *imamate,* or the sayings and actions of the twelve imams, descendants of the Prophet Muhammad through his daughter, Fatima. Fatima is the pivotal figure for both. She was a person, according to Shariati, who asked: "Who am I?" and found the answer in being herself.[2]

I recall my mother's experience of waking up one night, sitting straight up in bed, and crying out: "My God, who am I?" This question was with her for some time before the obvious answer arrived. The most basic part of herself, she realized, was that she was a woman. It was something she wanted to know more about, so that she could be the best possible woman she could be.

As Shariati said and my mother agreed: Women want to decide for themselves who they are. They want to be the midwife of their own lives without having society tell them who they should be or who they have to be. They want choices in order to be able to make conscious decisions.

I began to grow worried about my mother translating Shariati's book because his writings advocated socialism and were in opposition to Iran's monarchy. Some even said Shariati was a communist. She had been told that it was forbidden to read his books and now my mother was not only reading them but translating them. I was scared that the secret police who were arresting people for doing even less than translating forbidden texts might find out and arrest her.

The political situation in Iran was unstable in the late 1970s leading up to the 1979 Islamic revolution due to the activities of communists, socialists, and other anti-Shah groups who wanted to do away with the dictatorship of the Shah and the oppression of SAVAK.[3]

The government closed the universities while, on the other side, many government workers went on strike, including the workers in the oil industry. Aunt Shireen and Uncle Manoucher

were now jobless. There was no export of oil. Newspaper journalists went on strike. Electricity was turned off. The Iranian
people who lived religious lives according to the Islamic law
(*shariah*) had been suppressed for many years as the Shah had
tried to move toward modernization and secularization, but,
according to many people, it had been too quick and didn't give
the religious people a chance to accept new ways of life. They
simply felt their religious and political beliefs were being threatened as more and more students were arrested for political activ-
ity. In response, the government brought in military rule. The
military took over the radio and television stations and all government agencies while my mother was secluded at home translating Ali Shariati.

It took my mother six months to translate *Fatima Is Fatima*,
and, by its conclusion, to come to a revolution in her way of
thinking about women—namely, that in the West women are
misguided and used as a means to advertise a product, not for
what they know and who they are. I had come about with this
new sense, my mother wanted to give her spirit and strength to a
movement of women who would together assume the right they
had to rule over themselves instead of imitating the West or the
East. It had been up to the clerics, according to Shariati, to give
awareness, consciousness, and direction to the people, much like
leaders of the faithful of the past. Shariati believed the clerics
had let everyone down.

The method that Shariati promoted in his book was used by
the Prophet Muhammad; Shariati wanted to preserve his form
but contemporize the content. This was exactly what my mother

had first attempted to do when she embraced the spiritual path: She wanted to be proud of being a woman but also transform herself to embody and practice virtues like thankfulness, forgiveness, and repentance so that if God willed it, a spiritual transformation would occur. This was the mystical experience she was seeking.[4]

Shariati's book revealed to my mother that she had never formed her own identity because of natural circumstances—God's will, she called it, not her own will. There were pieces of her—mother, wife, student, teacher, lover—but they were only pieces, and she sought to understand her purpose: "her God-given nature" was still a question.

By the time she had finished the translation, opposition to the Shah's government in Iran was progressing rapidly. Our family did not participate at all nor did we know anyone who was, but every once in a while, someone would come into my mother's office and tell her the latest news of the protests.

In October 1978, Saddam Hussein deported the Ayatollah Khomeini from Najaf, Iraq. Khomeini and his family fled to the Paris suburb of Neauphle-le-Chateau. News began to infiltrate our home more frequently. Audiotapes of speeches by the Ayatollah Khomeini began arriving at my mother's office.

On December 2, 1978, the beginning of Muharram (the first month of the Islamic lunar calendar and Muslim New Year), the government instituted a curfew in all Iranian cities. My mother, who felt that she did not have enough command of the situation to venture out from our protected environment or let us do the same, was very concerned about our going to school in the midst of martial law and now a curfew. Then our neighbor, who knew that my mother lived alone with us, came and told her that that night, at nine p.m., the time of the curfew, everyone was to go to their rooftops and shout out: "God is Greater" (*Allah-o-akbar*). In the blackness of the night, standing on her balcony, raising her fist, she called out to the darkness, *"Allah-o-akbar!"* She had been undergoing her own internal search for spirituality at the same time that the country was undergoing its religious reawakening. To my mother, this seemed to be the direction she must take.

After that night, we began to hear from that same neighbor that some of our friends were leaving the country. My mother's mentor, Seyyed Hossein Nasr, and his wife had already left. It never occurred to Aunt Shireen, Uncle Jamshid, or my mother to leave Iran. Each had their own reasons, but in my mother's case, her American passport had expired; even if she'd had a current passport, she did not know where to go or how to earn a living, how to support us children.

On the afternoon of January 16, 1979, someone brought a copy of a newspaper to her office and the headlines read: "The Shah has gone." Just a year earlier President Carter had been in Iran celebrating New Year's Eve with the Shah and Empress Farah. Where was America *now?* How could the people have prevailed by peaceful marches and by raising their fists to the sky shouting: "God is Greater!" It all seemed like a bad dream. Although she believed in the spiritual awakening, the political manifestations scared her, for, like Helen and Abol, she was not a political person. Each day my mother would wake up thinking that things might go back to the way they were—but it was not meant to be. Without quite realizing it, we had all just lived through a revolution!

My mother thought that now that the nationalists were finally in power, the clergy would serve as advisers, which was only fair, she concluded, since the CIA ousted the nationalist movement in 1953, defeating Iran's elected leader, Mohammad Mossadegh. But on February 1, 1979, the Ayatollah Khomeini returned. When the live television broadcast of his return was abruptly canceled, my mother, brother, sister, and I joined the two million who flocked to see him, curious to lay eyes on the famous exiled leader of the Islamic movement against the Shah. Having grown up in a secular Iran, the militancy of recent events scared and confused me.

For my mother, the revolution was an extension of her own spiritual crisis. With everything beyond her control, all that was left was for her to submit to the situation. The thought of this was somehow easier to accept when she recalled her ancestors fleeing England and its religious intolerance. But it became harder when she thought about the America, founded on religious freedom, that she grew up in and loved. She thought: Perhaps her Iranian ancestors could rest in peace knowing that their descendants were now free to practice their faith in Iran.

Like grandmother Helen, she was completely trusting of whatever situation she found herself in, trusting and passive because she realized she was living through a process which was beyond her control. Just as my grandmother had been excited about taking the Bakhtiari migration, my mother was perhaps naively overtaken by the idea of "living through a revolution." She began wearing the veil and spending hours translating the works of Shariati. Looking back, I was a bit embarrassed by her and wasn't sure why she was changing outwardly.

The new revolutionaries began imprisoning and brutally executing members of the Shah's cabinet. Hostages were taken at the American Embassy. It did not make sense to us, and we began to fear for our future. Those who could left the country.

I was facing a turning point in my life and had to make a decision. My father had begun to make arrangements for us to leave Iran for a summer vacation in America. Would I stay or return to Iran at the end of the summer? After a few months, it became apparent that our school, Iranzamin, would never be the same. Revolutionaries sprayed "Death to Irvine" (our school principal) graffiti on the walls of the school and deemed subjects like art and music un-Islamic. Mr. Irvine recalls his wife, our music teacher, defying "a revolutionary committee's effort to kidnap one of the children." Mrs. Irvine even had to throw "a Molotov cocktail out of a classroom one morning." Iranzamin was eventually turned into an Islamic school for boys. While I had finished my sophomore year, my sister had graduated high school in June 1980 and was getting ready to go to America for college. I was not ready to submit to the revolution as my mother had, nor was leaving Iran an easy decision for me. I feared for my mother and brother if I left them, but having no school to go to left me no choice. I reasoned that if I no longer had Iranzamin, I would have to start over in a new school anyway so it might as well be in America. I decided to go to America to live with my father and his new wife in Boston.

· ❖ 8 ❖ ·

America and Back to Iran,
1980–83

Walking along Bigelow Street in Cambridge, Massachusetts, my sister and I found the brownstone where our parents had lived and where my sister had been conceived. It was almost therapeutic to retrace the steps our parents had taken and get a glimpse of their lives in Cambridge when my father had attended Harvard.

We then went to the Freedom Trail in Boston. It was not Paul Revere's house or Christ Church or even the Bunker Hill monument that drew my attention, but Faneuil Hall, where my father's architectural firm was housed. Standing inside Faneuil Hall, or, as John Adams had called it, the "Cradle of Liberty," I sensed the history of these cobblestoned markets.

The Declaration of Independence came about because Americans had rebelled against Great Britain's imposed authority. "Our forefathers, inhabitants of the island of Great Britain, left their native land to seek on these shores a residence for civil and religious freedom. . . . With an humble confidence in the mercies of the supreme and impartial Judge and Ruler of the Universe, we most devoutly implore his divine goodness to protect us happily through this great conflict, to dispose our adversaries to reconciliation on reasonable terms, and thereby to relieve the empire from the calamities of civil war." I was amazed that the result of the American struggle was religious freedom for all in the "Cradle of Liberty." This was what I felt was missing in the Islamic Revolution in Iran—where was the liberty?

I had lost Iran and gained America yet Iran was still all I knew. Where were the Alborz Mountains we used to see from our hall window? I felt so distant from Iran's heat, dust, fire, light, and cleansing rain. In my life, to this point, I had traveled over mountains, rivers, and deserts. I wondered when I would be able to find a place to call home. I used to lose myself in thought as I watched the wind playing hide-and-seek with the trees outside our home, caressing every leaf, allowing the whole tree to dance like a person in a trance. It felt like I was in a trance of my own, waiting and wishing, hesitating and lingering.

The sense of anticipation flying to America and away from Iran and the revolution had been tremendous—as was the apprehension that brought in its wake questions, doubts, hopes, and fears. Although my brother Karim came to Boston for a brief visit that summer to see our father, he returned to Iran at the end of the summer so that my mother wouldn't be alone. What would happen to them now that I was here? And my father was now remarried. How would I cope with that?

I wrote to my mother in August of 1980 after being in Boston for a month.[1]

I hope you're fine and everything in the office is going well. I miss you like I never have before and I feel so bad sitting here when I know I could be with you now. I love you and I feel so close to you. You have been the best mother ever to me and I want to thank you. As I have said many times before, you are unique, and honestly I'm proud that you're my mother. I have always loved everything that you taught me and I shall remember all of what you've said. Mommy, when you write, please write sayings from the Prophet or from Hazrat Ali because they help me.

My father, his wife, Shahla, and my baby brother, Ali Reza, lived in Fisher Hill in Brookline, Massachusetts, a suburb of Boston. Built in the 1850s as a summer retreat, this beautiful Georgian colonial house was situated on top of a hill. Altogether there were seventeen rooms on three stories, with a basement and an elevator. The sunroom had many double-hung colonial-style windows that let the light stream in, but there was also privacy and views of lush green trees. Having just come from Tehran—with its electricity outages—the contrast couldn't have been greater. My father had bought the house in the days before the revolution in Iran, which would ultimately have such an impact on his career.

I spent many hot days that first summer swimming in the pool and sunbathing in the beautiful garden, the cool breeze reminding me of summer homes we had visited in Shemiran in northern Tehran. Next to the house was a museum devoted to Mary Baker Eddy, the founder of Christian Science, beside which was a reservoir where I would go biking and jogging in the afternoon. It was surreal to think of my close girlfriends back in Iran who didn't have this freedom and were ordered to wear the veil in public.

But in Boston I saw graffiti on the streets with the words "BOMB IRAN." I felt out of place, lonely, and ashamed. I decided to drop my first name and use my middle name, Davar, which means "arbitrator" in Persian. I was named after my great-grandfather, Ali Akbar Davar, who had chosen his last name after consulting the poems of the mystic poet Hafez.[2]

My first day at Brookline High School I found myself standing in a courtyard surrounded by yellow school buses and the American flag at half-mast in solidarity with the fifty-two Americans still being held captive in the American Embassy in Tehran. Later that day a jock passed me in the hallway and said, "What's up?" I had no idea how to answer. Maybe: "Oh, I just fled a revolution"?

Although I was completely intimidated by the American high school experience, I found a way to fit in by joining the drama club, performing in a high school play, and dating Bill Summerville, a good-looking member of the school's swim team. As Billy and I grew closer, his family began to think of me as part of the extended family, but they also sensed my depression and tolerated my temper flare-ups. I was learning to survive in a very different culture without any real family support. My grades were now suffering. I found myself turning into a parrot, repeating my class notes without stopping to think, which caused me to make mistakes. "How long will it take me to control my mind?" I thought. "To realize my potential?" Detached from my emotions, it was hard for me to do more than merely react to what was going on around me.

Life at home with my father and stepmother was not pleasant, mostly because I felt if I got too close to my stepmother I would be disloyal to my mother. My sister, the Libra, was much more levelheaded than I was about my father's new life. Instead, I sought solace on many occasions at the home of the Ladjevardi family, who had known me from early childhood. Their three children had also all attended Iranzamin and moved to the Boston area after the revolution. They were the only real connection I had to Iran. Their eldest son Mahmoud and I formed a deep and loving friendship yet the pain of separation eventually did not allow me to get close to those who cared about me the most, including Mahmoud.

After my father was forced to sell his Fisher Hill home, due to lack of funds from his Iran–contracted work, my father set my sister and me up in an apartment on Lanark Road in Brookline, while he and his new family moved to a smaller home. Setting us up on our own may have been prompted by my growing animosity toward him. I was still in high school and my sister was in college. Perhaps most teenagers would have loved the independence, but I saw it as being pushed away, the third breakup of my family.

A girlfriend at Brookline High signed up for a beauty contest, and I signed up with her, coming in second-runner-up at the Miss Boston Camera Club Contest, the prize for which was a modeling shoot. At the shoot I posed like Brooke Shields in her

Modeling a la Brooke Shields (Photograph by Dan Alex, Boston, 1982)

famous Calvin Klein ad. The idea of a career in modeling—the very thing teenage girls dream about—was for me just another sign of my disguise.

Although I had been accepted at Boston College and had received offers from family friends to help pay my tuition, in 1982 I decided to move to Los Angeles. I had secured an invitation from Aunt Lailee, my mother's oldest sister, and my cousins Soraya and Dina that was too good to pass up. I was born in California but had left when I was six months old. It seemed to me that the West Coast was more relaxed and I might have a better time finding a way to fit in.

MY AUNT LAILEE PRACTICED MEDICINE IN LOS ANGELES. Through the years, Iranians had gravitated to her and her home in southern California. In 1978, a large number of Iranians fleeing the revolution chose to settle in Los Angeles, among them many performing artists. One of my aunt's patients was Manouchehr Bibiyan, one of Iran's most successful music producers. Two years after the revolution, my aunt helped Bibiyan and countless other performing artists launch *Jaam-e-Jam* Television from the living room of her Bel Air home. The station carried cultural as well as political programs, the latter extremely critical of the Islamic government in Iran. The comedy sketches of Iran's clerical leaders were aimed to insert humor in the lives of many who were in the process of starting their lives over again.

Jaam-e-Jam took its name from the mythical Persian king Jamshid, from whose cup or grail (*jaam*) the world could be viewed. On the broadcasts, famous singers such as Hayedeh and Homeyra could be seen descending Aunt Lailee's staircase. One Noruz, my aunt decided to rent two goats to roam around in her garden as a backdrop for the set. This was all fine and lovely until the goats started eating all the flowers, so they were quickly returned to their owner.

Lailee was the doctor for the first group of expatriates from Iran after the revolution, many of whom could not believe that they had found a doctor who spoke Persian, as so few of them spoke English. My aunt helped awaken them from the past as they tried to move into the future. For them, one reality simply stopped and another began without any relation between the two. The first generation was steeped in traditions and culture they had inherited from centuries before. The new generation they left behind was steeped in change alone.

Change without a past brings chaos. These exiles believed that change must come slowly. It is part of their heritage and they believed it would happen again. They believed that the revolution in Iran would change and the old system of the Shah would be reinstated.

Once settled in Los Angeles, I thought about how comfortable my family had been in Iran. Then, suddenly, the divorce and the revolution, and we were forced to experience the opposite. When I thought about it, I began seeing many things in terms of contradictions and paradoxes. There is God and there is the opposite, Satan; there are the affluent and the needy; cold and hot; wet and dry; courage and cowardice. Time began to wax and wane for me. While to my aunt and cousins and others, I appeared to be fine, inwardly I felt constrained in a dark world, passive to events around me. It was as if I had lost the ability to possess my own will, unable to reflect my true self or bear witness to others. It was a time of contemplative withdrawal. I had set out from Iran to defeat some foe who had broken my unity only to come to think that the foe was within me.

My father had always been there in the past and in a child's mind that guaranteed a future of the same. But I was no longer a child; my child's body was changing into a woman's. I reflected the loneliness with my need to be desired.

I soon realized that I attracted men, and that once around me they treated me differently than I had been accustomed to as a child. I loved this power and even discovered the pleasure of making men nervous when they would talk to me. I became a "tease," breaking the hearts of those who couldn't fill the void my father had left in my life; the hole that had developed in my father's absence had become a chasm that I could not easily fill, so my next great frontier would be seduction.

HE WAS THE NEPHEW OF THE SHAH OF IRAN AND MANY YEARS my senior and we met at my aunt Lailee's house, where he had come with his mother for a gathering. We went out for dinner alone on a Saturday night. He was charming, animated, and glamorous, and I shared little about myself, not wanting him to know I was only eighteen. I loved being mysterious, pretending to be happy and well-adjusted.

"Are you *real*?" he said to me once after kissing me passionately. I melted into submissive silence. Did he know how lonely and insecure I was? Damn, I told myself, so much for the mystery girl. I felt so humiliated for myself, for what was I doing—pretending. I wanted to run out the door right then, but his smile let me know that I was still welcome. But the table had turned.

That night I had a dream that I was at the edge of a spectacular waterfall. I tried to throw a rope across it but failed and I began to fall. It wasn't a long fall, but at the end I could see there was a wall. As I thought about how to avoid the dangerous wall, I woke up.

I spent the next day driving around Los Angeles trying to find the home where my mother and grandmother Helen had lived forty-five years earlier; 821 South Holt Avenue, just off Wilshire Boulevard near Beverly Hills was where Papa and Grandma Nell cared for my mother when she and Helen arrived from Iran in 1939. I couldn't find their home but I imagined Grandma Nell singing Christian songs to my mother in their front yard. Maybe it was those religious values that helped my mother get through so much suffering in her life.

I DRIFTED INTO A STATE OF PASSIVE SUFFERING. I GRABBED A handful of sleeping pills, but as soon as I swallowed them I called for help. Fortunately, I had enough presence of mind to know I had gone too far. This was not the way it was meant to be. While I was struggling, trying to find some meaning in life, I contemplated the existence of God. I felt that as my Creator He was the one who had taught me to hear, to see, to taste.

And then I thought of the genuine Iranians I had met as a child in the villages. Pious and down-to-earth, they were happy with fresh-baked bread, goat's cheese, homemade yogurt, fresh greens, and tea. Here I am living in America, I thought, with its wealth and plenty—all the amenities one could ask for—and yet

I was searching for more. I felt myself spiritually lost, living in Los Angeles. Would I ever find balance and be satisfied with it? I wondered. I tried to engage in my environment, but my heart was still detached. Those around me thought that I was living in heaven. They did not know that inwardly I was in hell. My name is Iran, but I could not even tell people. I felt vulnerable, lost, and alone. I was faced yet again with a momentous question: Where was I to go now?

The only answer for me was to return to Iran to join my mother and younger brother. The only words that consoled me were my mother's. She asked me to come back by sending me a poem that resonated in my soul:

> What is to be done, O Muslims? for I do not recognize myself.
> I am neither Christian nor Jew nor Zoroastrian nor Muslim.
> I am not of the East nor of the West nor of the land nor of the sea.
> I am not of nature's mint nor of the circling heavens.
> I am not of India, nor of China nor of Bulgaria nor of Spain.
> I am not of the kingdom of Iraq nor of the country of Khorasan.
> My place is the Placeless. My trace is the Traceless.
> It is neither body nor soul for I belong to the soul of the Beloved.
> I have put duality away. I have seen that the two worlds are one.
> One I seek. One I know. One I see. One I call.[3]

Longing to find a part of me that I had lost, I agreed to return to Iran. I donned the veil, left the Western world, and flew back to revolutionary Iran to be with my mother.

· 9 ·

Tehran,
1983–87

I left in daylight in America to return to night in Iran. I found everything at home just as I had left it three years before. The T-shirts in my closet were still folded as I had left them. The string of pearls my father bought me on a trip to Japan still sat on my dresser. I heard music in the sounds that had filled my days in Tehran—the fruit vendor walking down the middle of our street peddling his wares, the *bahrfi*, or snow shoveler, who would roam the streets in the winter, the call to prayer from a mosque. It was not only song and prayer that I heard, but the recitation of poetry—mythical, mystical, modern—every time I would turn on the television or listen to the radio. It seemed like rhythmic sounds were part of the Iranian soul.

While home had not changed, I soon realized that I had. Once again, and even at home, I had no idea who I was. I was suppressing my feelings and identifying too strongly with others around me; yet if I gave in completely, I could be rejected. Rejec-

Brother Karim, Davar, and Mom, Tehran, March 1983. (Author's personal collection)

tion, separation, and abandonment had torn my soul apart; I couldn't afford to risk it again.

I had never really been interested in practicing my religion. Now eighteen years old, I wanted to learn more about my Islamic heritage. I remembered my aunt Maryam, my mother's half-sister from grandfather Abol Ghassem's second marriage, who had taught me the prayers when I was a child. She was a complete contrast to my mother in all but their religious beliefs. Aunt Maryam had grown up in Iran with Iranian though not religious parents. She had married into an Iranian-Turkish family who strictly followed the tenets of Shia Islam, so she learned everything from her pious mother-in-law. She had a happy family life with four daughters of her own, who became my friends. All of my old friends had left Iran by then.

Aunt Maryam and her husband, Mohammad, had been active in the revolution. Because they felt that their religion was little understood in the West, they encouraged my mother to translate books from Persian into English—although not the works of Shariati, who remained controversial after the revolution—books on the practice of Islam, such as prayer and fasting. My mother eventually translated a book with my uncle Mohammad on the five daily prayers.

I had wanted to learn more about religious women. Aunt Maryam told me about two women who both lived in Mecca and were role models in Islamic tradition. She hoped to inspire me with their stories—stories of married women who also had their own careers.

Hagar of the Old Testament plays a pivotal role among all the children of Abraham. As it is today, Mecca was surrounded by desert, fifty miles inland from the Red Sea, and had only one well, Zamzam, which still exists today and which was discovered by Hagar, the second wife of Abraham, and their son Ishmael. Hagar had been an Ethiopian slave whom Abraham left in Mecca with their infant child. While Hagar ran between two hills looking for water in what was then a wasteland, her infant began to cry and kick the ground, thereby uncovering the well. Hagar then began to trade water for food and other goods with passing caravans, and this trade marked the beginning of the city of Mecca, founded by a woman. In honor of Hagar and the sacrifices she bore as the mother of the Arab tribes that trace their lineage to Abraham through Ishmael, pilgrims to Mecca today run seven times between the same two hills. I was amazed to hear that a woman had been the founder of a city that now welcomed two million people a year for the annual pilgrimage.[1]

The second woman was Khadija, a widow who at the age of forty was one of the wealthiest women in Arabia. A savvy businesswoman, she hired many caravans consisting of hundreds of camels that she would send out twice every year. In the wintertime, when water would be available along the caravan route and the weather was cooler, her caravan would go to Syria; in the summer, she would send a caravan to Ethiopia. She eventually married the Prophet Muhammad, to whom she proposed, and became the mother of his daughter Fatima.[2]

It seemed strange to me that in this culture that I had always thought was male-dominated, a woman could ask a man to marry her. While I had not yet considered marriage, this story somehow made me think that if I did meet someone, I would be able to ask him to marry me.

I began attending weekly Friday prayers. At times, the crowds inside Tehran University were so large that people would put down their prayer carpets on the streets surrounding the campus, up to just beyond where we lived. I would fold my prayer mat, inside of which I had put my prayer stone and prayer beads, and join the women's section, which also included most of the children. The men prayed separately. At first I wondered why men and women were not performing the prayer together, but then I remembered that before the revolution, even at family parties, women somehow always drifted to one another and the men to the other men. It just seemed to be part of the social custom. Listening to the cleric's sermon, I began to feel guilty for leaving Iran in its time of need. Iranians were still defending themselves against Saddam Hussein in the war with Iraq.[3] The war had given postrevolutionary Iran a cause to come together as a nation.

AT EIGHTEEN, I WAS LOOKING FOR A ROSTAM, A HERO WHO would set my soul free, but all whom I found caused me to weep. Eventually, I bowed my head and allowed myself to be led. The old wives' tale of "marriage will save her" rang through my mother's ears. The traditional Persian love stories I had grown up reading revolved around the concept of the unknown beloved, where a hero falls in love with a girl just by hearing a description of her or her name.

The idea of marriage appealed to me because it seemed like a package deal: with it would come a house, eventually a family, some jewelry, maybe, and a sense of having moved beyond being a daughter. I would have responsibilities as a wife, and my husband would take care of me. I would be part of an extended family, loved and cared for.

Given that my mother was a single divorced woman with no social life to speak of, not to mention still unfamiliar with both Islamic and Iranian customs, there was a very small circle of men from which to choose my husband. One of the few religious clerics who spoke English was an adviser to the women's magazine *Mahjubeh*, which was produced by my mother's printing shop. The cleric, Haji Agha, mentioned that his wife's brother was looking for a wife. He described him as twenty-nine years old, tall, dark, and handsome.

I met Karim during Noruz of 1983. Haji Agha brought his family to visit us for Persian New Year and my mother asked if I wanted to meet him. Before I met him, the intention behind our introduction was for us to be married. Knowing that, I said I would meet him. Karim came from a family of five sisters and one brother. We were told by the family that he was a very good Muslim, that he knew how to read the Koran and would be happy to teach me.

With the decision to become a "traditional wife" before me, I thought about the consequences as I had seen or understood them in the West. I thought about what the head nurse had told grandmother Helen—that Iran was a country where women had no rights. I also remembered that grandmother Helen did not listen. Imagining myself a modern woman who had chosen to succumb to tradition, I was determined to make this marriage work.

· 10 ·

Married Life in Revolutionary Iran

When my family and friends in America heard of my decision to agree to an arranged marriage, it seemed to them that I had lost all reason. While I knew that I should consider my decision carefully, I also did not want to go through a slow process. After my parents' divorce, I had decided to rely only on myself, to become fiercely independent in my drive for personal freedom. I did not realize, of course, that these very characteristics I prized in myself would become threatened as a result of my marriage.

The first meeting went well and I liked Karim, but the family never left us alone. We were wined and dined, so to speak, invited to his family's home for every possible occasion. In typical traditional style, they had a ten-foot tablecloth, or *sofreh*, laid out on top of a Kerman Persian carpet. Everyone ate around the *sofreh* sitting cross-legged on the floor. Marziyeh, the only other daughter-in-law, and my *jari* (women married to brothers) would portion out the main dish. Guests were served first, then my soon-to-be father-in-law (he got the chicken breast); then the two sons, and, finally, the five sisters received whatever was left. The warmth and hospitality of Karim's family overwhelmed my mother, brother, and me, as our life in revolutionary Iran was very secluded—both from tradition and religion.

Custom dictated that Karim and I not be left alone, though I remember casting glances at Karim every chance I could; almost as if from the beginning I was the lover and not the beloved. In Persian mystical poetry, it is the females who are the beloved, the ones to be desired. In Persian when you say you are in love, you also say, "*Ashegam,*" or literally, "I am the lover," which is who I had become.[1]

I thought of my grandmother Helen falling in love with Abol Ghassem, and my mother falling in love with my father. In each case, they had dated before marriage, while I was getting married the "traditional" Iranian way. Each glance at Karim brought with it more curiosity about what he was really like. The third time we met, he proposed, and without hesitation I said yes. The family was overjoyed.

I was told only later that prior to my engagement, Karim's brother-in-law, Haji Agha, had performed a divination with the Koran. Holding the Koran in his left hand and while thinking about a marriage between Karim and me, Haji Agha put the fingers of his right hand at the top edge of the Koran, opened it at random, and read the passage on which his fingers landed. The verse was a positive one, the grounds on which Karim based his decision to propose to me.

The month and a half that preceded the wedding was, as is customary everywhere, filled with activities. The groom-to-be had to provide a trousseau for the bride-to-be. In my case, this meant daily trips with my mother-in-law-to-be to the seamstress.

Karim's family followed all the traditions of an Iranian wedding, the first official ceremony of which was *sigheh mahramiat*. Only at the end of this ceremony was I allowed to take off my head covering when in the company of Karim and his father. Karim's family filled my mother's house with sweets and flowers, including a heart-shaped Valentine cake to be served while all his family surrounded us during the ceremony. As Haji Agha said a prayer, I removed my scarf in front of the women and Karim. Everyone cheered.

One by one my mother and I familiarized ourselves with the sheer array of customs. For example, it was traditional for the groom's family to send a suitcase full of clothes for the bride as well as the bride's family. To reciprocate, we had to do the same. My mother had some beautiful silk fabrics in her antique Kuwaiti chest and we put them all in a suitcase for my new in-laws.

We then decided that the wedding would be held in our courtyard with the fountains turned on and tables set around it. Many years before my parents had bought a beautiful flower-embroidered Egyptian tent when we were in Egypt that we hung over the courtyard so that when the guests looked up, they saw a garden in the sky.

Preparations for the wedding began with what is called *band andazi*—a folded thread rubbed across the face to remove all extra hair. My eyebrows were plucked. I asked what else was in store for me and they said white powder for my face, *sormeh,* or black eyeliner, for my eyes, dye for my eyebrows, and, finally, a black perfume consisting of musk, ambergris, and a special oil. Not being familiar with most of these elements, I declined the traditional makeup and insisted on doing it myself.

I had chosen to wear my mother's bridal gown, which raised objections from my in-laws who wondered if that would be a bad omen given that she was divorced. Without thinking twice about it, I proudly displayed her gown and veil as I arrived at my family home for the wedding ceremony.

Everything was a blur—literally—because my contact lenses were giving me trouble. I remember walking into my mother's living room and not recognizing anyone. I could hear the sounds of "*dombaks*" or drums, beating and women who looked like Russian babushkas with tiny head scarves and rosy cheeks singing traditional wedding songs. I realized they must be from Karim's family. Across from them was my father's family. My paternal grandmother Mani joone seemed very solemn and quiet. I would later discover that she did not approve, yet her presence there gave me strength of heart. One by one, as each of these guests came up to tell me how beautiful I looked, I still couldn't recognize them.

I was led to a small room where the *aqd* or marriage contract would be signed. Sitting in front of a large Persian tablecloth containing all the symbolic elements for a happy marriage, we began the first part of the ceremony. There was a Koran for God's blessing, a mirror for happiness, and, on either side of it, two candlestick holders with lit candles. One candle was lit in the name of Karim and one in mine. At the end of the ceremony, I snuffed them out and preserved them to be lit when our first child was born. On the tablecloth was also a glass of honey for sweetness, a large loaf of *sangak*—a flat bread baked on small stones—on which was written "Allah" with cinnamon, and a needle and thread to symbolically tie up my mother-in-law's tongue (she herself prepares it, to symbolize that she does so willingly). There were other plates containing wild rue, nuts, two sugar loaves, and another needle threaded with seven colors of thread.

Karim came and sat next to me and we looked at each other in the mirror as my sisters-in-law held a muslin cloth over my head. Two women, each of whom had been selected because they had been married once and had not suffered misfortune, rubbed the two loaves of sugar together over me. Another woman of the same description then picked up the seven-color-threaded needle and, knotting it for good luck, began to sew. When asked what she was sewing, she said, "Love and affection."

The cleric then came and stood where he could not see me— this was the signal that we were ready for the contractual part of the ceremony. I was asked by the cleric, "In the Name of God (*bismillah*) do you consent based on the dowry mentioned?" I had been told by my friends that the dowry, or *mehr*, was important because if he were to divorce me, he would have to pay me my *mehr*; if I ever wanted to divorce him, I would be able to do so by giving back my dowry to him. I did not realize then that I could have asked for additional conditions at that time—a kind of prenuptial agreement—but lost as my mother and I were in the excitement of it all, it never occurred to us to do so.

The only men in the room were Karim, his father, and my brother, who was then fifteen years old. My mother and Karim's parents had previously agreed upon the dowry: a mirror, two candleholders, a Koran, and two hundred fifty thousand tomans ($35,000). The cleric asked me if I was willing to marry Karim for this dowry. I had been warned that I should not answer until the third time so as not to appear too anxious. When I finally agreed, the celebrations began immediately, but not before two witnesses signed our marriage certificate. And with that Karim and I were married. All the women chanted "hurray," "*Kel kel kel,*" as sweets were passed around and each of my in-laws gave me a piece of jewelry.

As the bride, I had to supply the *jihaz* or furnishings for our home. My mother had sold her silver to buy me the refrigerator, stove, washing machine, and living room, dining room, and bed-room furniture—basically everything from pillowcases to china and toilet paper. My father and in-laws had given us carpets.[2]

The night of the wedding, family members accompanied us to our new home, a rented apartment in an affluent part of Tehran. All of Karim's family and my mother and brother came by and had pastries and tea. As a sign that they had modern views, my in-laws had made it clear that they would not be ask-ing for the traditional chastity test after the wedding night. But I was also told that part of my duty was to please my husband's sexual desires, which I couldn't begin to understand. My mother was the last to leave and I remember asking her: "Now what?" She hugged me and said: "Now you begin your new life." I thought to myself: "Let my fate do with me as it will."

Our first night was clumsy and awkward. Karim was scared and so was I. We were both dissolving into a marriage like gam-blers casting their dice. I resolved to myself that I would allow

Davar's first wedding, Tehran, May 1984. (Author's personal collection)

this stranger to take me. As my fear gave way to obligation, that gave way to love, not passion, but a sweet and kind love for the confused and insecure man I had married.

FOR THE FIRST TIME I FELT IN CHARGE OF MY OWN LIFE. I wrote a long letter to my father and family in Boston describing the wedding and my feelings:

Dear Dad, Shahla, Mani, Ali Reza, and BOSTON!

Today is our one-month anniversary. The reason why I write you so late is not because I was not thinking of you or that I did not care to. It was simply because I am going through a lot of changes and I need to adapt. That is where it is hard to find a few moments of spare time!! I hope you are all well and that you are leading a good and happy life.

Being back in Iran I felt that I had found a home forever. I felt my faith would ensure that my future life would not only be a happy one but also a very stable one. I was proud of the fact that I was able to accept my religion back so easily. While in America, I had forgotten all the beautiful rituals and prayers that one is obligated to do for God and I felt peaceful. In America, I gave in to the rumors about Iran and I truly had become alienated from my own homeland.

I had the choice to come back to the States. I had the choice to come back to a land where there is plenty of everything, a land of entertainment and a land of bliss, but to me that land remained foreign until the day I came back to Iran and it still remains a distant place. I searched and searched but I could not find my fate there. I could only find momentary love, momentary wealth, and momentary security. I was not born to live in the United States and I was not born to accept their mentality, which lives on buying the minds and faith of its people by making a society that lacks nothing, nothing but one thing, the most important thing, *God*.

I saw Disneyland, I saw the Red Sox, I saw Brooke Shields, and I saw Dan Rather. I saw Boston College. I heard Alan Parsons and I heard Reagan. I experienced Brookline High and I experienced Los Angeles. I tried working and I tried modeling. I sang and I danced. I swam and I ran. I was happy—I thought I was happy—but I was sad and empty. I was alone. I was in the wrong place. America and all its opportunities were not for me. My faith and country were to be the only two things that would allow me to have a fulfilled life.

Everyone chooses her own way. Everyone sees life in his own way. No one person is right or wrong. Everyone is right in their own minds, but we must never forget God and all His blessings and all the things He has created for us, all the basic things that we seem to overlook, like the water we drink and the air we breathe. If only we could sit and think about the fact that all He is asking for in return is for us to be aware that there is a Day of Judgment and that we must program ourselves for that day. We must be ready and alert. We must not give in to unhealthy desires. We must remain pious and we must remain as His servants on earth until the day we die.

Another reason for my happiness is that I have found a husband who was truly destined to be mine. Our aims and goals in life are the same. We see our future together so bright that that in itself brings us happiness. Although we do not come from the same kind of family, I mean, they are much more traditional then you or Mom ever were, we live a very harmonious life together.

There is still a lot of time for us to get to know each other, but as I said to you when I got married, "I know he will be my future husband so it does not matter that I do not know him so well before the marriage." He is a very affectionate, loving, and caring person. He has a strong character and yet when you see him with a little kid he is so gentle and kind. Some of my characteristics or ways of thought are new to him, but he is gradually learning some of my ways. And for me, it is the same. I am learning a lot about his way of life and his family. I do not agree with everything his family does, but I maintain the respect because I love Karim. As I told you before, he has five sisters and one brother and it is my task to keep them all happy and in smiles; sometimes that is difficult, especially with a person like me who is not too keen on giving compliments to everyone every two minutes.

I have cooked a lot of delicious foods for Karim. He cannot believe that I know so much at my age. He always tells me that he views me as a twenty-four-year-old woman. Once I made a really delicious chicken dish and Mommy was there to visit me. She did not stay for lunch, but when my husband came home and ate the chicken, he could not believe I made it. Later he told me, "You do not have to try so hard to make me happy. You did not have to tell your mother to cook that chicken." I was so mad because he would not believe that I had made it so I went straight to the kitchen and I cooked the same dish for him right in front of his eyes. He was impressed!!!

It is now the month of Ramadan. I was fasting for the first two days then I got a certain allergy and I kept sneezing and my nose is running and it is sort of irritating so I have to drink water. Hopefully by next week I will resume fasting.

On Eid-i Fitr we will all gather together and I will wear my dress again and we will take pictures together. Then we will send you the pictures. Well, I must go for now. I want to thank you Daddy for the beautiful rug that you gave me. Everyone loves it and it looks beautiful in our apartment.

If you have any questions about Karim or me or anything else, please write me because I do not know what else I should say. Take care and do not worry about me, Karim or the other Karim or Mommy or Mani joone. We are all well. We are eating well and we are surviving just as well as you are in the States. With all my love to you. Iran.[3]

I YEARNED TO LEARN MORE ABOUT KARIM'S VILLAGE, HIS CUS-toms, and Islam, so that I could become a better practicing Muslim. His family came from a small, picturesque village called Shahmirzad. A three-hour drive from Tehran, it is just north of the city of Semnan in northwestern Iran. It is a mountainous region and summer retreat, and I fell in love with the place the first time we went there.

Shahmirzad was where Karim's extended family went every summer for several months to get away from the summer heat of Tehran and, in the years I was there, to get away from Saddam

Hussein's perpetual aerial bombing. It was a frightening experience when we heard the air-raid sirens. We would crouch down in an area without windows at night, wondering if when we woke up the next morning, one of us would have died from the bombing.

Double doors led into the family courtyard in the house in Shahmirzad. In the center was a pool fed by a mountain stream. Their house was on the second floor and consisted of eight rooms, including three bedrooms, a family room, a formal living room, and a kitchen. All the rooms opened onto the porch, which protected the rooms from the high summer heat. The floors of the bedrooms were covered wall-to-wall with Persian carpets; neatly arranged in the corners were quilts, mattresses, and pillows. The house always contained enough bedding for twenty people. The bedroom where Karim and I stayed had a mirror on the wall and a few colored pictures taken from Persian magazines. As always, there were no chairs or tables. Everyone sat and slept on the floor.

Shahmirzad, which is right at the base of a mountain, is the first village to receive the pure mountain stream. The town square, a small open space surrounded by towering trees, included the local mosque, teahouse, bathhouse, and telephone company, where I would call my mother and friends.

The people I met in the village all had a quick wit and a natural sense of humor. In the early morning there was a trip to the village center for fresh cream (*sar shir*) and hot baked bread. This was where I learned the local gossip. Everyone I met, including all of Karim's family, was friendly and offered the typical Persian hospitality. Another thing that impressed me about the "pure"

Iranians I met in Shahmirzad was their politeness. They would begin a sentence with, "Your humble servant . . ." or, "This servant and your honor. . . ."

I noticed a square, short table at the side of the wall in the living room. I asked if it was a *korsi*. It was. Here in Shahmirzad, hot coals were placed under the table and a quilt laid on top. In the wintertime the table was moved—presumably, everyone sat, ate, and slept around this table, warmed by the heater and quilts. In Shahmirzad there was no other source of heat in the wintertime.

On Thursday evenings everyone in town would go to the public graveyard to pray for members of their family buried on the hill. Watching the entire village ascend the hill and sit in prayer for their ancestors was a dramatic sight indeed.

THE CLIMATE IN SHAHMIRZAD WAS BEAUTIFUL. LOFTY WALNUT trees and narrow village streets led to streams of pure drinking water. I picked up the Shahmirzadi dialect and learned how to cook Shahmirzadi food. My favorite was a chicken with plum sauce that is both tart and sweet. I wanted to be a Shamirzadi woman like my sisters-in-law. I tried hard to learn how to be exactly like them so that they would accept me as their own.

It was an Islamic holiday in Shahmirzad and my father-in-law, who was a well-known businessman, was holding a feast. Each year he prayed for the health of his family and in turn had vowed to feed the less fortunate on this holiday. I was very happy to be a part of the festivities. The act of making a vow (*nazr*) and giving charity is part of the Iranian way of life. When God is asked for a favor, in return a gift must be offered to the poor or some such—something must be given back for having received the favor.

Many women make a vow to give an offering in return for their prayers being answered. One such occasion is the *sofreh-yi* Abol Fazl. The women would sit around a tablecloth (*sofreh*) and participate in a generous meal while listening to a woman preacher speak about Islam and recite from the Koran. The event was held in honor of Abol Fazl, the uncle of Imam Hossein. It was he who had tried to get water for Imam Hossein on the plains of Karbala. Because Imam Hossein and his army were denied access to water, giving someone or something water to drink took on great religious significance in Iranian life. This is why the shrines to Imam Hossein we saw in Isfahan display vessels with water and why before any animal is slaughtered it is first given water to drink.[4]

On the occasion of my father-in-law's charitable feast, I observed my mother-in-law and sisters-in-law to see what role they played in the process. It seemed the women in the family were in charge of serving the food to the poor. They would stand beside the large brass pots of rice and lamb and give each person their portion. I felt I should be able to do the same thing to fulfill my obligation to God. But as I approached the food area, I felt a shield go up. My mother- and sisters-in-law turned their backs on me and immersed themselves in the confusion of the dozens of people in line to get food.

I was very hurt and, feeling ostracized, I decided to take my case straight to my father-in-law. I suppose my sisters-in-law saw this as disrespectful, given that in many cases traditional women aren't encouraged to speak their minds. Without beating around the bush, I told my father-in-law that I was very upset and felt left out. He was very supportive and said that I should not take it as a personal slight, that the others had been doing this for all their lives and that I would get my turn too. Well, I never did.

I was trying hard to fit in and keep my fieriness under control. I had a dream one night in Shahmirzad that would recur throughout my adult life. Circles of white and gray clay surrounded me. As I tried to mold them into a particular shape, a bowl, a vase, a plate, they resisted, always managing to form into a circle again and rise above my head. I reached up to grab them and they would slip in and out of my hands.

I WAS DOING EVERYTHING THAT WAS EXPECTED OF ME AS A wife. I baked, roasted, cleaned, and took care of the laundry, all the while working outside the home as a translator at different conferences. Between Karim and me there was never the rush of excitement when one of us came into the room, or youthful daydreams that would cause us to hesitate when the other was absent. Ours were days of family and nights of fulfilling my duties to please my husband. Two months after my wedding, I rushed to the emergency room thinking I had a stomach flu, but test results soon showed I was pregnant. It was expected of young brides to settle down and have children, and nineteen was not considered too young. I agreed because at the time I felt it was my Kismet—my fate.

Pregnancy put me into a state of acquiescence to whatever

occurred around me. I knew I had to deliver myself over to God and that my ego would have to stand by, unable to intervene in nature's course. At the same time, I was developing an overwhelming bond with the baby in my womb. I became both aware and attentive to each change within me; my feelings and intuitions were completely engaged in the process.

Being pregnant was a delightful time. Tradition held that the family was to satisfy all of the pregnant woman's desires. If I walked in when someone was eating a meal, I had to be invited to join immediately. If something was being cooked and smelled good, I had to be given some. Once the baby began to move, other women in the family would place their hands on my stomach and make a wish. If the baby moved at that moment, they knew that their wish would come true.

I WAS SIX MONTHS PREGNANT AND TRANSLATING AT A MEDICAL conference when an African American Muslim living in Iran came up to me and told me about auditions for a new English news program at the Islamic Republic of Iran Broadcasting. A week later, I was sitting in front of a camera and crew. I got the job of anchoring the four p.m. news every day. After my first appearance, the phones at the television station rang off the hook with men wanting to propose marriage. One day, my coanchor Judy Garland (yes, that was her real name) came out of the studio after reading her segment and answered a phone call for "the broadcaster." The woman on the phone asked if Judy was the young one or the old one. "Geez," Judy thought, "I'm only thirty." She told the woman if she wanted me for her son, she should get permission from my husband first. Needless to say, the woman hung up. One day, without realizing that the network camera was on, I walked on to the set with a pregnant hobble. The phones stopped ringing.[5]

Judy Garland was from Oklahoma. She was married to an Iranian university professor and was the mother of a little boy when I met her in January 1984. At first, she came across as cold and standoffish, but eventually we became the best of friends and shared many weekends together with our families.

A practicing Muslim, Judy was as American as she was Iranian, taking great pleasure in putting together a great Thanksgiving Day meal, albeit with the lean turkeys available in Tehran at the time. It is interesting how the two of us never really discussed the irony of our jobs as broadcasters of English news. Here we were, two American-born women, dressed in the veil, anchoring the afternoon news on Islamic Republic of Iran Broadcasting. I was only nineteen years old and thought of the job as fun and easy money even though I resented the fact that Judy got paid more than I did because she had a college degree.

Islamic Republic of Iran Broadcasting English News, Tehran, 1986. (Author's personal collection)

Every day around two p.m. a yellow jeep from the Islamic Republic of Iran Broadcasting would come to my apartment to pick me up for work. I was driven up Vali Asr Boulevard, formerly known as Pahlavi, to get to the station, which was located on top of the hill. Built in the 1970s during the Shah's time, it housed many of Iran's most famous news anchors, producers, and engineers, who had decided to continue broadcasting the news even though it was clear they were not fond of the Islamic regime. You could detect a certain rebellion in the way the women working behind the scenes wore their head scarves, ensuring that a bit of hair showed at their forehead. The atmosphere at the station was very collegial until the managing editor and the director of news appeared, both of whom were at some level connected or related to the ruling clerics and founders of the revolution.

The English broadcast newsroom consisted of one room with a large oval-shaped table in the center shared by translators, anchors, and production assistants. Our news director was responsible for pulling wire copy from the noon newscast aired in Persian, which would then be translated and handed to us to read verbatim. We had no say in the editorial content of the material we were given. For Judy, the newsroom was not as glum or foreboding as it was for me. Perhaps because she was older and fully American, she was able to cautiously laugh and joke with the young translators. I felt as though I was being watched more carefully, especially by the senior news managers, whose offices were down the hall.

On camera, we came across as just a bunch of amateurs trying to put on a fifteen-minute news program. We were stiff as boards sitting there in our scarves, afraid to smile or show any type of human emotion. We were perhaps an excellent propaganda point for the regime.[6] Article 175 of the Constitution of the Islamic Republic of Iran says, "The freedom of expression and dissemination of thoughts in the Radio and Television of the Islamic Republic of Iran must be guaranteed in keeping with the Islamic criteria and the best interests of the country." Furthermore, the constitution indicates that the head of the broadcasting station would be appointed and/or dismissed by the supreme leader and that "a council consisting of two representatives each of the President, the head of the judiciary branch, and the Islamic Consultative Assembly shall supervise the functioning of this organization."

The idea was to promote to an English-speaking audience not only the accomplishments of the Islamic Republic but also to highlight news from the Islamic world. This news was of particular interest to those Iranians who continued to wage an ideological battle with the United States following the revolution. With the Iran-Iraq war in full force, the news often began with the number of Iranians killed or wounded by Iraqi chemical weapons.

In February of 1984, Iran's foreign minister spoke at a disarmament conference in Geneva and reported at least forty-nine instances of Iraqi chemical attacks in dozens of border regions resulting in the deaths of 109 Iranians and the wounding of hundreds of others. It was at this time that Iran began a massive offensive toward Basra, Iraq, where it was alleged that poison gas was being used by Saddam. Eventually, the United Nations sent a team of experts to Iran and verified and condemned the use of chemical weapons by Iraq.

In addition, in 1984, the International Committee of the Red Cross confirmed that 160 wounded soldiers in hospitals in Tehran "presented a clinical picture whose nature leads to the presumption of the recent use of substances prohibited by international law." That statement by the ICRC was followed by a United States State Department statement that said: "The U.S. Government has concluded that the available evidence indicates that Iraq has used lethal chemical weapons." But Iraq continued to dismiss these international condemnations, calling them "political hypocrisy."

Although the news from the Iran-Iraq war dominated the news coverage, there was also great emphasis on news from the Middle East, particularly on the continued Israeli-Palestinian conflict. The civil war in Lebanon and the tensions there between Shia Muslims, Christians, and Israeli and Syrian forces were another constant source of news. The Soviet occupation of Afghanistan was also in full force at the time. Across the border from Iran, thousands of Afghan civilians were killed and entire villages were leveled by relentless Soviet bombings, while crops and irrigation systems were also destroyed. The news focused on the plight of the Afghan people and in particular the news of Afghan resistance fighters standing up to the Soviet occupiers.

And then there were the weekly, sometimes daily, stories of the Nicaraguan Sandinistas and their fight against the Contra rebels who were backed by the United States. In 1984, Daniel Ortega won the presidential elections in Nicaragua, but the

United States government saw the Sandinistas as a left-wing organization and were assisting the opposing group, known as the Contras. Based in neighboring Honduras, the Contras waged a bloody guerilla war against the Sandinistas.

The most unnerving aspect of the job was the fact that the television station was an obvious target for Saddam's aerial bombings. When the sirens, signaling an imminent aerial bombing, went off, we would take cover in the basement of the television station where the actual studios were located. These incidents became so ordinary that after a while we would go outside ourselves to look for the planes above.

It was on these occasions, when we had "down" time, that I got to know some of the other female employees at the station. Several were veteran television producers and directors from the Shah's time who had stayed on for the love of their careers and to continue earning an income, not because they liked the Islamic Republic. The revolutionary news managers tolerated them because they were good at what they did. So long as they didn't cause trouble, they held on to their jobs. We never spoke about politics—just about our children, or where to buy the latest manteau, he long jackets that we wore over our clothes to cover the shape of our bodies. One of them convinced me to try highlighting my hair. Even though we couldn't violate the standards of Islamic dignity by showing our hair in public, the blond streaks in our otherwise jet black hair lightened up our look and made us feel attractive when we lifted our veils at home.

· 11 ·

Becoming a Mother

My son Saied, whose name means happiness, was born on March 19, 1984. According to the custom of Shahmirzad, my mother-in-law had to give Saied his first bath when he was ten days old. When my mother-in-law took him from me, it was absolutely heart wrenching to hear him placed in the hot bath. I could hear Saied screech at the top of his tiny lungs. I kept banging on the bathroom door asking if everything was okay, much to my sisters-in-law's annoyance. Finally, I thought I'd just go in there and watch what she was doing. When she came out of the bathroom, my mother-in-law proceeded to faint out of frustration with me.

After Saied's birth, my father-in-law had recited the call to prayer in Saied's right ear and the declaration to perform the prayer in his left ear, as is the custom of all Muslims. His name was announced on the seventh day after his birth, the day when

Davar and Saied,
Tehran, 1984.
(Author's personal collection)

a lamb is sacrificed and food is given to the poor. My in-laws also attached a turquoise "eye" to Saied's clothes to keep away the evil eye.

Everyone was careful not to say that Saied was a handsome or beautiful child without first saying *"mashallah"* (God willing). One of his paternal aunts even gave him a gold necklace with *"mashallah"* engraved on a pendant in case someone forgot to say it and put the evil eye on Saied.

I loved that I was now a mother. The Prophet Muhammad had said, "Paradise lies beneath the feet of mothers."

WHILE I IMMERSED MYSELF IN MY NEWLY CREATED FAMILY life, my mother continued working on translating some of the lectures from the thirty-five volumes of Ali Shariati's writings and lectures. One day, one of her friends who knew about the clerics' objection to Shariati said my mother should go with her to Qom and ask a cleric there what he thought of the idea of her working on Shariati. My mother was aware that not all clerics accepted his Islamic point of view. My mother agreed. They went to Qom and there they met with one of the leading clerics of the city. Her friend explained to him what she was doing and, trying to dissuade her, he said: "If anyone reads a book you have translated from Shariati and kills a cleric because of what he reads, you will be responsible for the death of that cleric!"[1]

My mother could not believe her ears. Shariati's hundreds of lectures over a period of six years, lectures that drew thousands of listeners, had been instrumental up until his death in 1977, two years before the revolution, in preparing the Iranian public for a revolution which brought the clerics to power, although his intention had been to promote more of a nationalist Islamic movement rather than a theocracy. Here was a cleric who had come to power because of the effect of Shariati's lectures on the people now condemning Shariati's writings much as the Shah's regime had done. Here she had the best of intentions—feeling that the method used by Shariati to awaken the Muslim consciousness to social justice would be an invaluable service—and she was being told that she would be responsible for the death of people if she continued her translation. It was a very disappointing point of view and one she did not appreciate, knowing how much Shariati's work had brought consciousness within herself.

BEING CAUTIOUS, MY MOTHER HEEDED THE WORDS OF THE cleric and put her work on another Shariati translation on hold and began to think of other ways to bring in income. Most of the possibilities of English-language publications had dried up with the revolution. My brother, who had not seen our father in eight years, was about to finish high school and wanted to go to America for college.

My mother began looking for employment abroad. She had friends in London and thought that it would be a good place to start. She felt she had done what she could in Iran; she was ready to move on and go abroad with my brother. Maybe it was God's plan, she thought, that she migrate to the West once again.

My mother never really felt that Iranians saw her as an Iranian. Though she looked like her father, she sounded more like her American mother when she spoke Persian. While her fluency in English kept her in constant demand to translate letters and documents that did not interest her, opportunities for the worthwhile intellectual and literary pursuits that were her passions were not available. She felt the knowledge she had gained of Islam and the experiences she had of spiritual growth were being pushed aside in favor of tasks others were capable of doing. But by far her greatest battle was with loneliness.

My mother had not met anyone in Iran with whom to share her goals and dreams. As a divorced woman with guardianship of her three children she fell into the most undesirable category for women in Iran—a divorced woman with children who was not wealthy. The language barrier and different cultural upbringing only added further isolation to the mix.

Right around that time, my mother was offered a job at the al-Hoda Bookshop in London and she decided to take it.[2] With this move, she once again had to question her love for Shariati.

The experience with the cleric was enough to teach her that she had to let go of the Islam of Shariati and return to her first spiritual struggle brought about by her immersion in Sufism. She had to continue working on changing herself and realized the political implications in Shariati's works would only serve to distract her from her spiritual journey. She felt ready to test her faith to see whether or not her practice of Islam came about because she was living in an Islamic country or because she now fully believed in her faith.

When my mother was introduced as an adult to Islam and Sufism, it became an important goal for her to express herself through her beliefs, to experience and be what she said she was, and yet she had no idea at that point what being a Muslim meant. She wanted to learn the practices of her faith on her own. For her the question of leaving Iran—now as an American Muslim—came down to how her faith would fare in a secular nation where there is a separation between church and state as opposed to a nation that is based on one religion or another.

With my mother planning to leave, I began to think more deeply about the reality of the pious life. The two of us had become so close in Iran. It was as though when I had moved back to Iran I had taken up her psyche and way of life. Once she left, she would be free of Iran's revolutionary culture. Given my marriage, I would remain a part of it. She left me with a talisman that contained the entire Koran on twenty feet of vellum, each six-inch panel with exquisite calligraphy. This labor of love by some calligrapher in a remote village of Iran had been written to ward off the evil eye.

ON MY TWENTY-FIRST BIRTHDAY I WENT TO VISIT MY IRANIAN grandmother Mani joone, who still lived in Tehran. Two years into my marriage, Mani joone still disapproved of the match even though she'd had an arranged marriage as a young bride living in Iran in the 1920s. However, as I would only realize later, there was a significant difference. While she had lived a traditional life, it was in the environment of an educated, aristocratic family. I was experiencing it within a very different cultural setting. My mother-in-law, for example, couldn't read or write and my husband had only a high school education.

April 1, my birthday, was now an official holiday—the birthday of the Islamic Republic and the anniversary of the day millions of Iranians in a referendum voted yes for an Islamic Republic in 1979. On that day, I took Saied to Mani joone so she could see how her first great-grandchild had grown.

At seventy-four years old and now a widow after grandfather Abbas died of a heart attack eight years earlier, she lived alone. I asked her about her own arranged marriage. She said that she and my grandfather were engaged for eight months, during which time my grandfather would come in the evening to her home and they would sit together. She would put out sweets and fruit and tea would be brought by the servants. He would come by two or three times a week, when they would talk about their lives and future.

Mani joone's father, Ali Akbar Davar, was a minister in the court of the Shah and she was taken to her wedding celebration in the prime minister's car, where she sat with a veil over her head. My grandfather Abbas was sitting there next to her and someone sat in front of them holding a mirror to the backseat. The custom was to have a mirror in front of the bride so her husband-to-be could see her reflection.

She then described the dinner. At that time it was not customary to sit at a table to eat. At even the best parties, the hostess would spread a tablecloth on the carpets and everyone would sit on the floor. But grandfather Abbas had made arrangements for tables to be placed next to one another which resulted in a very large table set only for the women. Abbas was not allowed to come and sit with her; instead he had stood outside and gave the orders for the food. They ate dinner and some of the women began dancing for the other women. She added, "That was it, and in a few months I became pregnant and then Pari was born."

In 1935, Reza Shah passed a law that forbade the wearing of the chador. The women began to wear black scarves covered by a hat, which my grandmother thought looked silly. After the law was passed, she still wore a scarf when she went out on the streets in Tehran. By this time, my grandfather Abbas had gone to Europe to study; when he had been gone a year, he asked her to join him with my then four-year-old aunt Pari. She and her daughter accompanied another family to Europe as it was unheard of for an Iranian woman to travel abroad alone. Once they reached Baghdad and were ready to leave their hotel room for the first time, she looked at herself in the mirror. She had put on a very fashionable dress that had been made for her in Tehran before she left, and a hat. She said that she took one good look at herself and laughed thinking how she was actually going to go out in public looking like this. While she remained self-conscious and embarrassed, she eventually got used to it and went on. How amazing that, fifty years later, I donned the veil Mani joone had discarded.

STILL A STUDENT OF THE COUNTRY'S NEW ISLAMIC WAY OF LIFE, it was my responsibility to learn about Islam's history—information that I had not been privy to, having attended an American-style school during the time of the Shah. It was explained to me that there are two calendars in Iran—solar and lunar. The solar calendar is based on the twelve months named after Zoroastrian angels: Farvardin, Ordibehesht, Khordad, et cetera, which correspond exactly with the twelve constellations. The lunar calendar, on the other hand, is based on the Islamic calendar: Muharram, Safar, Ramadan, et cetera, each year falling ten days shorter than the solar year so that Muslim holidays migrate backward through the solar calendar. The first of each lunar month is calculated from the sunset immediately following the appearance of the new moon. When a day of mourning for the death of someone significant in Muslim history falls on a holiday in the solar year like Noruz, celebrations are limited—religious mourning takes precedence.

The year 1985 was perhaps the one in which I was most entrenched in the Islamic way of life. Each day it seemed we celebrated the birth or marked the passing of one or another of the Prophet's descendants.

During the month of Ramadan I began the fast from predawn to sunset. I found it difficult the first few days, but then got used to it as everyone around me was fasting. No one ate, drank, smoked, or engaged in sex from predawn until sunset. I felt the joy of following God's way while continuing to struggle to meet life's expectations. The Koran is divided into thirty parts so a person can read one part each day during the month of fasting and I followed this schedule of prayer.

Saddam Hussein was bombing Tehran even during the holy month of Ramadan. By the spring of 1985, there was an increase in the targeting of population centers and industrial facilities by the Iraqis. Iraq began more systematic attacks on Iranian cities and Saddam Hussein ordered the use of more chemical bombs on the warfront and against civilians in the border towns.

The twenty-first of Ramadan, one of the holiest days of the year, was a time for special prayers. That afternoon I was standing outside my father-in-law's house when a young woman in a black chador appeared at the door, her face looking gray—almost black. I felt death was practically in the air. She asked if she could tell my fortune. I was scared but said yes. She took my palm and said, "You will have four children from two men." I broke out in a sweat. My sisters-in-law, who were gathered in my home, started laughing.

We celebrated the end of the month of fasting, which is a lunar holiday throughout the Muslim world. My in-laws sacrificed a lamb for Saied, giving the meat to the poor as a charity. While I observed all the pious deeds that were required of me, I felt good, but my actions were becoming more a matter of routine than reflections of true belief. This could partly have been

Davar with son, Saied, in the village of Shahmirzad. (Author's personal collection)

due to the fact that my husband was not as orthodox in practicing Islam as I was led to believe. He never spent time reading the Koran nor did he attend Friday prayers on a regular basis.

BY JUNE, SAIED HAD BEGUN TO WALK. HE HAD ELEVEN TEETH and was speaking in full sentences. He was my joy in the midst of the great uncertainty in which we lived. One day an Iraqi missile hit near our house. It was horrifying and the thought of those killed and the lives lost raced through my mind. I remembered when I was in Boston I had heard about the death of a cousin who was killed when one of the Iraqi bombs hit her home, and now I thought of the suffering of the people who had to bury their loved ones. Could one of us be next?

Occasionally my father and sister would call from Boston to check on us. We had gotten so used to this way of life that we did not complain. We felt we were all on a mission, our faith and stamina regularly being tested, so I was as noble and brave as I could muster when responding to their questions and concerns.

While the occasions to mourn the loss of a religious figure were plentiful, in order not to be drawn into the depths of those sad emotions, I began to look forward to the pleasant times and happy celebrations, even if they were few and far between, to avoid falling into despair at the circumstances surrounding us. On September 10 I went shopping for gifts and food in preparing a party for my brother Karim's eighteenth birthday. Though I knew he would have to enlist in the army and potentially be sent to the front of the war with Iran, we knew we must celebrate this important day.

Walking in a crowded boulevard in Tehran, I heard the familiar sounds of the traditional Iranian martial arts rhythm of the *zurkhaneh*—translated literally *zurkhaneh* means "House of Strength." It was here that an ancient Persian sport similar to martial arts was performed. I had heard about these centers from my parents but never had time to venture into one, plus women aren't usually allowed inside. It is said that the Houses of Strength began early in Iranian history when Iran, occupied by foreigners, would train its young men to one day succeed in expelling those who had invaded their country.

I thought I could get away with going inside by pretending I was a tourist. The *zurkhaneh* had a large room with a pit in the center and room for an audience all around the pit. Eight or twelve men, wearing only embroidered knee-length trousers, entered the pit area and performed to the beating of the drum and the chanting of verses from the *Shahnameh.* In unison, they did push-ups and juggled a large *meel,* or wooden club, which they spun high in the air. Sitting above the center ring, I watched the session end with a wrestling match, the sport my grandfather Abol Ghassem had mastered. I could still hear him reciting Ferdowsi. Even in these tenuous times of war, I remained fascinated by Iran's vibrant culture.

I CONTINUED TO BE INTRIGUED BY THE PHILOSOPHY OF SHIA Islam less as a reflection of my integration into life in Iran and more because I sought a true understanding of the pillars and traditions of my faith. In the spring of 1986, on the occasion of the birthday of Fatima, the Prophet's daughter, we celebrated Women's Day. Judy and I were still anchoring the English news and were invited to visit the Ayatollah Khomeini on this day. This was not a private visit but rather a public viewing at his home in Jamaran, Tehran, for a couple thousand other women who had been invited to make this pilgrimage.

There was an electrifying feeling in the large hall next to his home as we waited for Khomeini's arrival. He was to appear on the balcony directly above us, the spiritual leader of millions of Iranians. As we waited, several hundred women led us in a chant, "*Allah-o-akbar, Khomeini rahbar*" ("God is Greater and Khomeini is the leader"). It was a chilling moment to hear the slogans all around you yet it did inspire me to say his name even louder and louder. The sheer power of our voices energized me. Then he appeared, somewhat shorter than I had imagined, waving his hand, and setting off more chants by the audience. Women began throwing extra scarves at him. I felt lost in that moment of the Islamic dream in which nothing could be more powerful than standing before the Ayatollah Khomeini. Many women had tears in their eyes, others wept incessantly, as he walked the narrow balcony and sat down to begin addressing the crowd.

He said as women we were to struggle just as Fatima "struggled to the best of her ability, during the short span of her life, addressing the government of the time and passing judgment on them." He said we were to imitate her life and follow the example of her virtuousness. As I sat there and listened to the man who had single-handedly changed the course of history, bringing a revolution to Iran in the name of Islam, I was asked to do as Fatima had done in seeking fairness and justice for her loved ones.

I strongly believe that the founding members of Islam, the Prophet and his descendants, had every intention to follow the principles of justice and fairness, but by 1986 many Iranians felt the erosion of justice in the public sphere. In October of 1986, one of Iran's most powerful religious bodies decreed that the supreme judicial council would be authorized to hire judges with "minimal experience." The law was as follows: "The Supreme Judicial Council is authorized to appoint persons who have been working in Revolutionary Prosecutors' Offices in judicial positions for more than three years as judges of the Prosecution Offices and Courts, without regard to the Legal Bill on the

Qualification of Judges, provided that they possess at least the High School Diploma or are approved by the Supreme Judicial Council, and provided that the candidates of either category are able to pass an examination on the Civil Procedure Code and the Islamic Penal Code."[4]

This meant that more and more judges came from the ranks of the hard-line revolutionary government, each harboring his own old cumbersome and patriarchal customs. Increasingly, the penalties imposed were gruesome and brutal. Under the penal code, the penalty for adultery for unmarried men and women was a hundred lashes of a whip. Married men and women accused of adultery could be stoned to death, a man while buried up to his waist and a women up to her neck. Newspaper articles printed reports of women being stoned from the holy city of Qom to the deserts of Kerman. Here and there I would hear of the execution of teenagers, not to mention of hundreds of prisoners, after summary trials.

After six years Iranians were growing weary of the Iraq-Iran war, but daily life became difficult as well. More families took on second or third jobs as poverty was on the rise. The revolutionary morality guards, or Komitehs, added a further element of intimidation and fear into our lives, pressuring society to conform to religious morals while they amassed tremendous amounts of wealth within their own private Islamic foundations. As religious observations increased, I noticed a rise in prostitution and addiction to heroin and opium, especially among the young.

In the span of our lives, my grandmother, mother, and I had

circled back and forth between Iran and America. In our personal journeys, whenever we found the possibilities in Iran limiting, we chose to invest in the other culture where our roots might take and actually blossom into fruit. While my mother and I both had sought out our Islamic heritage and were proud to have learned so much of its rich history, I had to admit, as my mother had, that the lens through which it was filtered and interpreted through the governance style of postrevolutionary Iran did not follow the principles it had taught us. I had learned from the Holy Koran, "There is no compulsion in religion" (2:256). But no matter how hard I tried to immerse myself in this Islamic Iran, while I had grown in consciousness and awareness of my surroundings, I was never going to be accepted as being "pure Iranian."

I sensed a kind of intolerance in others when they were faced with anything that did not fit into the exact patterns of what it meant "to be Iranian" or "to be Muslim." The culture wanted a woman to be childlike, helpless, and passive, which is how a female is accepted as being "pure Iranian"—obedient, submissive, someone who does not step out of her role. This realization came right out of the *Shahnameh*, the great epic poem of Iran, where a distinction is made between "foreign" wives and "Iranian" wives—Iranian wives have been persuaded to believe that they exist only to serve men. I had just enough "foreign" blood in me; my independence and "fieriness" would not let me fit the cultural mold.

Meanwhile, problems were brewing at the television station, where the director of the news division commented that I was too attractive. In an unrelated move, the station changed the veil that women anchors wore so that it covered more of the face. I began to see more hypocrisy in this new life I had chosen for myself. Having submitted myself in an effort to save myself, to be happy, I doubted that, in fact, I had been saved because in reality I was drowning in sorrow. Over the next year, life as I had come to know it would end. As I continued to be true to the tenets of my faith, I found that my husband was not.

In my letters home to my father and sister back in the States, I declared how happy I was to be a submissive wife. In truth, I was starting to dislike my husband and I wanted to escape. My husband had begun to change his opinion of me as well, developing a resentment of my Western upbringing, including the fact that I had had other boyfriends. I was always ridiculed about my parents' and grandparents' divorce. Where was the exuberance I had expressed in my letters and to my "self"? I thought I must redouble my efforts and lift myself out of my misery.

I went to the U.S. Interest Section at the Embassy of Switzerland in Tehran to renew my American passport. After the revolution, this was the office that looked after the interests of U.S. citizens in Iran. There, a counselor recognized me as the anchor of the English news and gave me some advice—quit your television job. She never said my citizenship was threatened but she did say that as an American, working as a mouthpiece for the Islamic republic might not bode well for the future. So I quit my job at the television station.

By the end of 1986, just three years after I arrived from Boston, I confronted my American grandmother's spirit. Knowing that there had to be more to my life, I turned once again to the *Shahnameh*, which taught me that women could act on their own desires and speak their minds. One story, that of Tahmineh and Rostam, came to mind. Perhaps shockingly, Tahmineh goes to Rostam's bed in the middle of the night offering herself to him. Those who love Ferdowsi and recite his poetry on all occasions do not object to this kind of behavior. On the other hand, Ferdowsi points out, there is a rule in the *Shahnameh:* "Our daughters have to behave, even if foreign daughters may not, and may be encouraged to kick over the traces in order to join 'us.'"[5]

Perhaps my husband and his family did in the end see me as a foreign woman. Probably with this in mind they talked Karim into going to the United States with Saied and me on the pretext that we could both begin studies at a university. My uncle Jamshid had moved to New Mexico and invited us to join him there. My mother and brother had simultaneously also decided to move to America. In the meantime my sister was getting married in Boston and I wanted to be able to attend her wedding. I realized that God was everywhere and I longed for my family to be in an environment in which I felt we could grow. I needed to move on.

A state of tranquility overcame me, one of free will. I did not have to give in to what I perceived to be my fate. The alternative now was to leave Iran—taking the archetypes I had come to love with me—and continue my education in the West. Now I would lose Iran but I would gain America. Once I realized this, the rest was easy. I left Iran for America in 1987 and never looked back.

Back to the West

At some point in Iran I realized that I longed for America once again. I missed her generosity, her democratic government, and as my uncle Cyrus had once said, "her undaunted courage, fortitude, and industry." I missed freedom. The myth of return, the urge to go back home, that so many first-generation immigrants feel after they have arrived in America, I felt in Iran. Once we arrived in America, I knew I had come home.

Our first stop on the journey westward was in London, where my mother was living and working and where my brother had just joined her. My husband had traveled outside of Iran just once, to visit Italy. London was a huge cosmopolitan city, full of diversity and adventure, steeped in history. We knew we would not stay there permanently, but it was a stopping point, a place to catch our breath.

My sister visited us in London. It had been four years since our mother or I had seen her, and seven years since she had seen my brother. Mani had been in college, and then because of the Iran-Iraq war, no one had come to see us in Iran. We had a mini-reunion of sorts and talked about our plans for going back to America. It felt good to see her again, for her to see my husband and son, and for us to share memories. As she was getting married soon, we talked about how the two of us had made our choices and had found our mates.

My cousin Jahanshah,[1] whose house we were all staying in, worked for the BBC Persian service. I was curious about his work and listened eagerly to stories about his life as a journalist. Often my cousin and his wife would entertain Iranians whom he worked with or whom he was interviewing. As he was living a religiously observant life style at the time, the men and women would be separated in two different rooms at these gatherings. I was curious to know what the "men" were talking about, since mostly the women took care of the cooking and talked about their children. I recall that my mother and I sometimes wondered what it would be like if we could be sitting in the room with the men, having intellectual conversations about life and politics. I couldn't wait to get back to America so I could begin to make my own decisions.

In August 1987, on our way to join my uncle in New Mexico, my husband, Saied, and I took a short trip to my sister's wedding in Boston. My father, whom I had not seen in four years, had not met my husband or seen his first grandchild. My mother and brother had also been able to come from London for the wedding. For the first time in seven years, my mother, father, and siblings were reunited.

Although we were all swept up in the excitement of my sister's wedding, it was odd for all of us to be together again. I remember my sister and I were worried about our parents seeing each other as well as how our mother and stepmother would react to each other, having never met.

My sister had asked me to put on her bridal makeup, and we were alone in her room getting ready. As we sat there, alone for the first time in many years, there was a sadness to the fact that this happy occasion was marked by these tensions. I eased Mani's mind by telling her about my own wedding preparations. In the end, everyone was gracious, and for my sister's sake, my parents were pleasant with each other.

This was my husband's first introduction to a Western-style Iranian wedding, where men and women socialized, ate together, and danced together. He seemed to be in a bit of cultural shock while I was thrilled to reconnect with my extended family of aunts, uncles, and cousins who had come for the wedding. Just a few months before, I was in the solemn country of Iran, where the sound of bombings was heard overhead and public displays of mourning were commonplace. Now here I was, smiling away, dancing and mingling in America, reunited with my family.

"THE LAND OF ENCHANTMENT," AS NEW MEXICO REFERS TO itself, would not disappoint me. The day we arrived, my uncle Jamshid picked us up from the airport and drove us along Tramway Avenue within view of the Sandia Mountains in Albuquerque. I thought I'd left the Alborz Mountains of Tehran only to find the Sandias.

I chose Albuquerque because of my uncle. Always a mythical figure in my life, much the way his father, Abol Ghassem, had been for him, I knew he would accept me as I was and that he would continue to show me unconditional love. Uncle Jamshid had become a psychiatrist and was the head of the department of mental health at the Lovelace Medical Center in Albuquerque.

As we began to get reacquainted after many years, I asked him why he had chosen New Mexico. He said he had been drawn there by its diverse history—Native American, Hispanic, and Anglo cultures. The climate, which turned out to be very much like Solomon's Mosque where he had lived in the early 1940s and I had lived as a child, was another draw. On some level, for my uncle, being in New Mexico felt like he was once again close to the essential nature of Iran.

Santa Fe, in particular, and its adobe architecture reminded Jamshid a great deal of the villages of Iran, especially the Saturday market when many of the Native Americans would come down from their reservations and homes to sell their homemade jewelry and their other arts and crafts. The Persian carpet shops in the city reminded him of the hours he had spent in the bazaars of Shiraz in southwestern Iran, when he had taught at the university. He recalled the crafts he had seen in Shiraz, the goldsmiths and silversmiths, the blacksmiths and leather makers, and how similar to theirs was the handiwork of the Native Americans.

Jamshid's journey to New Mexico came after a breathtaking escape from Iran in 1982 with his family over the Zagros Mountains and into Turkey. I first heard about this when I was living in Boston. First I was confused, wondering why he had wanted to leave Iran so much that he was even willing to go illegally. Now that I had also returned to America, some of that confusion had dissipated, only to be replaced with curiosity about his journey.

Uncle Jamshid had always been apolitical and continued to be, putting all of his energy into trying to help patients with their mental health issues and guide them to get in touch with their inner selves. Witnessing Iran's transition from a monarchy to a theocracy, he felt that the monarchy had been far from a representative democracy and that modernization and the influx of Western culture had happened at too rapid a pace for the average Iranian. The example he would give was of an art festival at the ancient ruins in Persepolis in the 1970s where the elite would come to see the Joffrey Ballet, with modern, alluring dance scenes, while at the same time chador-clad villagers from the distant hills would look on horrified at what they were seeing. Walking down the streets of Isfahan, where he lived with his wife and children for a few years, he would see people in traditional dress who seemingly overnight changed their style of clothing and adopted miniskirts. In order to accommodate Western workers, cabarets sprang up with dancing girls from Thailand, completely insensitive to the local customs. The outraged traditionalists were even more appalled when the Shah's government did not put a stop to what they saw as threats to their cultural norms.

Having observed all this as an American Iranian, Uncle Jamshid felt the people's patience was running short, that surely they would rebel, and then came the Islamic revolution. He had been hopeful, as my mother had been (although neither had heard of the Ayatollah Khomeini before), that some of the deep spiritual aspects of Islamic culture were emerging, bringing about a feeling of euphoria in the people which, however real, would not last for long. Once the new revolutionaries began executing members of the Shah's cabinet, Jamshid quickly became completely disillusioned. Within a few months the hostage crisis at the American Embassy in Tehran began and life for average Iranians got worse. Saddam Hussein began bombing Iran, and Iran's military draft stepped up its recruiting. Uncle Jamshid had thought about his son, then fifteen, and realized it would not be long before he would be drafted. He especially worried for his children because they were fair-skinned, blond-haired, and blue-eyed. His first wife had been American and his two oldest children stood out as "American looking" in a sea of dark-haired, olive-skinned, brown-eyed Iranians. With Iranian animosity toward America building up, he did not want to jeopardize their safety.

Soon after the war began, Jamshid took his family for a vacation to the Caspian Sea. Choosing to swim in an isolated area, his second wife, an Iranian, chose to wear the approved swimming dress code—a one-piece bathing suit with a long-sleeve shirt over it and pajama-style trousers—while his twelve-year-old daughter took off her trousers and swam only in her shirt and one-piece bathing suit. Suddenly Jamshid saw a military vehicle coming down the beach. He ran toward the guards and told them how sorry they were that his daughter had made this mistake and promised that she would put her trousers on top of her bathing suit.

Before he knew it, a young soldier got out of his vehicle brandishing a machine gun. Shouting at Jamshid's daughter, he aimed his gun and fired above her head to frighten her. It was just one shot, but on that deserted beach the sound was so loud that my uncle continued to hear it for many days afterward. Seeing his daughter terrified was enough for him to decide that they had to get out.

My uncle made plans to leave the country, but in doing so made the simple mistake of putting his belongings up for sale, making it known publicly that he intended to leave the country. Just before he and his family were to depart, three men with machine guns broke into their home in the middle of the night, removing Jamshid to the Central Committee Detention Center located in the middle of Tehran. Interestingly enough, his cell was in the old parliament building, the place where the 1906 Constitution had been born. The hallway of the building had been converted into a prison of single rooms or holding cells with eight or nine people in each area, sleeping on the floor. Several counterrevolutionaries were in that particular jail. Because he was a physician, my uncle's decision to leave was deemed illegal.

Although he was not tortured, neither was he offered legal representation or told what was going to happen to him. After enduring several hours of interrogation a day by a young man who had attended George Washington University and who had been an activist against the Shah, he continued to say nothing against the revolution or against Islam. His explanation for leaving was simply that he just did not fit there anymore. He said, "We cannot just change our identity overnight to something that we have not been all of our lives. I love Iran and I love Islam and I have respect for Mr. Khomeini, but our identity simply does not fit."

His detention continued for a few weeks and for all he knew this was now his existence. He volunteered to mop the prison floors at night in exchange for being allowed to shower. Eventually he got to know the guards, who learned by talking to Jamshid that he was a psychiatrist. They began sharing their dilemmas. They too were caught in the turmoil of the revolution. Some had lost relatives in the war with Iraq. Others suffered post-traumatic stress disorder; all of them seemed to have nightmares. The guards would ask my uncle what they could do about these feelings.

Jamshid asked those with whom he shared his cell to give him their life history and any important dreams they had so that he could interpret them. He still remembers one of his fellow prisoners—a very clever man who was able to extricate a pack of cigarettes from the guards. He would make a whole series of cups and dishes out of the silver foil inside the cigarette pack. He had actively resisted the revolution, including being caught with hand grenades in his bags and it appeared he was doomed. One night he told my uncle that he had a dream and asked for his help to understand it. He explained: "I was on a ship. We were traveling over the water. I slipped and fell into the water. I kept looking at the people who were standing at the railing. I asked them to please send me a rope to get myself out of the water. They threw a rope but it never reached me."

Obviously my uncle knew what that dream meant, filled as it was with such foreboding and a sense of doomed prophecy. The next morning the man was taken to the infamous Evin Prison where my uncle is certain he was executed for his involvement in the counterrevolutionary movement.

After twenty-eight days, the guards completed their extensive investigation into my uncle's background and records at the University of Isfahan only to conclude that he had not done anything wrong. Nonetheless, all the money from his bank account was removed before he was released on the condition that he would stay in Iran for at least five years.

Once he left jail, Jamshid was even more determined to get his family out. His wife, who was pregnant at the time, was just as determined as he was to leave Iran. Jamshid knew this time that he could not fail. Through some local contacts, he found a way to escape through Turkey and he went about preparing for it secretly. First he got his family into their car and left Tehran; from there they drove four hours to their first meeting place. Once there they changed cars and drove four or five more hours to the next rendezvous. At this point they were put on horses and rode two nights through the mountains, sleeping by day in caves where two sheepherders brought them food.

After two days in the mountains, they boarded a bus to Istanbul, where they stayed for a month, living off funds sent by family and friends in America until they got their papers in order.

Eventually they made their way to Washington, D.C., and later to Albuquerque, New Mexico.

THERE I WAS AT UNCLE JAMSHID'S DOORSTEP WITH MY THREE-year-old son, Saied, and my husband, Karim, who hardly spoke English. Perhaps because of my uncle's generous spirit and New Mexico's diversity, I felt that even a newcomer from the Middle East like Karim could start a new life with a minimum of culture shock.

Why had I not felt this way about Boston? Boston knew who it was and why and how it had developed. It was already formed; there was no sense that it might grow into something else.

Albuquerque and the rest of New Mexico, on the other hand, were discovered by Native Americans and settled by the Spanish before the pilgrims landed on Plymouth Rock. It was here that Anglo culture remained in the minority. Still not sure of my own dual identity, I realized now that searching for my identity must begin by respecting where I had come from. This made Albuquerque a much more vibrant and exciting place for me—I could dream of possibilities for self-discovery that were missing in Boston.

What drew me in first were the Native Americans. For my uncle it had been their crafts, and for me it was their art of storytelling. After all, storytelling was an art form in Iran as well. When I heard of Santo Domingo Pueblo Larry Littlebird and his hunting stories, I was taken back to my days as a child. Hunting was of course an Ardalan rite of passage, albeit one practiced only by the male side of my family. The Pueblos had the same unbroken rule as my family: They would only hunt what they could eat. This feeling of respect for life and for the Creator who gives sustenance came through in Larry Littlebird's story "Hunter's Heart."

"What had I done?" Littlebird says. "Who was I to take the life of this magnificent creature? What is this killing? My friend's words about the elk calling me echoed with a hollow ring. My eyes blurred as I saw how beautiful this creature was and the full force of what had happened hit me. Then his voice in the steady monotone of sound I had come to know as Indian praying caught my ear. Through my blur of tears I saw my friend kneeling by the elk's head. When I got to them, his prayer was in English for my benefit, I believe: Look at you, magnificent creature lying there. How is it that we, your poor human brothers, could be worthy to borrow your life? You honor us. You allow us to witness the power and the magnificence of the Creator. God has blessed your life and we see that. And thank God for the continued sustenance that is provided for all our relations: The sun, the clouds, the rain, the snow, the water, the air, the earth, and the mystery of fire. Now we are going to carry you home. You come with us easily. Our people will be happy to see you. They will make you welcome. You will live again in all our lives my brother.' And then, cupping his hands to his mouth, he breathed in all the essence living on that mountain. That day I think I saw the tip of the point of the arrow. Some day I will know the peace."[2]

Much as my Kurdish paternal grandfather and paternal great-uncles would retell the *Shahnameh,* Littlebird's stories helped me think of myself as a living link in a chain of humankind. His words served as a bridge between the lives of the people before me and the lives of my grandchildren yet to come, for I heard: "Cherish your family, heritage, and friends. Find common threads through storytelling. The stories of our people—whoever they may be—preserve who we are, make us unique."

I was determined to make this move to America work for my family and landed my first job with the *Albuquerque Journal.* Once a TV broadcaster, here I was just a few months later typing classified ads. In order for my new life to feel real, I had to start over.

My marriage up to that point had not been fulfilling; now I was motivated to find another way to make it work. Having first tried to become an accommodating individual, and to do everything everyone else's way, my inner voice now screamed to explain itself.

ALMOST EVERYTHING ABOUT THE *ALBUQUERQUE JOURNAL* inspired me: the tall glass buildings that housed their offices, watching real journalists at work, reading their columns. When I first arrived, I still lived my life much as I did in postrevolutionary Iran. On my days off from work, I chose to cover my hair by wearing the *hijab,* which led me to face similar problems as other Muslim immigrants: Where would we find halal meat (meat slaughtered in the name of God) to feed my family? Where was there a mosque? How would Saied learn about Islam?

In the midst of the small city of Albuquerque, we found a small, but very friendly Iranian community. It felt comforting to discover women who wore the *hijab* and who would tell me where Saied could attend Sunday religious classes. As we were setting down roots, Karim and I were trying to see if we could make our relationship work better than it had in Iran. I decided to get pregnant. My daughter, Samira, was born on July 26, 1989. Samira is the name of a desert flower but also means "one who talks long into the night," and was one of my favorite names for a girl.

I could never have realized the joy that having a daughter would bring me. Samira had my and my mother's big brown "Bakhtiari eyes." She was a sweet, sensitive child with a mind as curious and fiery as my own. Nothing gave me more pleasure than looking at Saied lovingly holding Samira in his arms as I went about my daily chores. By that time, my younger brother, Karim, who also attended the University of New Mexico, had come from Iran to Albuquerque for college and my mother had also moved to Albuquerque to get her Ph.D. in educational psychology at the University of New Mexico.[3] Uncle Jamshid had managed to gather a good part of our extended family around him and Samira was our newest addition.

IT WAS NOT LONG AFTER SAMIRA WAS BORN THAT MY HUSBAND and I realized that now he was gripped by the "myth of return." Though he truly missed his family and wanted to take us back to Iran, I vehemently resisted and we argued constantly.

I would reflect on my life at night when everyone in the house

Davar; daughter, Samira; and son, Saied, in Albuquerque, New Mexico, 1992. (Photograph by Karim Ardalan)

was asleep. There was not any one thing I could pinpoint as the source of my dissatisfaction; it was a process we were going through, one that needed quiet and darkness like a plant or fruit that grows at night.

By some process of inner illumination I came to stop listening to Karim's threatening tirades, to refuse to accept degradation, and instead demand respect. Our cross-purposes tested my moral fiber. I realized that I wanted him to support me to better myself and my children's lives through my own education. I repeatedly dreamed of an emerald serpent that appeared in every direction and would leap at me with its open mouth and prevent me from moving. In my dreams, I tried to shout but to no avail. I felt trapped.

In January of 1990, Karim left us and went back to Iran to visit his family, marking the end of our marriage. Even if the love of a deep romance had never developed between us, he must have wagered that if he left I would long to have him back or would not be able to manage on my own and would then be forced to return to Iran.

After he left, I dreamed that I was going on a trip. I had to first pass through a river of water, then climb a mountain before reaching a mountainside filled with pebbles and small streams. At first I wanted to go back, realizing it would not be easy. I began climbing up the mountain and although I got a bit wet, I actually made the ascent and descent. I had passed the test.

I was now unstoppable in my quest. While many of the Iranians I had come to know in Albuquerque were in one stage or another of their eventual plan to return to Iran, I now thrived on being an American in a multicultural environment.

My perspective on my marriage was based more on how things ought to be than how they were, which was part of the reason I was able to be absorbed into revolutionary Iran. As much as I enjoyed reaching toward the unknown, I also placed a high value on integrity and being responsible. Having not seen these qualities at work in my marriage, I pulled back, focusing instead on my own desire to grow as a person. Karim, showing little introspection, wanted to go back to his comfort zone and not press ahead in a new life as I insisted we do. At some point I realized that while I was trying to rescue him, I needed to rescue myself.

I began to realize that I had an inner Rostam to whom I could turn if there were no real, outer man.[4] I can do it on my own if I have to! This was my time of self-unfolding and now I had to turn to my inner guide for direction.[5]

My mother and brother lived on Harvard Drive near the university family housing, where I lived with Saied and Samira. We spent many a day in her backyard facing the Sandia Mountains talking about where we had been, and more important, where we were going. I had learned through experience that I had to remember where I had come from in order to know where I was headed, and I found the best person to share my recollections was my mother, who once again was there for me.

As we spoke, I realized that the only thing Islamic about my marriage had been my wearing the *hijab*. My former husband rarely practiced his faith even as I had inwardly grown closer to mine. Realizing that I must please and inspire him in every way, I also realized that little else was expected of me.

Talking with my mother helped me realize that wearing the

hijab in America called more rather than less attention to me, as opposed to wearing the *hijab* in Iran. In New Mexico I had met many Muslim women who did not wear the *hijab* but were still believers in their faith.

I remembered a story my uncle Jamshid had told me when he recalled his experience in prison. He knew that his physical presence, due to his years of playing football, drew people to him. At the same time, he had an inner world that none of the guards or fellow cellmates could touch. People who met him would only know the physical, the external, but nothing of his inner depth, values, and beliefs.

Having grown up with the same values and beliefs as Jamshid, the same desire to remove all inner veils covering my spiritual heart, I began to remove these veils, the outer one as well, because they prevented me from turning inward. I now was able to go much deeper inwardly and question who I had been, who I had become, and who I wanted to be.

I also came to understand that culture is an outward sign of inner faith. I could in my own fashion keep my faith in part by expressing my culture without. Although I lived in a secular world, I could continue to enjoy both culture and religion. This deep resolve was not something I had to share with others. And if indeed I were able to merge my culture and faith, I would not need to let go of either one in order to sense fulfillment.

MY UNCLE JAMSHID ENCOURAGED ME TO SEEK THERAPY AND I did. "You must become an audience to your own theater," he would say, and so I talked to a therapist on and off through the difficult year after Karim left. That first year there were plenty of tears and much soul-searching and a tremendous amount of suffering and self-doubt.

The process of reconstructing my life would not prove as difficult as I had imagined because I was surrounded by family and friends who loved me. My aunt Parvaneh and uncle Mozafar lived in Albuquerque as well. Parvaneh, my mother's half-sister, was studying to become a psychiatrist herself and she was an incredible source of comfort and unconditional love for me, Saied, and Samira. Relentless in her determination to protect me and get me back on my feet, Parvaneh was another strong woman in my life who saved me from becoming bitter and jaded.

I began taking part-time classes at the University of New Mexico. Eventually, a couple of my university professors became my closest friends, whom I would come to love and depend on. Among them, Amy Atkins, Maya Sutton, and their friend Valencia De La Vega came to my apartment at the student family housing complex to give me their blessings. Maya, a Celtic mythologist, brought drums and incense with her as a way to cleanse my home and bring harmony to it.

Amy and Maya told me that to clear a place meant to get rid of all previous spirits, vibes, energy, stored memories, and psychological baggage left behind by previous occupants. Before I moved into my new apartment, my friends gathered like-minded people who, in my case, were all women, and brought their drums and rattles. They went around the outside of the home making purposeful noises to awaken any sleeping spirits and make them aware that they were no longer welcome. Aloud and silently, they let all these energies know that this was no longer their home.

They put a special kind of protection on all four sides of my home. This comes from a Celtic and Druidic practice called "setting the *wards*." In Iran, it is known as removing the bad genie. *Ward* in English means "to protect and guard," as in the words *warranty, wardrobe, ward off,* and *beware.* Other female friends who had learned this practice went about setting protection around the outside of my apartment that could not be penetrated by anything harmful.

After entering into a procession around the outside of my apartment, they moved inside, each person rattling or drumming high and low around each room, particularly doorways and windows. They then opened all the doors and windows so just bad energy-dwellers could easily leave. They continued to rattle and drum into every drawer and closet, corners of ceilings, behind doors and furniture, in heating and cooling vents, refrigerator, and every other space where old vibes could be stored. They called out things like: "Be gone all you spirit dwellers. This is no longer your dwelling. Out! Out! That's it. There is the window and there is the door. Be gone!"

When everyone agreed that my new living space felt cleared, clean, and safe, they moved to the house-blessing portion of the ceremony, a ritual only an uninhibited woman could perform. They ran around putting notes and little signs everywhere so I would gradually find them in the kitchen, the bathroom, under chairs, in the closet, and more, loving messages such as: "May only true friends share meals at this table." "May you sleep with beautiful dreams." "What a life you have ahead of you!" "Read these books and think great thoughts, Davar."

As they left they handed me a pouch with crushed rue and anise to ward off negativity and evil, basil and oak for protection, rosemary for success and good memories, sandalwood and cinnamon for healing, and rose petals for love. In this way, my friends helped me redirect my life from my own center, and to unravel the hardships I endured so I could learn to succeed on my own. Then in a final gesture they revved up their drums and rattles in a vibrant celebration of this new phase of my life. Finally they felt I was safe, and I did too.

I ENROLLED FULL TIME AT THE UNIVERSITY OF NEW MEXICO. MY mother, brother, and I would often see each other on campus. I finally found a subject matter I loved and could see a career for myself in journalism. Although I was a wife and a mother, and older than most of the other students, I was struck by how much more determined I was than they were. I wanted an education then more passionately than I had at any other point in my life.

My newfound passion for journalism and communication had its roots in my past. On my travels as a child to historic sites, I saw how my parents were deeply involved with the philosophical and aesthetic considerations of ancient societies. Through them I became fascinated with the traditions and cultures of ancient civilizations. I wanted to play a major role in continuing the way of my ancestors, to report not only on the economic, political, and social conditions of cultures throughout the world but also on their traditions and beliefs.

In one of my first journalism classes, I was told to keep a diary, which in retrospect helped me reflect not only on my personal development but also on the development of my career.

On my first day as an intern at the local ABC affiliate, KOAT, I wore a navy suit with panty hose and navy pumps. Janet Blair, the assignment editor, gave us new interns a tour of the station. When we got to the equipment room she said: "We already have our *stars*. It's tough work for interns around here. You are going to have to carry around heavy tripods and cameras for the reporters so I do not want to hear anybody complain about tearing their panty hose!" Realizing that I was the only female she was addressing, the next day I wore pants and a nice sweater.

The next day was one of the last leading up to the Persian Gulf War and also the first day on the job for Susan Ramsey, KOAT's new weekend assignment editor. She seemed anxious as she tried to organize the day's events: rallies in Belen, Rio Rancho, and the Civic Plaza in support of the troops. Reporter Dan Monohan was assigned to cover the rallies and I went with him.

It was a day filled with sights of yellow balloons and ribbons, waving flags, and salutes and cheers for the men and women bound for the Persian Gulf. As I carried around my little flag, I felt very much a part of what was going on. I had just come from war-torn Iran and knew that someone had to stop Saddam's invasion of Kuwait.

Everyone at work monitored their televisions and the wires for the latest developments. Would Saddam withdraw from Kuwait? The deadline was twelve noon eastern time. Lisa Breeden, our news director, came in around nine thirty a.m. on her day off. She said she could not stay away from the newsroom.

As we all waited there in anticipation, one reporter even suggested starting a ground war pool. Susan Ramsey started to record the daily electronic feeds. Every few minutes a buzzer went off and we knew the wires were sending the latest information through. One piece of copy said: "As the deadline draws near, Soviet diplomats are still working on a possible diplomatic solution."

The deadline finally passed and with it no sign of an Iraqi withdrawal. In fact, several minutes before the deadline, Iraq launched a scud attack at Israel—another indication that Saddam was not sincere in his professed willingness to consider withdrawing from Kuwait.

By this time we knew that it was just a matter of time before the ground war began. All the TV stations were showing live shots of Baghdad being bombed. The allied raids were going on in full force. Analysts tried to shed light on what might happen next. At eleven thirty a.m. the wire services had reported Pentagon officials as saying the authority of starting a ground war had been given to the military leaders. The first President Bush had given the generals the okay to start the ground war whenever they deemed it necessary.

For a while there were some reports that Iraqi foreign minister Tariq Aziz had agreed to several parts of the U.S. proposal for

Iraqi withdrawal, but those reports remained unconfirmed and were later denied by Iraqi officials.

Susan asked me to call the offices of senators Jeff Bingaman and Pete Domenici and Congressman Steve Schiff and ask them where we could contact them for their reactions should the ground war begin. I called the press secretaries in Washington and left messages for them to contact the station.

Several reporters were also doing stories on the reactions of New Mexicans to the impending Persian Gulf War. By this time it was almost five thirty p.m. As I headed home there was still no sign of a ground war.

The next day, Janet told me to collate the morning report for the producers. I was to photocopy the wire stories she had chosen, along with the CNN rundowns, and place them on the producers' desks.

As I began photocopying, a name on one of the stories, an AP story on local reactions to the situation in the Persian Gulf, stood out to me. Of the several Muslims in New Mexico who they had interviewed, one was Mary Bakhtiar. I started reading my mother's comments and was relieved to find that she did not say anything controversial. I continued preparing the morning report.

Before I handed Janet a copy of the report, she said: "Davar, we need you to call your Middle Eastern contacts and get their reactions on Kuwait's liberation, et cetera." Then she added: "I do not think we have ever spoken to this Bakhtiar lady; do you think you can get in touch with her?" I had anticipated that someone would ask me this question at some point. I replied: "Yes, in fact she is my mother!"

Janet told me to contact her and see if she would speak to KOAT. At seven thirty p.m. that evening I brought her to the station for what turned out to be a very good interview. Reporter Rick Murray said this was the first time he had spoken to someone familiar with issues in the Middle East who knew what they were talking about (and probably who spoke English perfectly without an accent!).

After several months at KOAT, I came across an ad in the journalism department for a work-study position at KUNM, the NPR affiliate in Albuquerque. Something told me I should apply even though I knew very little about public radio. The news director, Marcos Martinez, sported a long ponytail and the reporters in the newsroom were practically hippies. The atmosphere could not have been any more different from that at KOAT. Marcos and I got along famously from that very first day. Meanwhile, KOAT had offered me a job as a teleprompter. I had to make a choice— work-study reporter at KUNM or teleprompter at KOAT. I think I made the right decision by sticking to public radio.

ONE OF MY COLLEAGUES AND GOOD FRIENDS AT KUNM HAD just begun research on a Catholic sanctuary in the village of Chimayo, ninety miles outside of Albuquerque. This same colleague taught me about several of New Mexico's religious traditions, including the Penitente and Our Lady of Guadalupe. Because my mother had grown up Catholic, I was curious to learn more.

Catholic families have made the pilgrimage to Chimayo for centuries. The sanctuary there was built by a Penitente in 1813 when a legendary crucifix was found in the healing dirt of

Chimayo. There the Brotherhood of Penitentes had formed what are known as *moradas* (places of worship), which tied the early Hispanic communities together and gave them a sense of social solidarity.

I realized that the Penitente ceremonies were very similar to those of the Shia in respect to the martyrdom of the third imam, Hossein, the grandson of the Prophet Muhammad—the passion plays I had witnessed just a few years earlier in Iran. These passion plays for Hossein began to flourish when the Sunni world held political rule under the Ottoman Turks. Previous to the sixteenth century, Iran was a Sunni country. With the rise of the Safavid Dynasty, the country became Shia. The rulers had wanted to distinguish themselves from the Turkish Arab world of the Sunnis to show that Iranians were different and would not be swallowed up by the Ottoman Empire.

While the Penitentes' special ceremonies relate to the reenactment of the passion of Christ during the lunar calendar of Holy Week leading up to Easter, for the Shias, their special ceremony relates to the ninth and tenth days of the first lunar month of the Islamic calendar, Muharram, the days of the wounding and death of Hossein.

The followers of Hossein would meet during the year at Hosseiniyehs. Most villages, towns, and cities in Iran have one and they are similar to the *moradas* or places of worship throughout northern New Mexico. The difference is that the Hosseiniyehs are open to anyone, no membership is required, while the members of the Penitentes had to be initiated. In either case, whether Shia or Catholic, each worshiper works to develop his or her virtuous conduct by performing religious ceremonies for the living and the dead, and expressing their own sacred ways with flagellation, prayer, and chanting.

The Penitentes embody the martyrdom of Christ in their bodies: his scourging, his crown of thorns, the burden of carrying the cross and being fastened to it, as well as resurrection from the earth; the Shias embody the martyrdom of Hossein, who was killed because he refused to give his allegiance to a ruling caliph who, while not practicing the faith he professed, claimed to be a follower of the Prophet. Hossein was ultimately killed for his beliefs.

The second Catholic tradition I learned about was that of Our Lady of Guadalupe, known as the Queen of Mexico or the Aztec Virgin Mary, who symbolizes compassion for Catholics. When she appeared to Juan Diego on Tepeyac Hill in 1531 she said to him, "I am the Compassionate Mother of you and your people here in this land, and of all the other people who love me, who call to me, search for me and confide in me." Her appearance is celebrated every year in New Mexico and elsewhere on December twelfth, with serenades from mariachis, which are performed in traditional style in front of the masses to celebrate the feast of Our Lady of Guadalupe.

I recalled reading the chapter on the Virgin Mary in the Koran. The Virgin is greatly honored in Islamic tradition and personifies the Divine Compassion. She also holds a special place among Sufis. Members of one Sufi order's prayers say, "Oh Mary, peace be unto thee, in the Name of God, the Merciful, the Compassionate."[6]

As I continued to learn about the culture of New Mexico, I realized that my instinctive comparisons to my own Iranian and Islamic heritage began to grow.

I searched for elements of Islam within New Mexico and found a remarkable one tucked away in the red rock canyons of northern New Mexico, a small Islamic community called Dar al Islam in the town of Abiquiu. Founded in 1754, Abiquiu is situated high over the Rio Chama and Perdenal mountains, a distinct mesa that looks like the top has been sliced off. Abiquiu was named after St. Thomas Apostle de Abiquiu. Georgia O'Keeffe loved painting the mountains here and referred to them as "my private mountain." When asked to explain why, she had said: "God told me if I painted it often enough, I could have it!"

The buildings in Abiquiu were designed by the well-known Egyptian architect Hasan Fathy, who incidentally had been a good friend of my father. Built in 1979, the mosque there is North African in style with white adobe walls, arches, and curved ceilings creating domes. The idea behind founding Dar al Islam was to build an ideal Islamic community in America.

The mosque functions in Abiquiu as it does everywhere: as a place of prayer. It is not only for Arabs, as one of the converts pointed out: "It is a common misconception that Islam exists only in the Middle East but actually one out of every five people on earth is a Muslim, most of whom are in fact from Indonesia, Malaysia, and Africa."

As I walked toward the mosque, a European convert began reciting the *azan*, the Muslim call to prayer. The blond-haired, blue-eyed man originally came from Holland and had converted to Islam. There were many American Muslims living there; some were of Hispanic origin, others were Arabs or Anglo converts.

Speaking with the Muslims at Dar al Islam, I felt an openness among them I had not felt in Iran. I thought that perhaps because they practiced their faith in a secular society, they were more intellectually in tune with their beliefs as well as more open to people of different backgrounds. While I was there, a noted Islamic scholar from Canada was holding Islamic history classes. The students attending his class were mostly from Christian and Jewish backgrounds. He explained that while most of the Muslim world had been in a state of social chaos for the past few decades, they must keep in mind that Western civilization has gained a tremendous amount from the rich history of Islam and its contributions to learning in past centuries.

In all my years in Iran, while I had Christian and Jewish friends, I had never thought to ask about their beliefs or to visit the places where they worshipped. As the students of Islamic history and I stood in front of this beautiful adobe mosque in Abiquiu, I sensed the deep excitement of the Muslim converts for their faith and for helping others understand who they were. It seemed surreal that there, as I stood next to someone who probably resembled my Irish ancestor James Mackey who had fought in the eighteenth-century American Revolution, I had found a Dutch convert to Islam.

Having lived through the twentieth-century Islamic revolution and returned to my American birthplace where I had found people of many faiths and cultures working and living side by side, I wondered if this could be a sign of another historic role for American Muslims. Could the progression toward an open and free society be an indication of the role American Muslims might play in reforming Islam? Would they perhaps be the leaders of a protest movement within the leaderless world of Islam?

THE ROADS OF NORTHERN NEW MEXICO BECAME FAMILIAR TO me over the next two years as I drove back and forth to Los Alamos, New Mexico, to report on a story that captured national interest. In 1991, concerns over possible health effects from decades of old radioactive substances in the area had taken over the quiet community of Los Alamos, home to the Manhattan Project and birthplace of the atomic bomb.[7]

Tyler Mercier, a local sculptor turned activist, claimed that radioactive waste from the Los Alamos National Laboratory could be related to a cluster of brain tumors in the area. Mercier stumbled onto this idea while doing an independent investigation into radiation levels in Los Alamos several months earlier, when he was startled to find radiation readings higher than those reported by the laboratory. And lab scientists said that for twenty years—from 1944 to 1964—large amounts of untreated radioactive waste were being dumped into an area canyon known by local residents as "acid canyon."

In producing the story for KUNM, I pulled together every skill I had learned in journalism. I spoke to scientists as well as to the affected residents. I interviewed scientists from the national lab, including a Department of Energy official who was leading an investigation into the lab's environmental and safety issues, as well as those who said they had been exposed to radiation.

On one of these interviews, walking through what was now called Acid Canyon, the lab's Alan Stoker pointed to an old pipeline where he said plutonium and other untreated radioactive waste had been discharged by the lab. Lab documents indicated areas containing high levels of radioactive waste in the canyon that were cleaned up once in 1967 and again in 1980. Although low levels of waste still remained in the canyon, Stoker said the residuals were within guidelines set by the Environmental Protection Agency.

Mercier, the activist, had gathered a list of seventy-nine names of people throughout the country who once lived and worked in Los Alamos who claimed to have brain tumors or other cancers caused by radioactive emissions. After Mercier went public with his findings, the lab decided to form a working group to see what, if anything, was going on. The group consisted of seven lab officials and seven members of the community, and focused specifically on the western residential area of Los Alamos where the initial reports of brain tumors originated.

In July 1991, at a meeting of the lab's working group, a local physician confirmed that over the past twenty-five years, twenty-one people on Mercier's list had died of a primary brain tumor. At the same time, he explained, there was no evidence to show that these brain tumors were caused by exposure to radiation. Mercier maintained that more investigation was needed.

The brain tumors were not his only concern, he claimed, going on to refer to a 1948 report completed by the National Safety Council that cited numerous safety concerns in Los Alamos.

After a four-month-long investigation to see if there was anything in the environment that could be causing the tumors, the working group said the results of their investigation showed no link between brain tumors and the environment in the western area. But the Department of Energy, unwilling to take any chances, decided to send a 150-member team of inspectors to review the lab's environmental, safety, and health programs.

Beyond the scientific and medical data were the stories of the affected people. Some fifteen miles down the hill from Los Alamos in Pojaque Valley in a little town called El Rancho, I visited the home of Joe Duran. Duran had a lot to say about the lab's operations. In 1954 he began working there as a custodian for the lab's maintenance contractor and spent the next twenty-four years there before being abruptly fired in 1978. He took the contractor to court and a federal judge awarded him one hundred thousand dollars in a wrongful termination settlement, but his battles did not end there.

In 1981, Duran had brain surgery to remove a tumor from what he contends was exposure to radiation. Duran's brother also worked at the lab, and in 1984, he died of stomach cancer. Although neither of the Durans blamed the lab for their health problems, Joe Duran said the lab's operations were dangerous. As a child, Duran lived near Los Alamos, and planted corn and beans there in the fields. He used to ride his horse through Acid Canyon. The farm boy grew up, went to work at the Nevada test site, but came back home to Los Alamos. He said he remembered seeing drainage coming into Acid Canyon from the various lab facilities.

After six weeks the Department of Energy concluded that there was no evidence to indicate a link between the cluster of brain tumors and exposure to radioactive substances. The report did, however, cite Los Alamos National Laboratory for lack of monitoring at the old waste sites, for not having warning signs in contaminated areas, and for having left radioactive scrap lying outside. Lab officials said they planned to implement what they called a "safety culture."

The news features and documentaries I produced on Los Alamos for KUNM helped me find my voice in radio journalism. The recognition and awards I was given by the New Mexico Associated Press made my thirst for national and even international radio news become ever more present. I implored unceasingly, "How do I get to the next level?"

BEFORE MY LAST SEMESTER AT JOURNALISM SCHOOL HAD begun, I started actively looking for work. I felt I had mastered whatever college could teach me about communications and now I needed good experience. It was then that one of my journalism professors very frankly suggested that I might have a hard time finding work as a reporter in New Mexico because I was—after all—the wrong minority. Not sure exactly how to heed his advice, I nonetheless searched for future job possibilities outside of New Mexico. "You need to be at NPR," the same professor said. "You know—with Sylvia Poggioli."[8]

In February of 1993, while at KUNM, I saw an application

228 · DAVAR ARDALAN

for a producer's symposium at the Public Radio Conference in Washington, D.C. The Corporation for Public Broadcasting (CPB) was looking for several multicultural producers to participate in a week-long training program. I remember looking at the application every now and then and thinking how great it would be if I was chosen.

After procrastinating for a month, I finally found the courage to fill out the application, write an essay, and send a sample tape of my work. In April I got a bulky package in the mail from CPB. Much to my surprise and delight I was one of twenty-five producers selected. A producer at NPR named Doug Mitchell had seen my application and insisted I be given a chance.

On May 5, 1993, just ten days before graduation, I flew to Washington for the conference. Opening night was spectacular.

It was a night of celebration, not only because we were kicking off the conference but also because it was Cinco de Mayo. National Public Radio had just begun a weekly news program called *Latino USA* and the first show would feature HUD Secretary Henry Cisneros, Transportation Secretary Federico Peña, and Hispanic congressional leaders who also attended the party. As if this weren't enough, President Bill Clinton made a brief appearance to congratulate NPR for all its diverse programming, and I got to shake his hand. It was a powerful moment.

The next day, we introduced ourselves to one another and exchanged stories about what we hoped to accomplish during the week. The majority of the producers said they hoped they would be able to learn from the production and writing workshops; others wanted to know how to pitch story ideas. When it came time for me to speak, I stood up and said, "My name is Davar Ardalan. I come here from KUNM radio station, I am a single mother, I'm graduating from college, and I'm here to find a job." I'm sure many in the audience, including the organizers from the Corporation for Public Broadcasting, thought that was a bit ambitious.

Before I even arrived I had decided to become my own public relations representative, printing a box of business cards with my picture on them. I went around with my résumé and business card to every station representative in the main exhibit hall. Program producers, news directors, station managers, reporters, and editors from NPR, the BBC, American Public Radio, the *Christian Science Monitor*—it didn't matter, I made a point of meeting and talking to them all.

By the end of my week in Washington I had been to the NPR offices several times, had met some remarkable journalists, and attended numerous workshops. I was confident that I had made the right connections. Saturday was our last day at the conference. At around four o'clock the multicultural producers got together for the last time to share their week-long experiences. As part of a writing exercise we were given fifteen minutes to write about one event or incident that had made a lasting impression on us. Because scheduling was getting tight we had to wrap things up, leaving only a few of us who got to read what we had written. A producer from Florida stood up and read a poem she had written about a woman whose persistence and ambitions had impressed her the most. She said, "There's something about the glitter in this woman's big brown eyes that tells me she is going to make it." I couldn't believe it but she was talking about me! I was touched.

Before I left Washington, D.C., Cindy Carpien, the senior producer of *Weekend Edition Saturday*, said she was willing to give me a job for two weeks. This was the only assurance I had but I was ready and willing to take the risk. I decided to move to Washington, D.C., with Saied and Samira. As fate would have it Uncle Jamshid had just bought a home in McLean, Virginia, which remained empty as he waited for his family to join him. He extended an invitation for the children and me to stay with him until we got our bearings.

Before I left New Mexico, I was selected by my journalism professors to give a speech at graduation. I was lucky to have both my parents, my sister, and my brothers there. I wanted them to see that I had persevered, that I was able to accomplish what I had set out to do, despite being a single mother. It was my opportunity to thank everyone who had shown me the strength and courage to carry on. I thanked Professor Charles Coates for believing in me. I thanked my friends and family who had been there for me during the most difficult times of my life. And I gave a special thanks to my two beautiful children, Saied and Samira, for giving me a sense of purpose and for always keeping me on my feet.

It was hard to say good-bye to New Mexico, which had sustained me both as a woman and as a journalist. This ancient land of Native American and Hispanic culture had paralleled so much of the Iranian culture with which I had grown up. The land and its people had given me an opportunity to fulfill my dream—to have a profession that I had come to love.

But I knew that I had much farther to go on my journey. A Sufi parable tells of two people wandering in a desert, dying of thirst. The first person dug out tens of shallow pits in the sand only to die of thirst. The second person found one spot and dug deep until he found water to quench his thirst. New Mexico was not my final destination; I knew I had to move on to find a place that would allow me to stay, dig deep, and quench my thirst.

·◇ 13 ◇·

Beginning a New Life

Like a novice *naqqal* or Persian storyteller, I roamed around the NPR headquarters in awe of everyone around me. I worked closely with Senior Producer Cindy Carpien, who had given me my first shot at temporary work as a production assistant. Watching her reminded me of the girls I had seen in Iran weaving an intricate Persian carpet. Her technical competency, the way she made edit marks on analog tape, rocking the tape back and forth while ever so conscious of the rhythm of the story as she was editing, were a marvel to look at. Cindy was known as one of the master producers. Her editing tricks were all in her head, fingers could only move as hers did because her heart was engaged—head and heart moving in unity to create a carpet of sounds.

I had always learned better through sounds than images. Not only do I remember sailing on the Nile as a child, I also remember the tranquil sound of the waves against our vessel. Maybe it was the years of hearing Mama Helen and my mother tell and retell family stories or hearing the tales of cities from the many travels we took throughout Iran that sharpened my ear and crystallized the innate sounds that distinguish one place from another.

My father had taught me to listen for sound that activates the sublime. A musician like Stravinsky does it, he would say, but so does a shepherd with his reed flute by the power of breathing life or his soul into an instrument. I loved the idea of sculpting sound images and fortifying the sense of rebirth through sound. I knew intuitively that it was only here at NPR that the creative conscience within me would find a way to slowly gather into a constellation of human stories I would be proud of. I was ready to learn everything.

Saied and Samira were delighted to hear we were staying at Uncle Jamshid's home, nestled in a wooded area in McLean, Virginia. It was of course a most timely coincidence that in June of 1993, Uncle Jamshid had decided to move back east to this upscale suburb of Washington, D.C. His home was still unfurnished and the air conditioning had not been turned on, but we made the most of our stay, enduring the hot and muggy summer days. The rocky rapids of Great Falls Park were a great diversion for Saied, Samira, and me. There was something symbolic about standing on the edge of the little cliffs with my two small children, watching the rushing waters go by. I thought about one of Mama Helen's favorite quotes from the Bible, "Behold, I make all things new,"[1] a testament perhaps to all the changes that she, my mother, and I had endured in our lifetime. Our yesterdays, todays, and tomorrows, it seems, were spent in constant change and new beginnings.

Insight upon insight filled my heart as I contemplated the mystery of our lives. Like my mother and her mother before her, I was a romantic idealist. "One can always succeed," my mother would say, "if only one has the will to do so. For when the will dies, the soul dies, and without a soul to appreciate the beauties of life, it is not worth being alive. The secret is to live and let live."[2]

I recalled that Mama Helen had moved to Washington, D.C., from Iran in 1946—a single parent responsible for seven children. It was hard to imagine how they all got by. Helen had no savings and little income. There were times when the milkman stopped delivering milk and when the children cried because there was no money to go to the circus. Helen was always behind on her bills and had to borrow from friends until my grandfather was able to send a few more rugs or wire some funds.[3]

When I got to Washington, I wanted to see for myself where Helen and my mother and uncles grew up. Uncle Jamshid remembered Mr. Nemazee's beautiful home in Potomac, Maryland, the one where my parents had been married. Growing up, they used to stock up on the goodies they found at Mr. Nemazee's home—pistachios, cashews, *gaz* (a Persian sweet, chewy candy made with pistachios) and fruit, filling their pockets as they said good-bye to their hosts.

My twin aunts Paree and Parveen had married Americans and had settled in the Washington area as well. Aunt Parveen was a remarkable artist who had six children. Her daughter

Lailee had her own television show called "Authors & Critics" on KCSM TV in San Mateo, California. Aunt Parveen's son Fred McNair IV was a member of the U.S. Tennis Team and won the French Open Doubles Championship in 1976.

Parveen had a beautiful home in Chevy Chase. Saied and Samira loved visiting her and were mesmerized by her Henri Matisse–style oil paintings with their vibrant Persian blue colors. Several of Parveen's paintings depicted a woman with dark hair and brown eyes—who the children thought looked like me.

My aunt Paree had settled in Hyattsville, Maryland. Her daughter, my cousin Shireen, offered to take care of Saied and Samira during those first summer months so I could work at NPR. The two weeks offered by Cindy Carpien turned into the assurance of months of work as a temporary production assistant. For several weeks, I drove an hour from Uncle Jamshid's house in northern Virginia to Greenbelt, Maryland, until we decided to move in temporarily with Shireen. The children loved her generous spirit. Her house was filled with artifacts from her mother's beatnik years in San Francisco, intermingled with Persian tapestries and artwork she had collected when she visited us in Iran.

It was here in Washington that I became even more conflicted about my Iranian and American heritage. Being born of the East and of the West, my heart and mind wandered in both directions. Uncle Jamshid and I often talked about our mutual life experiences and I was fascinated to learn of how he and his late brother, Cyrus, had completely different outlooks regarding their dual heritage.

Uncle Jamshid was an idealist about America and a realist

about Iran while Uncle Cyrus was the reverse. Jamshid felt that his ideas, education, and reactions were purely American; America could offer him the best future as a free and stable society. Uncle Cyrus, on the other hand, was a romantic at heart when it came to Iran. He wanted to live just like the average Iranian lived, savoring the same food and even becoming a nomad! Leaning toward his Eastern side, Cyrus's principal belief became fate or kismet; when leaning toward his Western side, he became a believer in free will—"where there is a will, there is a way."[4]

Uncle Cyrus felt that life was too easy in America. In America, a person does not have to match wits with the fruit or vegetable seller as in the bazaars of Iran. Here all you do, he would say, is drive to the supermarket and buy some frozen products. In Iran, Cyrus would declaim, you have to keep on your toes—survival of the fittest—but in America a person had a tendency to become double-chinned and pot-bellied at the age of forty! He felt that he had learned from Abol Ghassem the benefits of clean, simple living, the activation of the imagination by great poetry, and the blessedness of good health through exercise.

Intimations of destiny raced through my mind as I drove alongside the Potomac River near National Airport where Uncle Cyrus's life was cut short on Christmas Day, 1974. Cyrus was a champion swimmer and athlete. The sole survivor of the freak boating accident recalled later that at one point in the cruise, Cyrus wanted to go home but the others persuaded him to stay. Later, as they tried to pull the anchor, a gust of wind capsized the boat, Cyrus decided to swim to shore to get help, but he died in the frigid waters of the Potomac some five hundred feet from the airport.[5]

Uncle Cyrus's most poignant observations on our lives in between the worlds of Iran and America stay with me to this day:

> I will never, as long as I live, forget my Iran. You can have America and her milk shakes, her cakes, her television sets, her Cadillacs, and even her capitalists; I would much rather be sitting in a tea house drinking tea while I listen to those melancholic, tear-wringing, sorrowful tunes on the radio. . . . I love the rough, snow-capped mountains; the green valleys where a shepherd is always found leading his flocks; the camel caravans; the clang and clamor of Persian bazaars where purchasing an article is an art. I love the magnificent culture of Isfahan and Shiraz, where perfumed gardens scented with the exotic aroma of Persian roses are plentiful, and palaces of kings still stand as a monument to a once great and fabulous nation; where mosques, with their ineffable majesty and beauty, add a profound religious atmosphere to the city, their myriad colors and patterns painting a subtle, peaceful picture. These edifices of incomparable beauty are symbols of the Iranian devout faith in God . . . So I would have to put up with the beggars, the thieves, the opium, the open water ways along the streets. So what! Those only add color to the design, making it however paradoxically more intricate and mysterious; and yet, signifying something greater still. Iran is starving for improvement.[6]

NOW THAT I WAS IN WASHINGTON, I HAD MADE YET ANOTHER daring decision for my future and that of my children. First I left Iran in 1987 in order to think freely, further my education, and give Saied a chance for a brighter future, and now with Samira almost four years old, I was beginning my career at one of America's most important journalism institutions. I lost myself in journalism both for practical reasons—to be able to support my family—and self-fulfillment. My sense of destiny was stronger and motivated me beyond all other responsibilities in life. I would just have to make it work.

I knew that every stage from this point forward would require even more sacrifice. I had the responsibility of raising my children and so there was no room for self-indulgence. While in New Mexico, I had been in a state alternating between loss and discovery, between being and beholding. Now, I had to urge myself to give up the idea of separation—the feeling of being alone in the world. My quest was for seeing the oneness of humanity no matter what the culture. I wanted to plunge into the ocean of humanity and hear it pulsating.

The Carnegie Commission on the future of public broadcasting refers to the need to illuminate "the dark corners of the world and the dark corners of the mind" so that we may "add to our understanding of our own inner workings, and of one another; and we must reveal how we are different and what we share in common. . . . As future communicators we have the added challenge of being a bridge between different cultures."

The fragmentations that faced me, especially those between the countries of my origin, Iran, now the Islamic Republic, and America, were increasingly part of life in the twenty-first century. For my tree of life to continue to grow, I felt there must be profound communication between these two divided cultures.

Many of the Iranians I met living in Washington, D.C., had immigrated here after the Iranian Revolution in 1979 and were now successful members of society with high-profile jobs at Westinghouse, IBM, and AT&T. Many came from wealthy families and all had a tremendous sense of pride in their ancient Persian culture, their language, their cuisine and history. But nearly all grappled with a sense of alienation and a struggle to overcome the cultural death they had experienced leaving their homeland. What was profound though was that no matter how difficult and confusing their lives were, they transcended all the difficulties and maintained a sense of honor and pride in their new homeland.

One of the first Iranian women I met in Washington, D.C., was Mahnaz Afkhami. She was the former Minister of State for Women's Affairs under the Shah. Her life in exile had begun on November 27, 1978, when she was in New York working with the United Nations to organize an international training and research institute for the advancement of women's rights. The Iranian Revolution soon followed and she never returned. Through her travels in Iran in the 1960s and '70s she had helped build an infrastructure to support the needs of women, including child-care centers, health-care clinics, and what she called "consciousness-raising groups."

Women in villages and factory workers alike told her that women's rights and legal protections were irrelevant unless Iranian women were able to be financially independent. For example, Afkhami heard about a woman at a textile factory in Isfahan who locked her four children in the house for ten hours at a time in order to be able to go out and work. Afkhami and other women activists created the concept of "Houses of Women," where they worked to establish vocational classes, job counseling, and family planning across Iran.

Even in exile, Afkhami continued her work promoting the rights of Muslim women. In 1996, she directed the publication of a progressive manual, *Claiming Our Rights: A Manual for Women's Human Rights Education in Muslim Societies.* Published in half a dozen languages including Persian and Arabic, the manual was an instruction book to help women discuss their various rights under Islam. Afkhami's hope was for women to engage in grassroots dialogue.

Her work was inspiring in that through her nonprofit organization, she encouraged Muslim women to demand "egalitarian" legislation especially in the area of family law. But she lamented that advancements in the rights of women in Islam often went unnoticed "as militants and fundamentalists dominated contemporary images of Islam."

I WAS COMMITTED TO THE IDEA OF PERSONAL SACRIFICE BUT I had not given up my dream of finding love and happiness within an Iranian family. As a divorced, single mother, I was told not to expect too much. As my mother found out fifteen years before, most Iranian men were not keen on marrying someone who already had children. It was surprising, therefore, when after attending a family wedding, one of my second cousins and I began a courtship.

Our grandfathers were brothers, the same brothers who spent many weekends on hunting excursions in Iran. Faroukh was a few years older than I, charming and handsome. Being related to him meant that I did not have to explain my mixed Eastern and Western background, and that our families understood each other. He accepted my children.

Our parents thought we should wait awhile. But in our hearts, we really felt this was right. After a short courtship, we decided we could not wait for very long.

The wedding took place on Memorial Day weekend in May of 1994. It was a weekend of two weddings and a birthday. Uncle Jamshid was turning sixty and as was tradition in the Bakhtiar family, a big celebration had been planned. My brother Karim was set to marry his first love, Susan Khalili. I had introduced Karim and Susan to each other in Iran when they were teenagers. It felt good to me that both Karim and I were getting married at the same time. Since weddings are like family reunions, the two weddings combined to bring out all the Bakhtiars and Ardalans. My mother, father, stepmother, both brothers, and my sister attended. It was heartwarming to see them, because only my brother Karim and my mother had been able to attend my first wedding in Iran. In addition, my aunts Parveen, Paree, and Shireen and several Bakhtiar cousins were in attendance.

My wedding took place at the home of my in-laws in Vienna, Virginia. They had a beautiful lawn that served as the setting for the American part of the ceremony. We stood side by side, with Saied and Samira at one side, as the justice of the peace stated our vows. Looking back I saw every member of my extended family cheering us on. The last time the clans came together was the marriage of my parents at the home of Mohammad Nemazee in Potomac, Maryland. And so it was that once again the Ardalans and the Bakhtiars came together to celebrate the union of two cousins!

This wedding celebration was quite different from my first, in that men and women danced the night away together. The food had been deliciously arranged by my mother-in-law, including the requisite *shirin polo,* which is a sweet rice, prepared with saffron, pistachios, almonds, and orange slivers. All of us had a wonderful time. We took a huge family picture, with all my Ardalan and Bakhtiar relatives. I recall my grandmother Mani joone, who had moved from Tehran to Vienna, Virginia, to live with her daughter Pari, looking at us approvingly this time.

Over the next few years, Faroukh and I were to have two wonderful boys. For me, marriage to my second cousin was a reacquaintance with my father's family. As such we decided to name our first son, Aman, in memory of his grandfather Amanollah Ardalan. Both my husband and I were listed on the Ardalan family tree that dates back thirty generations. And for this, we named our second son Amir, meaning prince or leader, in memory of many of the same Ardalan ancestors who were statesmen.

IN JULY 1994 I WAS HIRED PERMANENTLY BY SENIOR PRODUCER Robert Malesky on *Weekend Edition Sunday.* There, I began working with the host of the show, Liane Hansen, on my very first music piece. Producers Walter Watson, Ned Wharton, and Fred Wasser helped get me oriented. This was particularly challenging since I had never heard of singer/songwriter Joe Jackson, my assigned subject, before.

With no cultural reference, I began researching his background. It was my first test as a producer. I listened to the music over and over again, imagining in my mind how I could make the piece represent the authentic man. I listened for the right moments to blend in the sounds of the interview, as though they were lyrics to a song, creating a melodic segment that hopefully gave the listeners an accurate picture of him.

What was most curious about this first collaboration between Liane and myself was the way she nurtured me, as she knew I had never produced a music piece before. She was not judgmental, only encouraging, and that is one significant lesson that I learned early on about the women in NPR's newsroom. Nina Totenberg said to me later, "It has been one of the nicest parts of my growing up in this profession that I have gone from being all alone everyplace I have worked to having loads of female company. Those of us who were the 'firsts' didn't realize back then how lonely it was to be the pioneer or the only one." And Susan Stamberg, the first woman to anchor a national nightly news program back in 1972 when she hosted *All Things Considered*, has said, "Women certainly influence the way stories are chosen and told," and she says we've done it "by working longer, harder, showing up on time with our socks pulled up."[7]

It was correspondent Jacki Lyden who further helped me realize the power of radio, in particular, how well suited it was to women's stories. Radio, she would say, penetrates interior spaces where women have many opinions but little place to express them.

In 1995, Jacki Lyden asked me if I would go to Iran with her. The last time I was in Iran was for a brief visit in 1989. Jacki was interested in seeking the pulse of the society and for that she knew we had to speak to the women. In particular we had heard that both conservative and liberal women had been challenging interpretations of Islamic law and demanding improvement in the treatment of women. Within days of the revolution in 1979, the clerics took control of the country's institutions. They took over the justice system and instituted a strict version of Islamic law—they made women wear the veil, brought back harsh punishments, and denounced everything Western. Sixteen years after the revolution, there was a sense that reforms were desperately needed. This was before the election of reformist president Mohammad Khatami. At the time, the divorce rate in Iran was rising, more women were working outside the home, and they were demanding better pay and equal rights to educate themselves.

As much as I was longing to go back to Iran, I could not join her. In 1991 I obtained an American divorce from my first husband, but he refused to grant me an Iranian divorce. If I had traveled to Iran with Jacki to report this story, I would have stood the risk of being refused permission to leave the country. I could still be considered my husband's wife. If I were to go, I would have needed his permission to leave, and I knew he would not have granted it. Since the divorce, we had barely heard from him and he had stopped child support payments.

Over the course of the next ten years, Jacki went to Iran several times and although I was not physically with Jacki in Iran, as she reported the pieces, I shaped the sound and gave the stories life from my edit booth in Washington, D.C. Together we produced numerous stories that examined how criticism and self-expression were reemerging in Iran.

It was surreal. As a producer stateside, I logged all the tape and took each voice as if it were wool dyed in brilliant colors and together with Jacki began weaving them into a larger tapestry. I could not see the faces of the women she interviewed, but I heard their voices and the ambient sounds of Iran. I saw before me scenes of places I had visited as a child. Hammer pounding on copper trays—yes, we are at the bazaar—and there is the sound of the designer etching—and here is the shrine and the sound of people in prostration and prayer—*Allah-o-akbar*—I could see the motion of their hands—and there are the huge wooden doors opening up into a *caravanserai* where rugs were piled high. I had the rhythm and I was in ecstasy.

My edit booth became the courtyard in which I sat, surrounded by women—traditional and modern, young and old, religious and secular, debating the fundamental questions of life, loss, and liberty. Strewn across the edit booth were yards of analog tape, each labeled to correspond with a voice, a thought, a moment in time. And then, each voice began to echo like a shadow from my own past. Each tale was like a metaphor for the dynamic patterns in the life of this Iran.

The voice that catapulted me farthest in time was that of a young Zoroastrian girl reading from the *Gathas*, the Zoroastrian holy book. As she read, "Let us all become of the people who renewed this life and the world," I was a child again in Takht-i Sulayman, the ancient site known as Solomon's Throne, with its mysterious fathomless lake where my sister and I had bathed. It was here where the early rulers of Iran who followed the religion of Zoroaster were crowned king. Prior to the seventh century and the advent of Islam, Iranians were Zoroastrians. This included the great dynasties of Cyrus and Darius the Great, but today only about thirty thousand Zoroastrians remain in Iran.

This particular story was called "Keepers of the Flame" and was set in Yazd, Iran, the spiritual home of the Zoroastrian faith. The prophet Zoroaster preached the existence of one God. Legend has it that the three kings who visited the infant Jesus were Zoroastrians. I fast-forwarded past the recitation of the *Gathas* to the sound of a wooden door opening up and Jacki entering the nine-hundred-year-old Temple of Nush. From this chamber, she described the center of the temple where fire burns continuously, but ironically the story we told was of all the young people leaving the birthplace of this religion. These dying villages in Yazd where Jacki was visiting were being tended by the very last keepers of the Zoroastrian flame.

And for the next story, I recognized the deep and penetrating voice of Farah Pahlavi, the only woman to be crowned empress in thousands of years of Persian history. I remembered seeing her in the carriage taking her to the coronation ceremony, before the revolution, when my mother, sister, and I were attending an international women's architectural conference near the Caspian Sea. Her voice now came to us not from Iran but on the phone from her home in exile in Paris. This was the twentieth anniversary of the Iranian Revolution.

We asked her if looking back she was surprised by the rapid turn of events in Iran's history and if she would comment on her husband's rule, the prosperity and modernization but also the loss of liberty and the suppression of democracy, including the paucity of human rights in dealing with his opponents. "If we had different political parties, people would have been organized and there would be some organized forces against the forces of destruction, and this is one of the mistakes of that period," she replied.

"All of us Iranians—we are Monday morning quarterbacking and just saying what happened, what could be done, what went wrong. I mean, there is no end to it. And, of course, many groups who were against the monarchy like many of the commoners, some of them even today say we should have supported the Shah for the positive things he was doing and criticized him for what we thought was wrong."

The one thing most Iranians will agree on—even if they had a disdain for the Shah and his brutal secret police who were responsible for the torture of thousands of political prisoners—was the fact that they loved their queen. She had been called "Empress of the Arts" given her passion for Iran's cultural heritage. Empress Farah was the driving force behind the preservation of Iran's ancient art and a great supporter of my father's contributions to Iranian architecture. She believed in the emancipation of women and encouraged them to actively participate in public life.

Empress Farah mentioned that whenever she is homesick for Iran, she picks up the phone and dials a random number in Tehran and invents a question, just to stay in touch. And then she said: "I have just to tell you one story. I drink my tea with dry mulberries, which we do in Iran. And one day I had a piece of sand in it. I was first worried I might have broken a tooth, but then suddenly I realized that I had a piece of sand and the land of Iran in my body. You know, it was such a strange feeling of love and belonging."

So many thoughts raced through my mind after that interview when she was still on the phone, especially after the empress said to me, "You know, I still have your mother's book on Sufism." It was again surreal to be sitting in a studio in Washington, D.C., producing a segment featuring the former queen of Iran on the telephone from her home in exile in Paris. Not only that, but to then recall these personal connections with my family. In 1949, for example, when the young Shah was on a visit to Washington, D.C., he had met my mother and introduced my grandmother Helen to President and Mrs. Truman.[8]

Most of my older Ardalan relatives in Washington were unable to go back to Iran given their prominence in the affairs of the Iranian government during the time of the Shah. What surprised them and most Iranian expatriates about our series, *Iran at the Crossroads*, was how candid women activists were about the need for change within Iran's legal system even as Iranian society at large remained unclear about how to bring it about. After the revolution, the Islamic state mandated everything related to daily life. There was even a government-approved list of acceptable Islamic names for newborns.

But, in the privacy of their homes, Iranians had found a way to express themselves. Satellite dishes were a pervasive means of entertainment. It was amazing to hear recordings of people in their living rooms watching *Oprah* and *Baywatch*. Westernized teenagers started jazz bands in their basements. Away from the watchful eyes of the authorities, they fostered a double life.

Listening through headphones, I heard another familiar voice—that of Azam Taleghani, the daughter of a prominent revolutionary ayatollah. Azam was a practicing Muslim and covered from head to toe in a black chador. In 1995, before the election of Mohammad Khatami, Taleghani, along with eight other women, had put their names down as presidential candidates. Running a settlement house for poor women at the age of fifty-eight, Azam Taleghani said that she knew the ruling clerics would not allow a woman to run, but she said other women were thanking her for speaking out and demanding that women be considered for such a position.

This interview stays with me for a very interesting reason. The translator who was with Jacki was male. Even though he did a competent job of translating Taleghani's answers, they had nowhere near the passion and zeal that came across in her choice of words and energy. Taleghani was on fire. I translated her words verbatim and did the voice-overs myself to include her affect. At one point, referring to the ruling clerics she exclaimed, "Let them be silent, I won't be silent. And even if I remain silent, the women won't be silent. . . . Our government officials have been put on notice," she said. "Our movement will continue."

Taleghani further explained that it was important for women to become involved in politics. At the beginning of the revolution when the constitution was being discussed in the parliament, she began contemplating the decision to run. She studied the Koran and books on jurisprudence. She spoke with religious scholars. She came to the conclusion that there is no reason according to Islamic law why a woman could not run for president.

But in postrevolutionary Iran, not even Azam Taleghani, the daughter of a prominent ayatollah, knew the reason why women were banned from running for this office. These decisions were made at the highest level within the patriarchal clerical establishment.

Even on audiotape Tehran came across as a severe city. With the talk of need for reform, the revolutionary rallies seemed just as fervent as they were in the days of the Shah. The drumbeats pulsated in my headphones. I turned up the volume to take notes on the chanting. Marching across the microphone and in the distance all you heard was "Death to America." And yet, in its own way, activism persisted. This was a particularly sensitive time for writers and intellectuals. Some had died under mysterious conditions. Others had received death threats.

My life in Iran in the early 1980s had been spent surrounded by traditional women—daughters, wives, and mothers. Yet clearly another quality was present in these women that we now heard as they and others opposed the clerical status quo that had replaced the unjust rule of the Shah. Khadija, Fatima, and Zaynab, the wife, daughter, and granddaughter of the Prophet Muhammad, were women who were aware of their surroundings. Nothing stopped them from opposing what they felt would weaken their children's future.

An extraordinary woman from the tradition of Fatima whom Jacki interviewed was Shahla Sherkat, editor of the muckraking magazine *Zanan,* meaning "Women." Sherkat exemplifed a group of religious female journalists challenging their traditional roles. On the cover of a back issue of her magazine was a drawing of a woman cowering in front of a man holding a stick with the headline: "Sir, have you ever beaten your wife?" Another read: "Why should women only be receptionists?" or, "Is your nanny your husband's doll?" Sherkat, a practicing Muslim, used moral persuasion as a means to counter the patriarchal mind-set that surrounded her.

Sherkat's magazine was partially funded by the government, and when the government warned her that some of her stories were disrespectful and disruptive, she published the warnings in her magazine. It was clear from her articles that in Iran more and more women wanted better education and better pay, and they were speaking out about wanting more independence.

One of the contributing writers at *Zanan,* who had been a leading voice in women's rights in Iran, was attorney and writer Mehrangiz Kar. In an interview with Jacki in 1997, before she left Iran as a political exile, Kar spoke about the fact that at every level of society—even in the Islamic schools—reformist clerics and politicians were talking about the need to change some of the old customs and laws that were on the books that were holding women back in Iran as the world entered the twenty-first century. Kar spoke about the need to change the age of marriage that then stood at nine for girls. She spoke about changing divorce laws and making inheritance laws more equitable. The level of activism in the area of legal rights of women was astonishing.

Perhaps the most iconoclastic of all the women Jacki interviewed in Iran was a little-known literature professor named

Azar Nafisi, who later wrote the popular book *Reading Lolita in Tehran*. Visiting her university classroom in Tehran, Jacki recorded Nafisi and her students as she challenged the system through the writings of Vladimir Nabokov, Jane Austen, and Henry James. Nafisi's stamina and courage were impressive. I could not picture what she looked like, but her voice was commanding and melodic. She could have been a heroine out of the *Shahnameh*.

Nafisi spoke to her students about the importance of personal freedom and using one's imagination in a society that enforced strict public conduct. She told Jacki that she found her life in postrevolutionary Iran "irreal." "I've tried to coin this word," she said, "because when you talk about unreal or even surreal, you're presupposing a sort of reality. But for me reality is so much created in a void, that every morning I get up I invent my reality, you know." Nafisi continued, "Fiction is much more real to me than reality."[9]

In her graduate-level class, you could hear her students discuss Jane Austen's *Pride and Prejudice*. "The fact that the novel begins with concentrating on these women who rebel against the way their lives have been shaped for them or defined for them, that is very important for my students," Nafisi said. "You have to define your existence, because you don't have a society, one society, to define it for you, you know. I felt that while I was in the States I was defining myself through the dream of Iran, through my language, my culture. And now that I'm in Iran, I've discovered that I can't forget James or Joyce or Nabokov or any of them. They're with me, part of me. And the way I communicate with my own society, ironically, is through these people."

I met Nafisi in May of 1996 when she was on a visit to Washington, D.C. She came to our studios and brought with her some of her students' diaries. The most touching entry came from one of her female students writing about the invisible woman. Nafisi read it for us on the air:

I'm not invisible/I touch the russet fall of the leaves and feel the scent of the last light upon the sky/The crushed sound of the bygone leaves I hear/The last song of the sparrows deep down the sycamores I see/The breeze taking the lifeless leaves I taste/I am not invisible/The night hears me engulfing my voice/The shadow of a cypress sees through me covering my look/The gray of the clouds cloaks my skin all over/The veiled sound of a cricket bears my breath/The silence of the dark carries my cry/Stretch your hands, I am in the wind/Call me, I am in the echo of the veils/Follow me, I am in the last vanishing notes of a seagull.

Today, almost three decades after the revolution, the ruling hard-line clerics in Iran are baffled at societal corruptions that have caught them off guard—street prostitution and drug addiction, to name just two. These excesses of modernity were precisely what clerics blasted during the time of the Shah as a sign of declining moral values. Now in the midst of their theocracy the same social ills are prevalent.

In the summer of 2000, I came across a surprising report published by a local government official (Tehran's head of cultural and artistic affairs). A reformist cleric, Mohammad Ali Zam, reported: "Drug addiction is the rage among schoolchildren, prostitution has increased 635% among high school students and the (growth) rate of suicide in the country has exceeded the record by 109%."[10]

Even Iran's holiest city, Qom, was not immune from street prostitution. To stem this tide, several high-level conservative clerics in Iran proposed a plan. Their idea was to create so-called chastity houses, where under Islamic law, men could temporarily marry women for a few hours. The theory behind this was to "eradicate social corruption" by legalizing this type of sexual relation. In Shia Islam, there is a code of law that allows temporary marriage between a man and a woman. To legalize this marriage, a verse is read from the Koran and there is an understanding as to how long the marriage will last. This relationship can last as little as a couple of hours or as long as a lifetime.

One of the hard-line ayatollahs who supported this plan was quoted as saying: "We face a real challenge with all these women on the street. Our society is in an emergency situation, so the formation of the chastity houses can be an immediate solution to the problem." However, critics—including women's groups—argued successfully that the creation of such "chastity houses" would only encourage impoverished women further into prostitution. The plan to create these "chastity houses" was subsequently dropped by the government.[11]

Whether through a religious or secular prism, Iranian women like journalist Shahla Sherkat, women's rights activist Mehrangiz Kar, literature professor Azar Nafisi, and Azam Taleghani, the activist daughter of an ayatollah, have constructively shined a light onto the predicament of women in Iran. Their hope is that by telling these truths they can generate discussion in the areas where women are denied their equality. Their hope is that other daughters and sisters will pass these stories along and stay active in the cause for a better future.

IF JACKI TAUGHT ME THE ART OF STORYTELLING ON RADIO, NPR's Daniel Zwerdling and Steve Inskeep taught me to have tenacity as a journalist. Whether we were on an aircraft carrier examining how it was built or darting through the streets of Atlantic City reporting on the history of gambling or hanging out

Davar and NPR's Jacki Lyden (*at right*), chasing a story on Long Island, New York, January 2003. (Author's personal collection)

with actor Paul Newman at his Connecticut office for a look at his philanthropic side, Zwerdling and Inskeep were relentless in their pursuit of drawing out the perfect anecdote. In fact, after spending three hours with Paul Newman, playing Ping-Pong with him, and interviewing him as he tested his latest salad dressing, Zwerdling still requested more time to follow him for the rest of the day, to which Newman responded gracefully, "You just got three hours of material to work with!" That might have been the longest time Newman had set aside for a radio interview.

Paul Newman was interested to know about my background. He wanted to know about my name and where I was from. He was intrigued to learn about my Persian heritage. When I asked to take a photo, he pulled out a chair and asked me to sit in front with him and Zwerdling standing behind me. Newman put his hand on my shoulders—a throwback to that famous portrait of him, Robert Redford, and Katharine Ross in their 1969 classic film *Butch Cassidy and the Sundance Kid*.

In late 1999, Zwerdling helped create of one of the most unusual literary adventures NPR had ever embarked on, a project I would later inherit from one of my colleagues. Along with Brooklyn-based novelist Paul Auster, he came up with the idea of having NPR listeners tell their stories. Paul Auster asked that listeners send in brief, true stories that represented a significant moment in their lives or, as Auster put it, "the revelatory stories that transformed them or the stories of synchronicity that belied skepticism." The result was the National Story Project.

Over the course of two years listeners sent in over five thousand submissions; more than a hundred were selected by Auster and read on the air on the first Saturday of each month.

For more than a year, I helped put the listener segments together. In July of 2000, given that some of the stories coming in were whimsical and lighthearted, I decided to find a fun summer venue away from the studio for Paul Auster to record them for the show. I thought no other place in America says leisure like Coney Island, with its ferris wheels, cotton candy, and hot dogs. My grandfather Abol Ghassem had taken his sweetheart Helen there for day trips in the late 1920s, and I knew she'd been mesmerized by his tales, so it seemed like the perfect spot where generations had come and gone.

So amid the sea gulls, the hot knishes, pizzas, and cold beer, Paul Auster read some of his favorite slapstick stories. "There is a kind of a Laurel and Hardy quality to almost all of these stories," Auster said on the air, "people stumbling, falling, tripping. And if nobody gets too badly hurt, it's finally quite hilarious."

The story project stimulated even more stories in myself, and as one listener put it, I started paying attention to the memories and writing them down for myself and for those that come after me.

BY THE SUMMER OF 2002, AS I GAINED CONFIDENCE AS A JOURnalist, my personal life was unfolding in a way that I had not anticipated. This time the difficulties in my marriage did not stem from differences in cultural backgrounds or a language problem. Though my husband and I had both matured in the

West and spoke English, these commonalities did not ensure compatibility. Because we had married quickly, we had not had time to sort through our personalities prior to marriage. It was like mixing oil and water; everything about us was different.

Being immersed in an area with many relatives, going to family gatherings and hosting parties was in effect a big distraction from our problems. Aside from the logistics of everyday life, our personal connection with each other was beginning to fade. Neither of us wanted to stay in denial of the situation. We felt it would be a much more positive experience for our children if we faced our unhappiness with honesty rather than living a lie and pretending all was well. Again, I was in a state of external and internal conflict. Faroukh and I decided to put aside all disguises and stop living our lives based on "what will people say?"

My husband and I separated, and then were eventually divorced. In time, we learned to maintain an amicable relationship for the sake of the children, to whom we are both committed.

After this last setback I became more aware of the importance of self-responsibility, self-sufficiency, and self-reliance, as I alone am responsible for my own destiny. I had found that I had the habit of expressing the weaker side of my personality first while I held back my true feelings because of wanting to "fit in." I had done this with both the families I married into. Now I know that the sheer power of my personality is what supports me in whatever I undertake and that my pioneering spirit gives me self-definition and awareness.

What was this legacy of loneliness that Mama Helen, my mother, and I shared? Growing up in Los Angeles during World

War II with Helen and without her father, my mother remembers every night of the first few years of her life spent in blackouts. When she was old enough to understand what was happening around her, she had to check in her closet and under her bed with her flashlight before going to bed, terrified that the Japanese would come for her. Mama Helen's nights were spent working as a nurse during the war and in the daytime earning her B.S. as a public health nurse at UCLA.

Later when they all moved to Washington, D.C., Helen had five independent-minded teenagers living at home and was unable to cope with earning a living and giving them all the time they demanded. She decided to send the youngest three, my two uncles and my mother, to Catholic school. Perhaps Helen thought the nuns would somehow put the fear of God in them. My mother was eight years old.

In the moments when her older brother, Cyrus, could no longer cope with the loneliness that he felt being separated from their father, he would tell my mother that she was "an accident." My mother said that the first time she heard this she was shocked. She was speechless. Not planned! Accident! Unwanted! Unloved! No father! Then her reasoning ability, undeveloped as it was, somehow told her, "Well, so what. Sticks and stones . . . maybe my parents had not planned to have me, but God had because I am a reality!"

By the age of thirty-eight my mother thought that she had borne such great sorrow in her childhood that surely there would be a rest from God testing her. But then, her husband of sixteen years, the father of her three children and her coauthor of *The*

Sense of Unity, asked her for a divorce. She said that nothing in her life—before or after—prepared her for the pain of that separation.

And with that separation, I entered a dark oblivion. I felt my heart lost in an expansive sea, lost as I approached a painful place with my mother alone and my father away in America. Outwardly, by the fall of 1978, at night I could hear sounds of protesters denouncing the Shah, chanting "God is Greater" (*Allah-o-akbar*). There were power outages. My sister, brother, and I studied and did our homework by candlelight. There was a shortage of heating oil so we all slept with a kerosene space heater in one room. During the long winter nights when we did not know what was happening around us, we prayed for our mother to have the strength to get us through each day.

And now, at the age of thirty-eight, I, too, confronted the same loneliness. There was nothing I could do but live through it and show my children how to overcome the pain of uncertainty. I realized that in both my marriages, I continued to grow and improve personally. I had undergone intense periods of cultural learning. In each relationship, I had been the one who searched into my soul, who delved deeper, and who asked more questions. Both times I had been the one inspired, the one who treaded on exciting waters, the one who searched for answers to the mysteries of life. In this way, spiritually, I was always alone.

· 14 ·

Crisis of Identity

After my second divorce, I moved into a rental apartment with my four children. With my older children with friends and my two younger sons with their father, I was left alone my first weekend in our new apartment with rooms filled only with unpacked boxes and a large couch in the living room. I put on some music, placed my Persian pillows on the couch, and sat down in the middle of the room with a cup of coffee.

It was an agonizing weekend. I cried for the people I had lost and for people I had hurt and for the sense of unity that I still longed for. I knew that because my marriage to my second cousin had broken up, I would be ostracized by some of my father's family in much the same way my mother had been after her divorce. I had to find a way to rise above it all, to overcome the sorrow and sense of abandonment that seemed to run as a thread throughout my life.

Davar's four children (*clockwise*), Saied, Samira, Aman, and Amir, Maryland, March 2006. (Author's personal collection)

While I had loved being a part of my father's family, I finally learned that some of them did not understand me. I could not thrive in an environment where I was not allowed to contribute new ways of doing things; I was independent. I expressed myself with great determination and found it difficult to adjust to things beyond my control. I was caught between trying to be diplomatic while being fairly entrenched in my own perceptions. These were all good qualities but hard to get away with in the patriarchal mind-set of my father's family.

The first crisis in my life was my parents' divorce, which during my life left me emotionally "locked up" and resentful, making it difficult for me to stop or change once my fire had been lit. I knew my "fire" was my Achilles' heel, but that was what ultimately grounded me. I could have drifted into my creative endeavors and lost myself and my children, but that same fire reminded me of the daily treasures of reading a bedtime story or going to a child's soccer game, in short, finding balance in my life. Amid all the exhaustion, it is the fire within me that wakes me up, gets me back into the car, and on to the work of helping create the sounds and symbols that people wake up to on the radio.

I realized that I had to break with the myths of the past to find myself and declare: Iran is Iran. Grandfather Abol Ghassem had the *Shahnameh*. Grandmother Helen had Abol Ghassem and Iran. My father had Lou Kahn and architecture. My mother had Sufism and her children. I had my children, who like God's flowers were wonderful expressions of love, light, and life. And I had journalism, yet I felt like a stranger—the unusual one—in the Iranian American community.

Setting aside traditional expectations of a woman, I wanted to be a doer, a creator who is inspired and not limited by cultural norms. My girlfriends and colleagues at NPR, including producer Tracy Wahl, helped me search for my self-confidence as a woman. They sensed in me an energy that was waiting to be unleashed, an energy linked to my urge for freedom of expression. With each change, painful as it may have been, they helped me have the confidence to search deeper into a more profound side of my nature.

One of my favorite quotes is from the writer Rainer Maria Rilke, in *Letters to a Young Poet,* who said: "Someday there will be girls and women whose name will no longer mean the mere opposite of the male, but something in itself, something that makes one think not of any complement and limit, but only of life and reality: the female human being."

· 15 ·

Discovering a Great-Grandfather

On October 10, 2003, Aman and Amir woke me early in the morning. I turned on the radio and heard that Iranian human rights lawyer Shirin Ebadi had won the Nobel Peace Prize. I could hardly believe what I was hearing. I knew Ebadi had been working tirelessly to change many of the oppressive laws in Iran. As an attorney, she fought for due process and the rule of law within Iran's theocracy.

Finally, I thought, Iran's nightingale can herald the dawn of a new day. I wanted to be a part of this, so I decided to find Ebadi. I tracked her down on the telephone and Robert Siegel interviewed her for *All Things Considered.* As she does not speak English, I translated for her on the air. Just before the interview began, I was able to give Ebadi my congratulations in Persian.

Later that day, an Iranian scholar posted an e-mail to a listserv I belong to. He explained that throughout Iran's modern history the question of the rule of law, the relationship between secular and religious law, and concerns about due process have been the main preoccupation of many lawyers, judges, and law professors. Nobel Laureate Shirin Ebadi, he explained, "is only the latest fruit from a big tree with deep roots in modern Iranian history starting with Davar." Ali Akbar Davar, Iran's minister of justice in the 1930s, was my paternal great-grandfather, and the person for whom I was named. I was stunned when I read this entry. I knew then that I had to be the one to tell this story.[1]

I was to pursue a story that no one had ever considered as a way of speaking for my great-grandfather. In fact, Davar's life was never talked about in our family, I presumed because of the way he had died. He had committed suicide in 1937, but why?

As a way of answering this question, I began to research Iran's battle for justice and the rule of law. I turned to my editor at American RadioWorks and NPR, Deborah George, and also to sociologist and Middle East analyst Rasool Nafisi. Rasool had spent many years in and out of Iran speaking to reformers and hard-liners as part of a book on reform in Islamic laws in post-revolutionary Iran. To trace a bit of this history, Rasool and I went to the Library of Congress to research hundreds of documents and articles on Iran dating back to the early 1900s.

The atmosphere surrounding me that day in November of 2003 was as intense as it was inspiring. I learned that my great-grandfather Ali Akbar Davar was born in Tehran in 1885. His father, Kalb-Ali, was a personal treasurer to Nasser-e-Din Shah, the Qajar king who ruled Iran for fifty years. The Shah stood in great favor with the Europeans by further opening Iran up for business and trade. In fact, Nasser-e-Din Shah was the first king to initiate "official visits" to England, where he met Queen Victoria, and also to Russia, the Netherlands, and Austria. Kalb-Ali, Davar's father, stood in great favor with this Qajar king.

As I glanced through other entries on Davar, a sudden rush of joy filled my whole being. The curator of the Persian Collection was eighty-six-year-old Ibrahim Pourhadi, a frail sage of Iranian origin. He took us through the maze of eight hundred thousand books and showed us a copy of Iran's Constitution of 1906. The constitutional revolution of 1906 was the first of its kind in the Middle East, which guaranteed Iranians fair representation and political rights. The constitution, which limited the role of the clerics and established a monarch as head of state, was a first attempt at secularizing Iranian laws while maintaining an Islamic identity.

The constitution was created when Iranians came together to limit the role of the monarchy, giving rise to an elected legislative assembly or parliament. Freedom of the press soon followed, allowing for the constitutionalists to spread their message. After protests by Iranians of all walks of life against the Qajar Shah's mishandling of revenues and the foreign domination of Iranian assets, the Shah signed a new constitution that effectively limited the power of the monarchy.

This new revolution, however, did not limit the role of the clergy. Conservative cleric Sheikh Fazlollah Nouri succeeded in 1907 in amending the constitution, giving a council of five

Islamic jurists the ability to invalidate laws that conflicted with Islam. Furthermore, the constitution reflected that the Shah and his ministers had to be Shia Muslims.

It was in this climate that my great-grandfather, Davar, entered politics. At the age of twenty-four, he was appointed the nation's first public prosecutor, but he soon realized that the country did not have a formal judicial system with laws that he could defend. He realized that in order to make a difference, he needed to go abroad for his higher education. He went to Switzerland in 1911, and spent the next ten years getting his law degree.

In 1921, Davar was finishing his doctoral thesis when he abruptly returned to Iran after a coup ousted the last of the Qajar monarchs. Nationalists were up in arms that Ahmad Shah, the Qajar king, was considering giving more of Iran's oil revenues and commercial interests to the British. Fed up with Britain's influence in Iran, nationalists staged uprisings and Iran was on the verge of chaos when a military officer named Reza Khan from the Cossack Brigade staged a coup and eventually became prime minister. By 1925, Davar became a member of parliament and helped pass a bill making Reza Khan the new ruler of Iran. Reza Khan chose the last name of Pahlavi, the language spoken in Iran before the advent of Islam, and crowned himself Shah, or king, in 1926.

Davar belonged to the generation of Iranians and secular intellectuals in the region who sought law and order as a remedy for underdevelopment. At the time, neighboring Turkey, under the leadership of Mustafa Kemal, known as Ataturk, was undergoing major political, economic, and social reforms. Ataturk was a secular nationalist and had a disdain for Islamic culture. He banned Islamic dress, shut down religious schools, introduced the Western calendar, and initiated a new Turkish script based on Latin to replace Arabic.

By 1926, after Reza Shah came to power, he and intellectuals like Davar were determined to secularize Iran. They believed that political maneuvering, in the parliament especially, could bring an end to tribal ideas and old customs and bring about a modernist country. Iran's "New Order" included a massive redevelopment plan and brought with it the expansion of the railroad system that in turn revitalized industrial growth, creating an urban middle class. Oil revenues went toward the creation of more manufacturing plants and a modern educational system.

Being an ardent nationalist, Davar believed as did many other intellectuals of his time that Great Britain's dominance in Iran was another cause of Iran's underdevelopment. For a time, as the editor of a magazine called *Mard-e-Azad*, or "Free Man," he penned articles exposing the exploitative role of England in Iran and worked hard to get rid of "Capitulation" (the treaty that granted extraterritorial rights to British citizens in Iran). In this way, Davar crusaded against British hegemony in Iran and on May 9, 1927, the law of Capitulation was abolished.[2]

DAVAR WORKED WITH REZA SHAH PAHLAVI FOR WHAT HE thought would be a reform-based yet autocratic Pahlavi monarchy. At the time he felt that he could bring about a constitutional monarchy and eventually a democracy through this monarchy. He was idealistic in his thinking that those in control would cede their power for a democratically elected government.

Davar's great grandfather Ali Akbar Davar, Justice Minister, Tehran, 1927. (Author's personal collection)

In 1927, when Davar was appointed minister of justice, he set in motion his own fundamental changes within the judicial system. Scrolling through microfilms at the Library of Congress, I found official notices from Davar himself—one specifically on

changing the laws on punishment. Before 1927 strict interpretations of Islamic Sharia law as well as tribal customs dominated
Iran's system of justice.

Davar was able to recruit a few learned men who had
obtained their degrees from universities in Europe, but for the
most part he had to hire clerics who were well versed in law and
jurisprudence. In order to give his ministry a uniform appearance, Davar persuaded the clerics to dress in suits and wear a
European-style hat instead of turbans.[3]

Between 1927 and 1932, as Iran's minister of justice, Davar
dismantled and reorganized the ministry, which was primarily
run by clergy and the laws of Islam. He put an end to the practice of retribution, or *qesas*, meaning "an eye for an eye, a tooth
for a tooth." He replaced the centuries-old law of retribution
with a new penal code, borrowed from legal codes in Belgium
and France. He envisioned Iran as a country based on modern
laws and a system of justice based on human rights. As such he
abolished harsh Islamic punishments such as stoning and lash-
ing, which basically victimized women. He and his colleagues at
the ministry also drew up a civil code that combined Western
legal precepts and the law of Sharia.

But in some cases, his reforms contradicted centuries-old
Islamic canons. He reduced the social power of the clerics by
putting secular lawyers in charge of registering all legal contracts
and documents. Furthermore, he created a new justice system
that included local courts, regional ones, and a supreme court.
He gave state judges the power to decide which cases should be
handled by the clerics.

In this way Davar was not without controversy—entries in books on the reign of Reza Shah point to protests that were triggered by the enactment of Davar's secular laws. The traditional clerics protested and general strikes were organized in major Iranian cities, while prodemocracy intellectuals criticized Davar for promoting the authoritarian rule of Reza Shah.

The Shah was a military man who used force to unify what he saw as Iran's diverse people, end foreign influence, and emancipate women. Reza Shah imposed European dress on the population. He opened the schools to women and brought them into the workforce. In 1936, he forcibly abolished the wearing of the veil. In fact, he held a public gathering where he introduced his wife and daughter without their veils. The clerics and religious leaders were incensed. A revolution could be in the making, but Reza Shah was enjoying wide support. He had restored order, unified the country, reinforced national independence, and implemented economic and educational reforms, all of which bore Davar's handprint.

But with this new power came the erosion of some of the democratic reforms that Davar had sought for so many years. Reza Shah's notorious police chiefs began arresting opponents and suppressing the press. Religious leaders were exiled or sent to jail. For his part, Davar felt that his proposed legal reforms were so revolutionary that he needed to have the backing of a strong leader, even a dictator, because there would be tremendous opposition to his reforms.

But Davar would learn that bureaucrats who became too powerful suffered a similar fate. Reza Shah had recently jailed his friend Abdol Hossein Teimurtash. Teimurtash was the Shah's powerful minister of court. He was a charismatic politician and together with Davar and another statesman named Nosratdowleh, the triumvirate had shaped the rule of Reza Shah. Reza Shah became suspicious of Teimurtash after he returned from a trip to England via Russia. His suitcase had apparently been stolen and it included sensitive information. Davar was terrified by the arrest of Teimurtash. He told his daughter, "Haven't you heard? They have taken Teimurtash. I know that one day the same thing will happen to me." In October 1933, Teimurtash was murdered in prison.

Within Iran's religious establishment, protests of Reza Shah's reforms continued. In the summer of 1936, in the Holy City of Mashad, confrontations turned deadly. Dozens of worshipers were killed by government troops as they gathered in a shrine protesting against the reforms of the Shah. In addition, the Shah had arrested and imprisoned one of his most ardent critics, the ayatollah Hassan Modarres. Modarres was a member of parliament who in 1914 was sent to Iran from Najaf, Iraq, one of the centers of Shia Islam, to make sure the laws of parliament were in accordance with Islam. Reza Shah and Modarres, who interestingly was the teacher of a young Ruhollah Khomeini, never saw eye to eye.

By this time in 1936, Davar had left the justice ministry and was minister of finance, where he had succeeded in strengthening Iran's economy. He changed the country's tax laws and introduced the General Accounting Act of 1934–35, as well as a civil service code. He was working hard to break British domination over Iran and was looking to America as a partner in commerce. Davar's growing popularity with the people and his insistence on breaking free from the British began to arouse the anger of Reza Shah. The Shah would not allow any powerful or popular individual to dare rise above him.

On the morning of February 9, 1937, Reza Shah Pahlavi called Davar to his palace for an audience. Davar left his home in such a hurry he dropped his glasses on the way and arrived unable to see clearly. The Shah was visibly angry. Davar was immediately afraid for his life.[4]

Davar asked Reza Shah what he wished him to do. *"Boro gomsho!"* He said angrily to his old friend, *"Boro gomsho!"* (Go and get lost). Davar knew his fate if he were not to choose this path. The thought of running never crossed his mind. How could he live anywhere but here? How could he live without his beloved country? All he worked for and believed in was crashing down around him. Forty-nine years old and his dreams of democracy had failed. The only chance now for his family was for him to disappear silently into the night. Would anyone ever know of his struggles? Would they ever know what he tried to do?

That night, he sat down at his desk at home and began to write a letter to his family. He apologized for what he was about to do, but he wrote that he had no choice and that he loved them deeply. Then he made a fatal drink of opium and alcohol, swallowed the lethal combination, and went quietly into the night.

· 16 ·

Sorrow and Triumph

T
he morning after Davar committed suicide, my grandmother Mani joone was walking alongside Lalizar
Avenue, shopping with her friend, when a car began honking
behind them. She looked and saw her father's driver. He told her
that her father was sick and that he had been sent to find her.
She got in the car with her friend and went to her father's house.
She saw crowds of people outside his home and told her friend:
"Something has happened to my father."[1]

She said, "When we got out of the car and went into the garden, I saw that it was filled with people. I went into the room and
asked: "What has happened?" I asked a friend of my father's,
"What is it? What has happened? Has something happened to
my father?" He said: "Please do not make a lot of noise. The prime
minister is here and other ministers and many other dignitaries."

Because she was so anxious, she remembers being very
abrupt. She said: "I want to see my father. I do not care about

anyone else." She saw that they had laid her father out and covered him with a white cloth. She pulled back the cloth and became distraught. By that time his throat and stomach had become bloated because of the opium he had ingested.

"They pulled me off of my father's body and took me into another room. I saw my grandmother and my paternal aunts and friends had all come. When they took my father's body into the car to take him away, I fainted. Later I realized that they had lifted me and carried me back into the room. That night I was in a very bad state. I telephoned my husband. He came and was bewildered at what had happened. I told him to watch our daughter because I would spend the night there. I stayed there all night."

MY GRANDMOTHER MANI JOONE WAS MY ONLY IMMEDIATE LINK to Davar. For ninety-one years, she had buried her father's story in her soul and I longed to know every detail. I spent precious time interviewing her at her bedside. I could see her face light up as she spent hours with me talking and reminiscing.

My grandmother saw very little of her father once he'd returned from Europe. He worked long hours and ate very little. Every so often he would write letters apologizing for being out of touch. Once he wrote her a note: "A thousand pardons for not having come to see you and for not responding to your letter. Enclosed is thirty tomans, fifteen tomans for your mother and fifteen tomans for you for this month."

Although Davar was an absent father, Mani joone still inherited his sense of integrity and ethics, if not in person then through his sporadic letters. On October 19, 1928, Davar wrote to my grandparents Mani joone and Abbas: "I received a box of lemons in the mail. Unfortunately the sender is an employee of the justice ministry and I have a strict policy of not accepting gifts from people within the ministry or those who deal with the ministry. I feel it would be rude to send it back to my colleague in Shiraz. As such, I am forwarding you this box of lemons."

Davar was a lover of music and this also carried over to my grandmother. At a young age, she became interested in musical instruments and took up the tar, a classic stringed instrument. Back then, Ghamar Molouk Vaziri was a very popular singer and as such was very selective about where she would perform, but she had great admiration for Davar and would attend gatherings at his home. One night, Mani joone and her father were sitting next to the fireplace. After Molouk sang, Davar said: "Farangis, what about you? I understand you have learned how to play. You play for us." She played all the songs she had learned. Another musician played along as well. When they finished, Davar turned to the musician and said: "I hope you do not mind. You were Farangis's teacher but Farangis's fingers are sweeter than yours."

IN MEMORY OF MY GREAT-GRANDFATHER, AND REPRESENTING NPR and American RadioWorks, I traveled to Oslo, Norway, to cover the Nobel Peace Prize ceremony and meet human rights lawyer Shirin Ebadi. Iranians, who have seen both the fall of the

Shah and the rise of the first Islamic revolution, yearn today for more of a voice in their government and their courts. The Nobel Peace Prize that was to be awarded to Shirin Ebadi recognized this yearning.

Looking down from the airplane as we were about to land, I saw it was still early morning and dark. It was as if we were going to land on the moon. It was this unbelievable image, as if I were going to a whole other world. Once in Oslo, I arrived at the hotel where Shirin Ebadi was staying. I first contacted her good friend and renowned human rights lawyer Karim Lahiji. He was in Oslo to help honor the soon-to-be Nobel Laureate. Before the world knew Shirin Ebadi, Karim Lahiji was considered Iran's most well-known human rights activist. He had been one of several scholars who was asked by the Ayatollah Khomeini to draft Iran's new constitution after the revolution. But when the new revolutionaries felt he was too secular, they marginalized him, and eventually he fled Iran and now lives in Paris. Lahiji provided tremendous background on the early struggles of lawyers like Davar who wanted to take Iran toward modernity.

I met Lahiji in his hotel room. As I interviewed him, the phone rang and it was Shirin Ebadi. After a couple of minutes, I interrupted Mr. Lahiji and said, "Can you please ask Mrs. Ebadi if I can interview her while I am here?" Mr. Lahiji said, "Shirin, Ali Akbar Davar's granddaughter is sitting here. She is a journalist from the United States I think we owe a debt of gratitude to Davar—perhaps it would not be a bad idea if you spoke to her." Mrs. Ebadi asked me to meet her the following day after her interview with the BBC.

Meanwhile, it was the night before the peace prize ceremonies, and Shirin Ebadi's family and friends were having dinner at a restaurant at the Grand Hotel in Oslo. Lahiji had
invited me to come and meet Ebadi's family. Many of her family
members had come from the United States. There were physicians from Boston and New York. I first talked to her nineteen-
year-old daughter, who spoke about how proud she was of her
mother and yet how difficult it had been for them in Iran, especially in the last few months with the threats against their life.
Because they were not specific it was clear to them that they
were intimidation techniques more than actual threats. She and
her family continued with their daily lives.

On the day she received the Nobel Peace Prize, I arrived at
the press filing center at Oslo's City Hall, along with hundreds
of other journalists. As the international sound system was being
tested for broadcast and the orchestra got in one last practice, the
hall started filling up. Looking down from the press center I saw
some familiar faces walking in to honor Shirin Ebadi.

One of them was Parastou Forouhar. Her parents, Dariush
and Parvaneh Forouhar, were well-known intellectuals and
prodemocracy activists in Iran. The two were brutally stabbed to
death by agents of the Islamic Republic in 1998. Since then,
Parastou has been trying to bring her parents' killers to justice in
Iran's criminal courts and Shirin Ebadi is her attorney. I then
saw human rights lawyer Karim Lahiji proudly walking down
the aisle to take his seat.

On that day, Shirin Ebadi took her seat next to the royal family of Norway. The walls of Oslo's City Hall were adorned with

paintings featuring themes of wartime occupation, resistance, and liberation. Azaleas, ivy, and white roses adorned the main hall. And after some graceful piano music, the Nobel Laureate was serenaded with music from Kurdistan. Needless to say the hall was transfixed!

When it came time for Ebadi to take the stand for her acceptance speech, in a dramatic gesture she raised her right arm and said, "I am an Iranian—a descendant of Cyrus the Great— the emperor who at the height of his power said he would not rule over the people if they did not want him to." In her Nobel Peace Prize acceptance speech, she cited the Islamic holy book, the Koran, to make the point that people who know their rights are more likely to be free.

Ebadi has gone on record stating that some Muslim countries justify repressive governments by saying that democracy is not compatible with the teachings of Islam. Ebadi disagrees. Many have said that she is part of a larger reform movement in the Islamic world that wants to reinterpret Islam to prove that it is not just one monolithic set of ideas. Ebadi said: "The people of Iran have been battling against consecutive conflicts between tradition and modernity for over one hundred years." She believes Iranians should be allowed to have a part in choosing their own destiny.

Shirin Ebadi is a lawyer; she understands the power of words; she knows the danger of ideas. Throughout history, on the basis of these ideas alone, many have died and many more have been imprisoned. My great-grandfather Ali Akbar Davar came to know the power of ideas and their price.

When I returned from Oslo, I went to visit my grandmother Mani joone. I planned to give her a biography of Davar that Shirin Ebadi had generously inscribed. My grandmother was weak and in the last cycle of her life, but I wanted to honor her and her father for what he gave to Iran. For so many years our family had been silent about his death and his legacy. Aunt Pari, my father's sister, who was there said: "No, Iran, you should keep this book. You are the next generation."

· 17 ·

Finding Myself Through Love

As I began working on the radio documentary, my mind wandered through the vaults and corridors of my own experiences. Could the telling of this story about Iran's search for a lawful society also be my conscious quest for my own identity as Iran, the woman? With sunlight overhead, the shadows disappeared and I began to see my past clearly as if it were unfolding for the first time that very day. I mentioned to my editor Deborah George that my first name is actually Iran. Deborah looked at me and said, "That should be the title of the piece—My Name Is Iran." This came as a surprise to many of my American colleagues, many of whom never guessed at my past. Suddenly I understood that like so many Iranian Americans, I had been living in disguise. I had been afraid to share the Iranian side of myself with Westerners but I had also been afraid to express my individuality and rise above the cultural norms of my Iranian side.

It was as if I had become a woman warrior ready to do battle with my inner self, my false me. I was reminded of the great woman warrior of the *Shahnameh*, Gordafarid (female warrior). She was able to move out of the role culture had cast for her, take the divine mandate (*farr*)—the right to rule over herself—and rise to a level equal to men, on their own turf and on her own terms.[1]

I spent countless days and nights logging tape, listening back to interviews, editing sound files, sometimes so exhausted I would end up sleeping on the floor next to my desk. I realized I was going through a time of great creativity, longing and yearning to express, to communicate, to cause an effect in such a way that the effect would itself become a cause, for I had grown beyond the suffering, pain, and anguish of alienation.

Upon hearing the news that I was going to Oslo my father wrote me, "As your dad, I am deeply proud of you." My father was living and working in Kuwait at the time, designing buildings throughout the Persian Gulf. He wrote, "Look to the transitory aspect of this event from close up, and from a far vantage point. See the archetypal dimension of Shirin Ebadi as Ali Akbar Davar; as mythic Rostam against the *divs* or demons; and right versus wrong, as light and truth set against darkness and untruth. See this as a pivotal transformative event in your own life . . . this is what you have been prepared for, yet never experienced."[2]

Up to now my father had said, "I have seen a familiar repeat pattern in your life—it is a pattern of masks and shells—of Brooke Shields, bride of Khomeini, NPR producer, behind which the real Iran has yet to be revealed. Release yourself from your mother and father's persona, divorce, and any lingering shadows."

At the age of forty, I began cracking the shells to liberate myself from them. The pattern that now unfolded was one of a journalist interested in allowing a multiplicity of voices to speak for themselves and to build on them—whether of the place where the sun rises or of the place where it sets.

Listening back to the speeches given at the Nobel ceremony, I realized that one of the most meaningful symbolisms of Ebadi's peace prize was the uniting of the East and West. A woman from the East had been recognized by one of the most prestigious institutions of the West. Representing, as the two coordinates often do, fate versus free will, my mother had once explained the difference between the East and the West as put forth by French philosopher Henri Corbin. He had said that the East believes it must prepare itself to receive the divine mandate and even then, once prepared, depending on fate, it may or may not be granted. In the West, on the other hand, the belief is that humankind takes the divine mandate, much as Prometheus did, through willpower. It is there to be taken. My uncle Cyrus had mused on much the same issue. Even after he had read solutions offered by various sages of the past, he found them to be at best mirages in the vast desert of unsolved mysteries. He felt that while one may sense his thirst has been quenched, the sensation lasted only a few moments before one awoke to the reality that the question remained unanswered.

After further review and study, Uncle Cyrus found the answer right under his feet—a Persian carpet that his mother, my grandmother Helen, had given him when he had graduated from Harvard. My uncle moved often in America, but wherever he went, he would place his Persian carpet next to his bed so that when he stepped on it on rising in the morning, it became his bridge between East and West.

He reasoned: The carpet and its components came from thousands of years of history—plant-dyed colors from plants that have grown in the East for thousands of years; wool from sheep raised in the Bakhtiari mountains for thousands of years; patterns and designs created by artists that evolved over centuries.

Much like human life, the carpet's colors are its genes inherited from thousands of ancestors; its wool-like flesh formed at conception; its patterns evolving from its environment and nurturing process.

I came to much the same conclusion about the carpet being a bridge between East and West the moment I saw the funeral of Pope John Paul II and the beautiful Persian carpet on which his casket lay. NPR's Renee Montagne was cohosting from the Vatican that day and I was producing the live broadcast on *Morning Edition*. As I listened to our show and glanced at the live television images, I felt that my Eastern culture was part of the carpet holding up the body of this great man of history. I thought about the stories of the people who had woven it in the East, and who had participated in his funeral in the West.

And then I realized that while the Persian carpet had been silent for my uncle, I heard the voices of the people who wove their stories into its creation. For me, the best bridge between East and West is storytelling—communicating.[3]

I thought about my parents, both creative people who had also suffered separation and a sense of rejection at points in their life, but they had still remained creative. I wondered: "What does it mean to be creative? Where do creative ideas come from? How are they learned or are they just instinctive?" I had so many questions, and for a change, time to find some answers for myself. I began with a kind of contemplative withdrawal from the outer world. I began with the past in order to make the present real.

One spring afternoon, through the grace of God, I came to meet a man who helped me shed the pessimism within me to approach the fuller possibilities life offered. His name was John Oliver Smith. He lived by the water in Annapolis, spending his free time sailing on Chesapeake Bay or taking walks on the local beach by the bay. He loved to sail east to the Wye River or south to Solomon's Island and immerse himself in nature. Of Irish ancestry, he had traveled widely, from Malaysia to Saudi Arabia, to Germany, and to Italy.

I wrote him a note telling him of my family's sailing trip on the Nile River, my love for adventure and, as we were both Aries, perhaps we would be dangerous together. But it was our quiet acceptance of each other and the joy our children brought to us that formed the basis of our strong friendship. We would joke about both being stubborn, although eventually we would find that we could be supportive of each other's faith, his as Catholic, and mine as Muslim, each realizing we had common religious origins going back to the Prophet Abraham.

He said his family were hardworking people from the Midwest who had persevered through difficult times because of the strength of their character. He admitted to skeletons in his closet, but said that it is how we deal with overcoming those mistakes and maintaining our kindness toward others that is our legacy, adding: "I have had some trouble in my life and it is the people who would be disappointed of my poor choices and most forgiving of those choices, who have provided me with a moral compass."

John then wrote me his favorite saying from Teddy Roosevelt: Far better is it to dare mighty things, even though checkered by failure, than to dwell in that perpetual twilight that knows not victory nor defeat. It was as if my grandmother Helen were

Davar and John Oliver Smith, May 2006. (Photograph by Samira Ghaffari)

saying it to me. I, too, through the splendor of my quest had become more of a follower of free will.

There were so many connections for me in what he wrote that my mind raced forward: Could fate finally be dealing me a good hand for a lasting relationship? He was an environmental engineer and lived near several of my mother's family, including my Aunt Parveen, who had moved to Annapolis from Chevy Chase. Her daughter, Lailee Bakhtiar McNair, who had traveled in the footsteps of Mama Helen in the Bakhtiari regions of Iran, lived nearby, as well. Lailee's great-grandfather Rear Admiral Frederick V. McNair was the superintendent of the Naval Academy. Furthermore, I had been investigating the possibility of specializing in environmental reporting at the time, and the Chesapeake Bay area seemed like the natural place to do so.

Divorced for several years, John also yearned to have a happy and stable family home. Depressed and lonely, he had retreated from life, only finding fulfillment in his faith and the times he would see his boys. For this, our connection was not just physical but spiritual. We would sit in a little Irish pub/restaurant near NPR and talk for hours, about our ideals, our children, and our families. From the restaurant we would drive to Georgetown in his old yellow Jeep and walk by the river where the lights of the Kennedy Center reflect on the water. As we walked along the Potomac River, we mused, which of our life experiences had belonged to the domain of the mysterious, the spiritual? Could we conceive and bring forth the natural and spiritual power of our ancestors, have them arise from the depths of the ocean of our unconsciousness?

We decided we would never be able to solve the paradox of light and darkness of soul and spirit. We said that we had stayed bound to the earth for the sake of our children and now perhaps we had found someone to journey with. I took his hand and pulled him close. I felt safe. For the first time in a very long time, I felt safe.

It never seemed to matter that he was raised in Lima, Ohio, and I in Tehran, Iran. We loved being together, alone and talking; however, John had four sons and with my four children those moments were going to become precious and few. His oldest, Zachary, was the ever ambitious and hard-working student, Mike, handsome and charming, was the sensitive mediator, Danny was smart and always ready with a joke or a smile, and Joey, the gentle and wise youngest child. They ranged in age from thirteen to nineteen and mixed harmoniously with Saied, our now creative entrepreneur, Samira, the princess/soccer athlete, Aman, the little philosopher, and Amir, our compassionate future engineer.

Since we are both professionals with demanding jobs, negotiating time for each other was going to be a challenge, so John and I decided to move in together in August of 2003. Our time became one of celebrating family and each other in our own oasis of serenity just off the Severn River. Sundays would begin with the preparation of our magnificent brunches. Each of the older children, who were home for the weekend, prepared different parts of the feast. When Saied was home, he and John discussed their faith along with exchanging jokes and family stories while John grilled his famous London broil. Someone made the

Belgian waffles, another the scrambled eggs and turkey bacon, and still another the home fries. Fresh fruit was set out, coffee made, and orange juice poured. In the warm months we would eat outdoors, in the winter we all sat around one large table. Dessert is always a milkshake made in the antique Hamilton Beach milkshake maker that John's father used to welcome John home from college in Ohio when he was young.

For the Fourth of July one year, John took Saied, Samira, and me out for a day of sailing down to Annapolis where we ate dinner and watched fireworks from the deck of the family sailboat. Aman and Amir spend weekends with their father, Faroukh, in Virginia, but on weeknights they love helping John on household projects.

We've made several trips to Ohio, which John says is the east of the Midwest and, although my grandmother Helen was from Idaho, which is the western edge of the Midwest, I feel there is a similarity in their culture. Their stoicism, warmth, and kindness are evident and through them I have gained an insight into my own Midwestern roots.

During the holidays our house has become the focal point for extended family gatherings. As was done in Iran, during the *dorehs* and Noruz festivities, we celebrate our family with tons of Persian food that I love to prepare. My mother, who by then had moved to Chicago, would come to visit and help John and me play host to her family. Aunts Paree and Parveen and cousins come from Annapolis and D.C., and, of course, Uncle Jamshid is there to entertain us, not by wrestling calves but with his wonderful stories of his life and our family. My aunt Parveen always has a new painting to show, and we have bought one with brilliant brown and purple colors. It is a painting of a bull and I told the children how it represented the animal Uncle Jamshid used to wrestle when he was a kid in Solomon's Mosque.

The Smith boys love spending Noruz with us as well. They have embraced the season and all love to stay for some exotic food. One year, John and his son Michael even tried on a classic Bahktiari tribal outfit that cousin Lailee had brought back from her trip to the Bakhtiari region of Iran. The two Irish-Americans looked so proud in the garb usually worn by the Bakhtiari tribesmen during local celebrations.

Just as John has learned about my faith, on occasion, I enjoy joining him for Sunday Mass at Saint Mary's, a historic Gothic-style Roman Catholic Church in Annapolis. I do this not only to show respect for his beliefs but because I have my own yearning to learn about the principles of the religion of my American forbears. This Gothic church was constructed in 1858 on the property of a Revolutionary patriot and signer of the Declaration of Independence, Charles Carroll. Carroll fought for religious freedom for Catholics who, until the nation guaranteed freedom of religion, were unable to worship publicly in Maryland.

John and I have both faced failure. This has changed us forever—has humbled us—and like a great teacher, our failures have taught us how to see what really matters. John seems to know me inside out, "You can never control a Persian woman," he says. He then says, "If you seek comfort, you will neither find truth nor comfort. If you seek truth, in the end you will find comfort." In the safety of this loving relationship and knowing that my children are being raised in a peaceful home, I have spent a good deal of time trying to develop patience.

Looking at John as he reads his book on sailing, I laugh. We are in our favorite bookstore in Annapolis, sipping lattes. Young midshipmen and old sailors wander in and out checking their e-mails, getting coffee, and just enjoying springtime near the water. John looks at me, smiles, shakes his head, and gives me a little kiss. "I love you," he whispers. Then it's back to his book.

I have found deep inner strength as if my emotions were profoundly linked to the stream of my life. My creative instincts focused my imagination, bringing me success at home and work. Thus a new day and a new Iran are born.

· 18 ·

My Name Is Iran

I t was not long after my documentary aired on public radio
that I lost my grandmother Mani joone. This was the first
time I experienced the death of someone close to me as an adult.
As her youngest granddaughter I had vivid memories of playing
in Mani joone's garden in Tehran in springtime and in the winter snow, the cherry blossoms that adorned the entrance to her
house, those carefree days when she taught us to leave an empty
bowl out in the cold to catch fresh falling snow and then drip
cherry juice on top for our very own homemade snow cones!

I saw my grandmother for the last time in the intensive care
unit at Virginia's Inova Fairfax Hospital in July 2005. Bless her
soul, at the age of ninety-two, she had just undergone heart surgery. I spent the night in her room checking her heart monitor
and blood pressure every hour even though there were plenty of
people more qualified already keeping an eye on her. She asked

for some juice. With a straw, I gave her a cup of cranberry juice and ice.

Mani joone asked me, "How is Saied doing?" I told her that he was working and thriving and that I was so proud of him for the great character and judgment he shows even as a young adult. She asked about Samira, and I said she is feisty and fearless and that I was organizing a surprise sixteenth birthday party for her at the beach near our house. "And Aman?" I told her he continues to say things beyond his nine years of age. He recently said he wanted to marry one of his younger cousins when he got older. Someone pointed out that you can't marry a cousin to which he responded, "My dad married my mom and they were second cousins." "And Amir?" I said Amir is my nature boy, who loves swimming and has a precious, beautiful, and selfless soul.

She dozed off. I kissed her hand and touched her angelic face. She opened her eyes and said, "Iran, your father called this morning from Kuwait and I said to him, 'Nader, I bid you farewell.'" She closed her eyes and went back to sleep.

I found myself once again considering the span of her life. Mani joone, the granddaughter of the personal treasurer of the Qajar Shah, daughter of Davar, wife of the deputy minister of finance, my grandmother. I felt I was in the presence of death but the heart monitor was beating strong and steady and so I kept on writing and kept on remembering that before me was the physical manifestation of my past. Now that I knew so much about her, I could live her legacy.

I had come to a favorable time in my life. I had looked inward. I was in touch with my soul, with that which measures time, with that which creates music and rhythm in one's life. I was full of ideas. I had moved into a new world, a world where the "self" gives birth to its "self." I was deep in the root bed where things grow and where lay my identity as a creative child of God. I was a soul in touch with its spirit, whole, unified, one. Through my life experiences I had touched the paradoxes of unity and chaos, of death and also of life. It was an organic growth for me because it related to my ancestors' experiences as well.

Today, I am fulfilled with the unconditional love for my children. As a daughter, I have come to learn to love and respect my father and Shahla. To this day, my mother and I are extremely close. She has constantly been at my side and my main support throughout my life. I asked my mother what she thought of my life journey, and she said, "I remember from the time you were very young, you had a self-consciousness about yourself. You had deep feelings, but were afraid to show them. However, from the time you began your career in broadcast journalism, you have amazed those who listen to your creations. The sounds of your radio stories move in waves."[1]

It reminded me of something that Rumi once said:

Do you not see how the spring breeze becomes visible in the trees and grasses, the rose-beds and sweet herbs? Through the medium of these you gaze upon the beauty of spring. But when you look upon the spring breeze itself, you see nothing of these things . . . those waves are subtle and do not come into sight, only through some medium are they revealed out of their subtlety. Likewise in the human being these qualities are hidden, and only become manifest through an inward or outward medium. . . . The wave is a commotion visible from within you,

Producing a story on Iraqi Americans and the FBI for NPR in Manassas, Virginia, March 2003. (Photograph by Jacki Lyden)

without an external medium. But so long as the sea is still, you see nothing. Your body is on the shore of the sea and your soul is of the sea.[2]

My name is Iran but being Iranian is not all of me. I am American, but being American is not all of me. I am a mother and a journalist, but these do not exhaust me. Finding the courage to tell my story, I have overcome my fear and replaced it with love.

Author's Note, April 17, 2006

A s I prepared to dive into the immense, uncharted sea of my life, I felt like an outsider, a stranger to my inner world. The desire was there but I was terrified and impatient with myself. Was I determined to embark? Should I write about the vice and villains or the virtues of living this blessed life? And then along came my mother, Mary Laleh Bakhtiar. Ever the Sufi, she helped me journey back in time to bring insight into this Iran.

As our family historian and archivist, my mother had sorted through thousands of family letters, photos, journals, notes, and newspaper clippings that had helped her when she researched and wrote two books about her parents, *Helen of Tus: Her Odyssey from Idaho to Iran* and *Abol Ghassem of Tus: The Epic Journey of Abol Ghassem Bakhtiar, M.D.*

What good fortune, then, when in the process of writing this book, my mother shared these treasured documents that reflected on the dichotomy of free will versus destiny in their lives. I began then to distill the past and present, in order to open the secret of my own life.

Like nomads on a journey of self-discovery, we went from letter to letter and story to story hoping to answer this unsolved mystery as old as time itself. Whether it was my Eastern grandfather's Sufi cloak, which he had inherited from his father, or my Western grandmother's American flag, which she had inherited from her father, I found my answer in the splendor of the quest.

· notes ·

CHAPTER 1: From America to Iran, 1946–66

1. Recollections of my father, Nader Ardalan, 2005.

2. Bakhtiar, meaning, "friend of good fortune." The Bakhtiari are a tribal group, many of whom live in southwest Iran, migrating twice a year between Solomon's Mosque in the province of Khuzistan and Chahar Mahal near Isfahan. There are two main branches of this tribe, the Haft Lang and the Chahar Lang. They speak Luri and claim to be descendants of Shah Fereydoun of the *Shahnameh*. Well-known among them in the West have been Soraya, the second wife of Mohammad Reza Shah, and Shapour Bakhtiar, the last prime minister of Iran before the 1979 revolution.

3. First International Conference of Architects, Isfahan, 1970.

4. It is said that the original inhabitants of Solomon's Mosque named their city Masjid-i Sulayman after the Achaemenid ruins they found there. The Achaemenids ruled Iran from c. 550–330 BC. They wrote in cuneiform script, followed the religion of Zoroaster, and were known as great builders. Cyrus the Great built a palace in Pasargadae, while other Shahs built palaces at Susa and the famous Persepolis Palace compound with great audience halls that the Shah approached through double flights of stairs. The sense of space and scale are distinctive to the Achaemenid period. Khuzistan is believed to be the most ancient of Iranian provinces. It had been called Elam and birthplace of the nation. It was here that Aryan tribes migrated after first having established the Median City of Ecbatana, present-day Hamadan, and ultimately settled and mixed with the Elamite population.

5. The Anglo-Persian Oil Company was founded in 1909 after oil was discovered in Solomon's Mosque. In 1935, once Reza Shah proclaimed Persia to be called Iran, the company changed its name to the Anglo-Iranian Oil Company. This was the name of the company when my grandfather was the chief surgeon for the company. During the early 1950s, when Iran nationalized the oil industry, the Anglo-Iranian Oil Company became the National Iranian Oil Company, which my father worked for; the former Anglo part, originally a partner in the oil discovered in Solomon's Mosque, became British Petroleum (BP).

6. My aunt Parveen McNair's article "I Can't Keep It a Secret Anymore," *Family Times*, December 21, 1990, p. 14.

7. Solomon of the Old Testament became a source of legend in Islamic culture, and it is said that he was the model for Shah Jamshid in the *Shahnameh*. Solomon is declared the successor of David in the Koran. Solomon was given a ring that had magical qualities in the Traditions. See Jay R. Crook, *The Bible: An Islamic Perspective: David and Solomon.*

8. Cyrus the Great, mentioned in the Bible as Koresh (Ezra 1:1–8), the founder of the Achaemenid Dynasty in Iran, united the two Iranian tribes of the Medes and the Persians. A great military leader, his empire at one time stretched from Asia Minor to the Indus valley. When he conquered Babylon, he had what came to be known as "the first charter of human rights" carved on a clay cylinder discovered in Babylon in 1879. He issued an edict allowing the Jewish people to return to the Promised Land.

9. Recollections of Nader Ardalan, 2005.

10. Collection of writings of my mother, Laleh Bakhtiar, January 10, 1966, to her mother, Helen.

11. Composed in the late tenth and early eleventh centuries AD, the *Shahnameh* re-creates the mythical and historical eras of Iran up until the seventh century AD. An epic poem seven times longer than the *Iliad* of Homer, it is an original national epic based on experiences of past generations of the Iranian people. In chronicling the Mythical Age, Heroic Age, and Historical Age, the poet uses pure Persian, and in doing so preserved the Persian language. The message of Ferdowsi, whose name means "Paradisiacal," is to strive for justice and truth and avoid cruelty and other vices.

12. Abol Ghassem Ferdowsi, *Shahnameh: Epic of Kings,* Reuben Levy, translator, p. 206. Gordafarid was the lioness who in battle disguised herself as a man to achieve victory over her enemy. Pourandokht is the woman who ruled as king in AD 629–631. See Dick Davis, "Women in the *Shahnameh:* Exotics and Natives, Rebellious Legends and Dutiful Histories."

13. Reuben Levy, translator, Abol Ghassem Ferdowsi, *Shahnameh: Epic of Kings,* "Poet's Introduction," p. 2.

14. Ibid.

15. Saadi, the thirteenth-century Sufi and writer from Shiraz, traveled extensively for perhaps thirty years during his lifetime, visiting Arabia, Egypt, Morocco, Ethiopia, Central Asia, and India. His two most famous works are the *Bostan,* in which he teaches moral virtues through poetic verse, exhibiting great wisdom, and the *Golestan,* mainly in prose, containing anecdotes and stories that became proverbial throughout Iran. The *Golestan* compares the destiny of those who depend on the mood of Shahs to the Sufi freedom from rulers. Saadi is known also as a poet of lyric verse; Iranians recognize him as the first Persian poet who illustrated the principles of love in lyric form. One of his most famous poems is carved on a column at the United Nations, a poem my grandmother Helen would quote in her 1958 radio interview in Charlottesville, Virginia: Human beings are all members of one body. / They are created from the same essence. / When one member is in pain, / The others cannot rest. / If you do not care about the pain of others, / You do not deserve to be called a human being. See A. J. Arberry, *Classical Persian Literature.*

The fourteenth-century Hafez—a favorite of my grandfather Abol Ghassem—was yet another famous Iranian master of mystical lyric poems, also from Shiraz in the southwest of Iran. Hafez's poetry, often sung by Iranian singers, has many levels and few can claim to understand them all. Arberry had this to say: "The magic of Hafez's poetry will continue to cast its spell, and men will still wonder at the inner meaning of his wonderfully melodious and simple but baffling words." A. J. Arberry, *Classical Persian Literature,* p. 361.

16. From the article "Social engineering and the contradictions of modernization in Khuzistan's oil company towns, Abadan and Masjed-i Soleyman," posted on Iranian.com on February 15, 2005, by Kaveh Ehsani, a member of the editorial board of *Goft-o-Gu* magazine.

17. Collection of the letters of my uncle Cyrus Bakhtiar, August 3, 1954. He was eighteen years old when he wrote this letter.

18. Built on four mounds, Shush (Susa), 125 miles north of Abadan, is one of the world's oldest cities and capital of Elam during the Elamite period around 3000 BC. It became a Greek city-state colony after the conquest of Alexander the Great. It was at Shush that French archaeologists in the nineteenth century discovered the Code of Hammurabi, dating from 1800 BC. A long document of over three hundred paragraphs, it contains sections on moral, religious, social, commercial, and civil law. Choga Zanbil was the religious center of Shush. Shush was abandoned around the thirteenth century CE. See Roman Ghirshman, *Persian Art: 249 B.C.–A.D. 651: The Parthian and Sassanian Dynasties.* Shushtar, historically, had been the capital of the province of Khuzistan. It had flourished in the Elamite period. It lies on the only navigable river in Iran, the Karun, which is well known for its dams and systems of irrigation; one dam is 550 meters long, built during the Sassanian times of the third to seventh centuries CE. See Roman Ghirshman, *Persian Art.*

19. For the similarities between Shah Jamshid and Solomon, see John Renard, *Islam and the Heroic Image,* p. 103. For Shah Jamshid proclaiming Noruz, see Ferdowsi, *Shahnameh: Epic of Kings,* translated by Ruben Levy, p. 6.

20. Spring cleaning, or *khaneh takani,* is a ritual that precedes Noruz. People try to clean every room in their house, wash the rugs and curtains, and polish the silverware. Everyone also buys new clothes to wear on that day. Houses are filled with sweet-smelling flowers like narcissus and hyacinth, and wild rue is burned to ward off the evil eye.

21. Each family follows their own religious tradition by placing their Holy Book on the table they sit around to celebrate Noruz. Some even place a book of Hafez's poetry there.

22. Collection of writings of my mother, Laleh Bakhtiar, January 7, 1968, to her sister Shireen.

23. Seyyed Hossein Nasr is a professor at George Washington University in Washington, D.C. He has been my mother's mentor most of her adult life, and I grew up with his children in Iran.

24. Collection of letters of Helen Jeffreys Bakhtiar, November 11, 1967, to her son Cyrus. Empress Farah was Mohammad Reza Shah's third wife, who bore him four children, two boys and two girls.

CHAPTER 2: West Meets East, 1927

1. Collection of letters of Helen Jeffreys Bakhtiar, no date, not clear to whom she was writing. She said that as her father would not let her travel alone across the country, he and her brother James accompanied her on the train from Los Angeles to Washington, D.C. Her father and brother were going to Paris to participate in the national meeting of the American Legion, the only time the meeting was held outside the United States.

2. My grandmother Helen recounted this story to my mother.

3. See Reuben Levy, *Shahnameh: Epic of Kings,* pp. 23–25.

4. Collection of letters of my grandfather Abol Ghassem Bakhtiar, summer 1951, dictated to his son and my uncle Cyrus Bakhtiar; Collection of letters of my grandfather Abol Ghassem Bakhtiar, November 20, 1956, to his son and my uncle Jamshid Bakhtiar.

5. Imam Hossein was the second son of Fatima, the daughter of Prophet Muhammad, and her husband, Ali, the first cousin of the Prophet. The Prophet had grown up under the care of Ali's father and then Ali grew up in the home of the Prophet and his wife, Khadijah.

After the death of the Prophet, the Muslim community was divided as to who should succeed the Prophet. One group said that the community should select a committee to elect the successor and another group said that the Prophet had chosen Ali to be his successor. Those who desired an election were in the majority and came to be known as the Sunnis. The Shias were in the minority. Abu Bakr, a close friend and father-in-law of the Prophet, was chosen the first successor. Umar was elected the second, and the third was Uthman. Ali was elected to be the fourth caliph. The first four caliphs are called "the rightly guided" caliphs.

According to Shia tradition, Imam Ali was killed during his caliphate and his oldest son, Imam Hasan, was chosen to succeed him as caliph. However, the governor of Damascus protested this election and Imam Hasan withdrew. Soon after that Imam Hasan was poisoned and died. The governor of Damascus also died and was replaced by his son, who then demanded allegiance from Imam Hasan's younger brother, Imam Hossein.

Imam Hossein, standing up for what was right and preventing what was wrong, refused to give his allegiance to a man who was not following the principles laid down by the Prophet. The people of Kufa, Iraq, invited Imam Hossein to move to their city and be their leader. He left for Kufa with his family and a small group of followers. Once he reached Karbala on the way to Kufa, he received word that the people of Kufa had withdrawn their invitation and that the caliph was sending an army thirty thousand strong to force him to give his allegiance. Imam Hossein and his small band of followers stood their ground of moral resistance even when the armed forces that opposed him cut him and his group off from water in the scorching heat of Karbala. Imam Hossein and his followers were all killed; Imam Hossein was beheaded and his head taken to Damascus to present to the caliph. Imam Hossein's sister, Zaynab, had witnessed the massacre and spoke out against the caliph once they reached Damascus. She kept the message of the death of her brother and his family alive.

The story of the tragedy of Karbala is marked every year by Shias through great processions and passion plays, the passion plays being performed in the *takiya* like the one in the front of my grandfather's home. Shia passion plays are comparable to ancient Greek drama. Both Shia passion plays and ancient Greek theater grew out of their respective nations; both are attached to religion or myths; both developed through religious rites and deal with religious subjects and religious legends; both use soloists and choirs, and the audiences sit around the stage. The medium in both cases is poetry and the audience is familiar with the plot so any emotional response depends on the actors. See Edmund K. Chambers, *The Medieval Stage*, pp. 64 *ff.*, in Mehdi Forough, *A Comparative Study of Abraham's Sacrifice in Persian Passion Plays and Western Mystery Plays.*

6. Letter from Sally Harris, Leland Rex Robinson's daughter, to Aunt Lailee.

7. James Mackey was not my grandmother's direct ancestor. Otherwise, she, my mother, and I would have been eligible to join the Daughters of the American Revolution!

8. "Ancestors of Davar Ardalan," researched by James Ransopher, sent December 15, 2004, p. 6. Helen's maternal aunt was Florence McRoberts, who married Christopher Ransopher. James is their son. Research on the Jeffreys family also provided by my cousin Janice von Schummer. Janice introduced me to James

Ransopher. Both Janice and James have spent many years on our family's genealogy and were kind enough to send me the information.

9. Letters of James Woodson Jeffreys, May 23, 1942, to Mrs. William Rummler.

10. Collection of letters of my grandmother Helen Jeffreys Bakhtiar, no date.

11. Collection of letters of my grandmother Helen Jeffreys Bakhtiar, no date, to her daughter Lailee.

CHAPTER 3: The Bakhtiars and the Ardalans

1. Collection of letters of Helen Jeffreys Bakhtiar, no date, to her daughter Lailee.

2. Reza Shah had been a member of the Cossacks before his rise to the throne. See Sandra Mackey, *The Iranians*, pp. 152–56.

3. My grandmother Helen related this to my mother.

4. Collection of the letters of my grandmother Helen Jeffreys Bakhtiar, February 1, 1942, to my grandfather Abol Ghassem.

5. Related by Lailee Bakhtiar and Jamshid Bakhtiar to their siblings.

6. See Sandra Mackey, *The Iranians*, pp. 180–82.

7. Related by Lailee and Shireen Bakhtiar, who remember their aunt Mary's visit to Tehran.

8. Shireen Bakhtiar, "My Time with Papa," *Family Times*, September 21, 1990, p. 6.

9. Collection of the letters of Helen Jeffreys Bakhtiar, February 1, 1942, to Abol Ghassem.

10. Collection of letters of Helen Jeffreys Bakhtiar, November 11, 1963, documenting my mother Mary Nell's U.S. citizenship.

11. Collection of the letters of Helen Jeffreys Bakhtiar, January 23, 1946–January 9, 1950.

12. Collection of the letters of Helen Jeffreys Bakhtiar, March 16, 1948, to Abol Ghassem.

13. My grandfather named each of his ten children with his Persian wife, Bibi Turan, names that were similar to those of his first seven children with Helen: Lili, Shirley, Parvaneh, Jomi, Pirooz, Gohar, Noruz, Sharbanoo, Afsaneh, and Abol Ghassem. Once my family had moved to Tehran, Bibi Turan's children would often visit our home, and Sharbanoo took care of my siblings and me when we were children.

14. Memories of my mother.

15. As one of the first generations of Iranian-Americans who lived at a time when letter writing was the best means of communication, we have a collection of thousands of family letters. My grandfather saved all the letters written to him in a famous file cabinet. Whenever one of his children from America would visit him for the summer, they would organize the file of letters. It contained not just letters that *he* had received; Helen would forward any letters she received for him to file as

well. In 1962 when my grandfather, then ninety years old, fell down in the shower, my aunt Lailee and uncle Jamshid rushed from America to Abadan and insisted he retire in Tehran. While they were moving him, the file cabinet of letters went to my aunt Shireen, who was living in Abadan at that time. She and her husband, Manoucher Javid, both worked for the oil company. They kept the letters until 1980 when Manoucher had died and she had remarried and was moving back to America. She gave the letters to my mother. When my uncle Jamshid left Iran, he also gave all the letters he had saved to my mother. My mother had not thought much about the letters until 1999 when she and my aunt Shireen (Rose) decided to write a book about Helen's life. My mother returned to Iran after an eleven-year absence and found the letters. She returned to Chicago with seven suitcases full of the letters and photos. She and my aunt Shireen (Rose) then wrote *Helen of Tus: Her Odyssey from Idaho to Iran.* Two years later my mother and my aunt Lailee wrote the story of my grandfather's life in *Abol Ghassem of Tus: The Epic Journey of Abol Ghassem Bakhtiar, M.D.* The books they wrote were based on the collection of letters.

16. In President Truman's January 20, 1949, Inaugural Address, in the fourth point, he said, "We must embark on a bold, new program for making the benefits of our scientific advancements and industrial progress available for improvement and growth to underdeveloped areas. . . . I believe that we should make available to peace-loving peoples the benefits of our store of technical knowledge in order to help them realize their aspirations for a better life." From William E. Warne, *Mission for Peace,* p. 16.

17. William E. Warne, *Mission for Peace,* p. 307. Also note that in this same book, Warne writes that the regional headquarters for the Point Four mission in Tehran was located next door to Dr. Mossadegh's residence. On one occasion, in February 1953, when a mob formed in front of Mossadegh's house, while still wearing his famous striped pajamas, he climbed a ladder with the help of one of his sons and sought refuge in the grounds of Point Four, pp. 124, 125.

18. Source: *Health Abroad: A Challenge to Americans. Iran: One of Many.* U.S. Department of Health, Education, and Welfare. Public Health Service Publication No. 349, 1954, came to me by way of Kristen Palmquist, daughter of Emil Palmquist.

19. William E. Warne, *Misson for Peace,* p. 143.

20. See Sandra Mackey, *The Iranians,* pp. 193–209.

21. Collection of the letters of Helen Jeffreys Bakhtiar, July 30, 1954, to Abol Ghassem.

22. Collection of writings of my mother, Laleh Bakhtiar, July 16, 1957, to her mother Helen.

23. Her pen name was Mah Sharaf Khanoom. Two of her best-known writings include a book of poetry called *Divan-i Mah Sharaf Khanum Kurdistani* and a history of the Ardalan family called *Tarikh-i-Ardalan.* According to Wikipedia, her

son, Reza Gholi Khan, was imprisoned by the Qajar king and according to Ardalan family oral history, was later poisoned in prison. After his capture, Mastoureh Ardalan fled Sannandaj for Suleimaniyeh, Iraq, where she is buried. In December 2005, a festival in Irbil honored her two hundredth birthday, and a statue of her was also unveiled. Source: *Hewler Globe,* English newspaper in Irbil, Iraqi Kurdistan, Tuesday, December 13, 2005, No. 36.

24. Source: family history from cousin Nayer Mostofi Glenn, prepared in March 2004, Houston, Texas. Nayer, an educator and linguist herself, is the granddaughter of Abol Hassan Ardalan. Nayer has written down all the Ardalan family stories from her youth. The tragic story of Reza Gholi Khan came to Nayer through her mother, Maryam Ardalan (1892–1963). Specifically, it was Maryam's nursemaid, Ahoo jan, who recounted the story of the poisoning. Ahoo jan was a trusted family aide who was later promoted to chief nurse. She had once traveled with my great-grandfather Abol Hassan Ardalan on a trip to Baghdad to visit the Shrine of Karbala.

25. Collection of writings of Laleh Bakhtiar, February 28, 1958, to Helen.

26. Collection of writings of Laleh Bakhtiar, March 19, 1958.

27. Collection of letters of Nader Ardalan to Laleh Bakhtiar, June 30, 1959.

28. Collection of letters of Nader Ardalan to Laleh Bakhtiar, August 8, 1959.

29. Ibid.

30. Ibid.

31. Collection of letters of Nader Ardalan to Abol Ghassem, July 1959.

32. Collection of letters of Nader Ardalan to Helen Bakhtiar, November 30, 1959.

33. Source: William O. Douglas, *Strange Lands and Friendly People,* p. 117.

34. Source: Ibid., p. 118. Justice Douglas knew a great deal about Helen's family. She would later recall their long conversations. There in Dastana, Justice Douglas extended an invitation for Helen and her family to visit him in Washington, D.C. Mrs. Douglas remembered meeting my twin aunts, Paree and Parveen, at the home of Mohammad Nemazee on the occasion of Noruz. Collection of letters of Helen Jeffreys Bakhtiar, August 13, 1957, to Abol Ghassem.

CHAPTER 4: My Childhood

1. Collection of letters of Nader Ardalan to Laleh Bakhtiar, July 1958.

2. Louis I. Kahn said in an undated letter about *The Sense of Unity,* "What they (Ardalan and Bakhtiar) are bringing to us is the recalling of the original inspiration which motivated building. What we admire and stand in wonder over in the works of old is the marvel of their beginnings when the desire to express sought the means. The human who primarily lives to express conjured up the record within him of how he was made which he found to be the non-conscious means of nature's growth structure forms-geometric; which, when discovered, had to be

honored as metaphysical. Another way of expressing this is the traditional man builds his expressions satisfying the unmeasurable spirit devoid of means, calling upon non-conscious nature which is the source of all means. This is so important now when the means sought to express directions to our human environment-building is in great part professionally based on statistics, surveys and technology. Times long ago had only meager means to go on. They were highly motivated by wonder which brought about the desire to learn, the profundity of which lay at the threshold of where the unmeasurable and the measurable met. This meeting was the moment of inspiration when the desire to express met the possible. Today as yesterday such moments are essential to man. This is the crux of their inspired and most worthy work."

3. See Nader Ardalan and Laleh Bakhtiar, *The Sense of Unity*, p. 68.

4. Ibid.

5. Mashhad, meaning "place of martyrdom," the second largest city in Iran, is the capital of Khorasan Province and has been the largest site of Shia pilgrimage in Iran since its founding in 823 CE. Today twenty million pilgrims visit annually. Mashhad is the burial place of Imam Reza. He was born in Medina, Arabia, during the caliphate of Harun al-Rashid of *A Thousand and One Nights* fame. Upon the death of Harun al-Rashid, his two sons divided up the empire. Caliph Mamun was given control of Iran and he succeeded in defeating his brother, insisting then that Imam Reza become his successor. It never came to pass because Imam Reza was poisoned and died in Tus before Mamun died. See Moojan Momen, *An Introduction to Shi'i Islam: The History and Doctrines of Twelver Shi'ism.*

CHAPTER 5: Mysteries of Life Unfold

1. Collection of letters of Nader Ardalan to Laleh Bakhtiar, February 20, 1973.

2. As told to my mother by Sulayman Nyang, professor of African studies at Howard University, Washington, D.C.

3. Jalal al-Din Rumi was born in Balkh, which is in present-day Afghanistan but at that time was part of the Persian Empire. His family migrated to Konya, in present-day Turkey, which was also part of the Persian Empire at that time. In addition, he wrote all of his poetry in Persian. That is why all three countries—Afghanistan, Turkey, and Iran—claim him as their own. Introduced to Sufism at an early age, he was thirty-eight years old when he met Shams, the man who changed his life. They were together for a few years and then Shams disappeared. It was after that that Rumi began to recite his Persian poetry as he whirled. Two important poetic works resulted, the *Mathnawi*, twenty-five thousand rhymed couplets, composed spontaneously, of which he never changed a single line, and the *Divan i-Shams*, forty thousand rhymed couplets. He was said to be "the greatest mystical poet of any age," by his translator, R. A. Nicholson, who found "a wealth of satire, humor and pathos" in the poetry. From A. J. Arberry, *Classical Persian Literature*, p. 241.

4. Jalal al-Din Rumi, *Mathnawi*, in *Rumi: Poet and Mystic*, translated by R. A. Nicholson, p. 47.

5. Abu Hamid Muhammad al-Ghazzali, *Revival of the Religious Sciences* (eleventh century) in Margaret Smith, *Al-Ghazzali, the Mystic*, p. 111.

6. Collection of writings of Laleh Bakhtiar, n.d.

7. This book is part of a series of books published by Thames and Hudson on art and the imagination. It describes the mystic journey through illustrations of art forms.

8. Collection of letters of Nader Ardalan to Laleh Bakhtiar, October 7, 1975.

9. This is a three-volume work titled *Al-Masjid al-Haram* commissioned by the Associated Consulting Engineers, Ltd., who were undertaking the extension to the mosque in Mecca that surrounds the Kabah, to be presented to King Abdul Aziz upon completion. This was the first significant addition to the mosque in over four hundred years. My parents wrote volume one on the history of the Kabah. Volume two contains the technical information for the building project, and volume three, the plans, detailed architectural designs, and as-built drawings.

10. Collection of letters of Nader Ardalan to Laleh Bakhtiar, May 29, 1976.

11. Collection of letters of Abol Ghassem Bakhtiar, February 4, 1954, to his son Jamshid Bakhtiar.

12. Helen was interviewed twice by Mrs. Brown at a Charlottesville radio station in 1958, and she described her love of Iran and work with Point Four.

13. Taped interview with my aunt Dr. Lailee Bakhtiar in 2005.

14. See Laleh Bakhtiar and Lailee Bakhtiar, *Abol Ghassem of Tus*.

15. Ibid.

16. Collection of writings of Laleh Bakhtiar, January 28, 1971, to her brother Jamshid.

17. Ibid.

18. Hafez, *Diwan i-Hafez*, pp. 347–48.

19. Translation paraphrased by Laleh Bakhtiar.

20. Collection of letters of Helen Jeffreys Bakhtiar, January 17, 1971, to her son Cyrus Bakhtiar.

21. Collection of letters of Helen Jeffreys Bakhtiar, May 27, 1968, to her daughter Shireen.

22. Collection of writings of Laleh Bakhtiar, July 9, 1973, to her brother Cyrus.

23. Collection of writings of Laleh Bakhtiar, July 9, 1973, in her diary.

24. Ibid.

25. Collection of writings of Laleh Bakhtiar, December 5, 1973, in her diary. *Irfan*, or gnosis—mysticism, experiential knowledge that aims at a direct experience between a person and God—is a word often used interchangeably with *tasawwuf* (Sufism) in English. In the Islamic world, clerics study *irfan* but never *tasawwuf*, because clerics categorize the followers of the latter as people whose following of the Divine Law is questionable. See Seyyed Hossein Nasr, *Sufi Essays*.

26. Collection of writings of Laleh Bakhtiar, in her diary.

27. There are some forty traditional Sufi orders in the Islamic world where a seeker on the way to experience God would find other disciples and a guide to the way. See J. Spencer Trimingham, *The Sufi Orders in Islam.*

28. Collection of writings of Laleh Bakhtiar, December 4, 1974, in her diary.

29. Collection of writings of Laleh Bakhtiar, December 27, 1974, in her diary.

30. Collection of writings of Laleh Bakhtiar, December 29, 1974, in her diary.

31. Collection of letters of Nader Ardalan to Laleh Bakhtiar, January 3, 1975.

32. Ibid.

CHAPTER 6: Struggling with Reality, 1976–79

1. Recollections of my sister, Mani Helene Ardalan Farhadi.

2. He had also been appointed to the founding steering committee of the prestigious Aga Khan Award for Architecture, which has become the equivalent of a Nobel Prize but in Architecture.

3. Collection of letters of Nader Ardalan to Laleh Bakhtiar, June 24, 1976.

4. Collection of writings of Laleh Bakhtiar, September 23, 1976, in her diary.

5. Ibid.

6. Collection of writings of Laleh Bakhtiar, September 11, 1975, in her diary.

CHAPTER 7: The Islamic Revolution

1. In addition to writing *Fatima Is Fatima,* Ali Shariati gave three important lectures oriented toward women: "Women in the Heart of Muhammad," "The Islamic Modest Dress," and "Expectations from the Muslim Women." In "The Islamic Modest Dress," a lecture given in 1976, three years before the Islamic revolution and a year before he died under mysterious circumstances in London, he proposes that Muslims follow the method of the Prophet Muhammad. The Prophet did not present all of Islamic practice in the first year, but rather over a period of twenty-three years. His method was to gradually present Islamic practices. "He first presented an intellectual worldview. When that thought grew and spread and took root in the minds of the people, a group became prepared. What for? For another type of practice. They were prepared to listen to something new" (Ali Shariati, "The Islamic Modest Dress," translated by Laleh Bakhtiar in *Shariati on Shariati and the Muslim Woman,* p. 40). In the opinion of Shariati, the concept of the modest dress must first be explained and its meaning analyzed for people "and then, without even telling them what they should do or not do, they'd know what they should do. The question of choice is important to them. Imposing or dictating what people should do causes them to offer resistance" (p. 42). He gives the example of Inidra Gandhi who did not feel humiliated or inferior by wearing the Indian sari. "By wearing the sari and traveling all over the world, she said: 'The West has been trying for four hundred years to make us similar to themselves, to assimilate us into Western culture, to alienate us, but by wearing the sari, I prove to

you all that their efforts and struggles have been in vain. I still maintain my own identity and being in both my outer as well as inner self'" (p. 48). Ali Shariati's view of how to present the modest dress was certainly not one accepted by the Islamic revolution when the modest dress was made obligatory.

2. Collection of writings of Laleh Bakhtiar, October 20, 1972, in her diary.

3. SAVAK was the Iranian security forces under the Shah formed to protect the Shah. With the help of the CIA in 1953, the Shah was returned to Iran following the nationalization of oil by Mohammad Mossadegh. See "SAVAK in Iran—A Country Study," Library of Congress, Federal Research Division.

4. Collection of writings of Laleh Bakhtiar, October 20, 1972, in her diary.

5. Recollections of Richard Irvine, posted on June 7, 2006 on a blog entry at The Atlantic Online. Entry: Our Experience in Iran, http://iran. theatlantic.com/blog/index.php?/archives/2006/06/07.html.

CHAPTER 8: America and Back to Iran, 1980–83

1. Collection of letters of Iran Davar Ardalan, August 1980, to her mother, Laleh Bakhtiar.

2. To consult the *Diwan-i Hafez* is a common practice among Iranians for any significant decision one has to make. Many just consult the *ghazal* poetry for spiritual guidance. Women in Iran are often named after flowers, names found in Hafez's poetry. Some men consult Hafez before they ask for a woman's hand in marriage and if her name appears in the poetry, it confirms their decision and they then feel that the marriage was meant to be.

3. R. A. Nicholson, *Selected Poems from the Divani Shamsi Tabriz*, p. 125.

CHAPTER 9: Tehran, 1983–87

1. A description of Hagar and the role she played in the Islamic culture of Iran can be found in Ali Shariati's *Hajj: Reflections on Its Rituals*, in which he describes the Kabah, the cubelike structure in the courtyard of the mosque in Mecca. Hagar was an Ethiopian bondswoman, the second wife of the patriarch Abraham, and mother of Ishmael, the half-brother of Isaac, the son of Sarah.

Sarah was unable to conceive, so she suggested to her husband, Abraham, that he wed her slave woman, who had been given to her by the pharaoh of Egypt, who would then bear his child. Abraham did so and Hagar became pregnant. At that point, Sarah grew jealous and asked Abraham to take Hagar away.

He did so, taking her to Mecca, where he left her and her baby, Ishmael. Mother and child became thirsty so Hagar ran seven times between two mounds, known as Safa and Marwa, looking from their heights for any sign of water. She found none but when she returned to her baby son, he, in his thirst, had kicked the earth and the water of Zamzam appeared, a spring that still provides water to the pilgrims and people of Mecca. Hagar then began to give water to passing caravans in exchange for food. This was the origin of the city of Mecca, founded by a woman.

According to tradition, Hagar is said to be buried near the third pillar of the Kabah. Only this woman, a female slave, is buried there, and millions of pilgrims each year on the annual pilgrimage (*hajj*) circumambulate the Kabah and her place of burial. According to the earliest biographer of Prophet Muhammad, Hagar "is the mother of the Arabs." Ishmael is thereby considered to be the father of the Arab tribes. Once Abraham returned to Sarah, Sarah became pregnant and gave birth to Isaac, the father of the Jewish tribes.

2. Khadija, a wealthy businesswoman in Mecca at the end of the sixth century CE, had twice become a widow and was older than Prophet Muhammad. She heard of him and asked him to lead her caravans to Syria and upon his return was so impressed by his honesty and trustworthiness that she asked him to marry her. He was twenty-five and she was forty. They were married for twenty-five years during which time he took no other wife. She was the first person to accept his message when revelations of the Koran began for him when he was forty, and from that time forward she spent all of her wealth to help propagate his message.

3. War was imposed upon Iran in September 1980 by the order of Saddam Hussein. The war lasted eight years and caused over a million casualties, many of the Iranian forces suffering from Saddam Hussein's use of chemical weapons.

CHAPTER 10: Married Life in Revolutionary Iran

1. The Beloved for Sufis and Sufi poets is God, but the image of the Beloved is female, because, for the Sufi, women show the Divine Qualities of beauty, compassion, and gentleness. As one Sufi points out, "In Rumi's view, their derivative beauty is the closest thing to True Beauty in the material world." William Chittick, *The Sufi Path of Love*, p. 286. Rumi also said, "The physical form is of great importance; nothing can be done without the consociation of the form and the essence. However often you may sow a seed, stripped of the pod, it will not grow. Sow it with the pod, it will become a great tree. From this point of view, the body is fundamental and necessary for the realization of the Divine intention." See Jalal al-Din Rumi, *The Mathnawi*, translated by R. A. Nicholson. Another Sufi, the founder of the school of *irfan*, or gnosis, Ibn Arabi, is quoted by Nicholson to have said, "Woman is the highest form of earthly beauty, but earthly beauty is nothing unless it is a manifestation and reflection of the Divine Qualities. Know that the Absolute cannot be contemplated independently of a concrete being, and it is more perfectly seen in a human form than in any other, and more perfectly in woman than in man." See Rumi, *The Mathnawi*, translated by R. A. Nicholson.

Sufis developed a technical language to express their love of the Beloved using aspects of women, such as, for example, her eyes and mouth. "Whereas the eye, the niche of light, is directed outwards, the mouth draws one inwards. One eats and speaks by invoking one of the Names of God. Through invocation, in a sense, one consumes the Divinity and, by doing so, is oneself consumed." Laleh Bakhtiar, *Sufi: Expressions of the Mystic Quest*, p. 68.

2. Whereas in the West, a woman would prepare her trousseau and place it in her cedar chest, in Iran the bride has to provide much more than that. She is responsible for providing all of the household items and, because of this, mothers of daughters start early buying items for her daughter's marriage. My in-laws had five daughters and each of them had an elaborate *jihaz* that they took with them when they were married including refrigerator, stove, washing machine, dryer, and living room, dining room, and bedroom furniture.

3. Iran's letter to family, June 1983.

4. Muslims slaughter their meat in a special way so that it becomes halal, which is similar to kosher meat of the Jewish people. In Iran, the animal is first given water and then the name of God is recited over the animal before it is slaughtered.

5. Memories of Judy Garland, now living in the United States.

6. Memories of Judy Garland.

CHAPTER 11: Becoming a Mother

1. The city of Qom is south of Tehran. A holy city for Shia Muslims, it is the burial place of Fatimah Masumah, the sister of the eighth Shia imam, Imam Reza. The city also houses the largest number of seminaries for the training of Shia clerics, only exceeded by Najaf, Iraq. My mother had gone to see Ayatollah Rosti.

2. The al-Hoda Bookshop on Charing Cross Road in London is an Islamic bookstore founded and funded by Iran although my mother was not aware of this when she started working there.

3. Lawyers' Committee for Human Rights, *The Justice System of the Islamic Republic of Iran*, pp. 18–19.

4. Dick Davis, "Women in the *Shahnameh:* Exotics and Natives, Rebellious Legends and Dutiful Histories." See Ferdowsi, *Shahnameh: Epic of Kings*, Reuben Levy, translator, for the story.

CHAPTER 12: Back to the West

1. We spent many memorable Noruz holidays in Abadan visiting Jahanshah, his mother, Aunt Shireen, father, Uncle Manoucher, and sisters, Soraya and Sue-san Ghahremani, and Iran Javid. They would often visit us once we moved to Tehran. My aunt's Bakhtiari hospitality always made us feel as if we were in our own home, and each day we would have different desserts that she had prepared.

2. *Hunters Heart* (audio cassette) by Larry Littlebird, December 1991.

3. My mother earned two master's degrees, one in philosophy with a concentration in religious studies and one in counseling psychology, before she completed her Ph.D. in educational psychology at the University of New Mexico in Albuquerque.

4. Some would call it my animus, not easy to find, for as Rumi had said: "Rare (*nader*) is it that a Rostam be born from Mary's womb." Jalal al-Din Rumi, *The*

Mathnawi, Book 6, line 1884. The verse seemed providential to me as my father's name is Nader, meaning "rare," and my mother often answers to her birth name Mary.

5. Typical examples of the animus, according to Emma Jung, are heroes of legend much like Rostam, "a man who accomplishes deeds in the sense that he directs his power toward something of great significance." Emma Jung, *Animus and Anima,* p. 3.

6. Mary is the only woman to be named in the Koran; there is also a chapter named Mary (Maryam) and she is mentioned more often in the Koran than in the New Testament (see Barbara Freyer Stowasser, *Women in the Quran, Traditions and Interpretation*). She plays a major role in Islamic culture as the Koran states that God has chosen Mary and purified her and preferred her above the women of all nations (the Koran 3:42) and she has special significance among Sufis as she symbolizes eternal wisdom or *sophia,* as the receptive form which gave birth to Jesus, the Word of God. In Arabic, a son is often known by the word *ibn,* son of—for instance, Abbas. In the case of Jesus, he is referred to as Isa ibn Maryam or Jesus the son of Mary.

7. The *Albuquerque Journal* and *Albuquerque Tribune,* August 1991 to June 1993.

8. My journalism professor was Miguel Gandert, born in Espanola, New Mexico. He is also a documentary photographer.

CHAPTER 13: Beginning a New Life

1. Revelation 21.5.

2. Collection of writings of Laleh Bakhtiar, diary, n.d.

3. Collection of letters of Helen Jeffreys Bakhtiar, June 16, 1949, to Abol Ghassem.

4. Collection of letters of Cyrus Jeffreys Bakhtiar, January 31, 1955, to his mother, Helen.

5. *Washington Post* article, December 27, 1974.

6. Collection of letters of Cyrus Jeffreys Bakhtiar, May 1954, to his mother, Helen.

7. In April 2000 I was asked to be keynote speaker in Santa Fe, New Mexico, at the fiftieth anniversary celebration for the New Mexico Press Women. Preparing for the speech, I interviewed Nina Totenberg. Susan Stamberg's quote is an excerpt from her book *Talk,* published in 1994.

8. Collection of letters of Helen Jeffreys Bakhtiar, December 27, 1949, to her husband, Abol Ghassem.

9. NPR, "Iran at the Crossroads." Alice Winkler conducted the interview.

10. BBC News, July 6, 2000.

11. Radio Free Europe, August 7, 2002.

CHAPTER 15: Discovering a Great-Grandfather

1. The listserv is Gulf2000, an online forum where specialists from across the world share insight and analysis on issues related to the Gulf region. The founder and executive director is Gary Sick, an expert on Iran and former member of the National Security Council.

2. Ironically, a similar law known as Consular Jurisdiction undermined the second Pahlavi monarch. When Mohammad Reza Shah granted diplomatic immunity to American servicemen in 1963, the Ayatollah Khomeini exploited it masterfully. A bloody revolt took place in Tehran in which scores of people were killed. This was the beginning of the "Rouhaniat," or clerical movement, that led to the downfall of the Shah in 1979. Notes/research of Rasool Nafisi.

3. Interview with Karim Lahiji, Oslo, Norway, December 9, 2003.

4. My father interviewed Davar's ninety-seven-year-old sister, Mehraghdas Maleki, on October 27, 2003, in Tehran. Mrs. Maleki said that her brother, Ali Akbar Davar, died on Dey 21, 1315 (January 11, 1937), but the biographers of Ali Akbar Davar and other scholars say that he died on February 10, 1937. Mrs. Maleki recalls the Shah angrily yelled at Davar, "Why have you put my reign in such danger? The British are offended by your decree to prevent them from the oil reserves!" Mrs. Maleki recalls that Davar had proposed a decree for the following day in the Majlis that would effectively nationalize Iranian oil. When the British heard of the decree, a message was sent to Reza Shah, "Either Davar or Monarchy." World War II was looming in Europe. Oil would be critical. The British were never going to agree to being thrown out of Iran. Mrs. Maleki said Reza Shah told my great-grandfather to "Go and die!" (*boro bimir*). Davar's biographers have said the Shah said, "Go get lost!" (*boro gomsho*).

CHAPTER 16: Sorrow and Triumph

1. My interview with Davar's daughter, Mani joone, July 2004.

CHAPTER 17: Finding Myself Through Love

1. See Dick Davis, "Women in the *Shahnameh:* Exotics and Natives, Rebellious Legends and Dutiful Histories."

2. E-mail from my father, Nader Ardalan, December 6, 2003. My father lived and worked in Kuwait from 1994 to 2006 designing waterfront developments, universities, shopping malls, luxury hotels, residential homes, banks, and company headquarters throughout the Persian Gulf.

3. Collection of writings of Cyrus Jeffreys Bakhtiar, "The Persian Carpet," a paper presented for one of his classes at Harvard University, 1954–58.

CHAPTER 18: My Name Is Iran

1. My mother is still an active writer as well as being president of the Institute of Traditional Psychology in Chicago where she offers computer-based training

programs on the Sufi Enneagram. She also is a resident scholar at Kazi Publications, founded in 1972, the oldest Muslim publisher in America. Along with the many translations she has done, she has also authored over twenty books on Sufism and Islam and is presently working on an English translation and concordance of the Koran.

2. Jalal al-Din Rumi, *Fihi ma Fihi* (meaning, *In It Is What Is In It*), translated by A. J. Arberry, in *Discourses of Rumi,* p. 74.

· bibliography ·

American RadioWorks. February 2004. "My Name Is Iran." Reporter/producer Davar Ardalan, coproducer Rasool Nafisi, editor Deborah George.

Ami Zaki, Muhammad. *History of Kurds and Kurdistan* (*Zebdeyeh Tarikeh Kurd va Kurdistan*). Translated by Yadollah Roshan Ardalan. Tehran: Toos Publishers, 2003 (1381). 2 volumes.

Aqli, Baghir. *Davar va adliyeh.* Tehran: Ilmi Publishers, 1991 (1369).

Aqli, Baghir. *Shahr hal rijal siyasi va nizami ma'asir-i iran.* Tehran: Maharat Printers, 2002 (1380).

Arberry, A. J. *Classical Persian Literature.* London: George Allen and Unwin, 1958.

Ardalan, Nader, and Laleh Bakhtiar. *The Sense of Unity: The Sufi Tradition in Persian Architecture.* Chicago, Ill.: University of Chicago Press, 1973.

Ardalan, Nader. "2004. Building in the Persian Gulf." http://archnet.org/library/documents/one-document.tcl?document_id=9391.

Ardalan, Nader. "On Mosque Architecture." http://archnet.org/library/documents/one-document.tcl?document_id=6138.

Associated Consulting Engineers, Ltd. *Al-Masjid al-Haram.* Mecca: King Abdul Aziz, 1975.

Avsati, Alireza. "Iran in the Last 3 Centuries." Tehran, 2003. Vol. 1. http://en.wikipedia.org/wiki/Ali_Akbar_Davar.

Bakhtiar, Laleh. *Shariati on Shariati and the Muslim Woman.* Chicago: ABC International Group, 1996.

———. *Sufi: Expressions of the Mystic Quest.* London: Thames and Hudson, 1976.

Bakhtiar, Laleh, trans. *Fatima Is Fatima.* Tehran: Ali Shariati Handami Publishers, 1980.

Bakhtiar, Laleh, and Rose Bakhtiari. *Helen of Tus: Her Odyssey from Idaho to Iran.* Chicago: Institute of Traditional Psychology, 2002.

Bakhtiar, Laleh, and Lailee Bakhtiar. *Abol Ghassem of Tus: The Epic Journey of Abol Ghassem Bakhtiar, M.D.* Chicago, Ill.: Institute of Traditional Psychology, 2003.

Bakhtiar, Laleh, editor. *Family Times.* Chicago: Kazi Publications, 1990.

Barks, Coleman, trans. *The Essential Rumi.* San Franciso: Harper Collins, 1996.

BBC News. "Drugs and Prostitution Soar in Iran." Thursday, July 6, 2000.

Bill, James A., and John Alden Williams. *Roman Catholics and Shi'i Muslims: Prayer, Passion and Politics.* Chapel Hill, N.C., and London: The University of North Carolina Press, 2002.

Carroll, Michael P. *The Penitent Brotherhood: Patriarchy and Hispano-Catholicism in New Mexico.* Baltimore, Md., and London: The Johns Hopkins University Press, 2002.

Chittick, William. *The Sufi Path of Love.* New York: SUNY Press, 1983.

Crook, Jay R. *The Bible: An Islamic Perspective: David and Solomon.* Chicago: ABC International Group, 2005.

Davis, Dick. *Fathers and Sons: Stories from the* Shahnameh *of Ferdowsi.* Vol. 2. Washington, D.C.: Mazda Publishers, 2000.

———. *Lion and the Throne: Stories from the* Shahnameh *of Ferdowsi.* Vol. 1. Washington, D.C.: Mazda Publishers, 1998.

———. *Sunset of Empires: Stories from the* Shahnameh *of Ferdowsi.* Vol. 3. Washington, D.C.: Mazda Publishers, 2003.

———. "Women in the *Shahnameh:* Exotics and Natives, Rebellious Legends and Dutiful Histories." In Sara S. Poor and Jana K. Schulman, eds., *Women and Medieval Epic,* forthcoming.

Davis, Dick, trans. *Shahnameh: The Persian Book of Kings,* by Abolqasem Ferdowsi. New York: Viking Press, 2006.

Douglas, William O. *Strange Lands and Friendly People.* New York: Harper and Brothers, 1951.

Ehsani, Kaveh, a member of the editorial board of *Goft-o-Gu* magazine. "Social engineering and the contradictions of modernization in Khuzestan's oil company towns, Abadan and Masjed-Soleyman," posted on Iranian.com on February 15, 2005.

Encyclopaedia Iranica. http://www.iranica.com/articles/v7/v7f2/v7f220. html. Entry: DAÚVAR, ¿ALÈ-AKBAR.

Fard, Camelia E. "She Found Prostitution among Iran's Holy Men. They Found a Way to Put Her in Jail." *The Village Voice,* March 28–April 3, 2001.

Farmer, Henry George. "Studies in Oriental Musical Instruments." In Pope, *A Survey of Persian Art.* Vol. 6. London, 1931.

Ferdowsi, Abol Ghassem. *Shahnameh.* Compiled by G. A. Atabaki. Tehran: Mahdiyeh Publishers, 2000 (1378).

———. *The Shahnameh: The Persian Book of Kings.* Translated by Dick Davis. New York: Penguin USA, 2006.

———. *Shahnameh: Epic of Kings.* Translated by Reuben Levy. Tehran: Yassavoli Publications, 2003.

Forough, Mehdi. *A Comparative Study of Abraham's Sacrifice in Persian Passion Plays and Western Mystery Plays.* Tehran: Ministry of Culture and Arts, n.d.

Ghani, Cyrus. *A Man of Many Worlds: The Memoirs and Diaries of Dr. Ghassem Ghani.* Translated by Cyrus Ghani and Paul Sprachman. Washington, D.C.: Mage Publishers, 2006.

Ghirshman, Roman. *Persian Art: 249 B.C.–A.D. 651: The Parthian and Sassanian Dynasties.* New York: Golden Press, 1962.

Guardian Unlimited. "A Revolution Crumbles." Saturday, October 5, 2002.

Gulshayan, Abbas Qoli. *Gozashteh ha va andisheha-yeh zindigi ya khatirat man.* Tehran: Einstein Institute, 1998 (orig. 1376).

Hafez. *Diwan.* Tehran: Anjoman Khoshnivisan, 1989 (orig. 1367).

"Health Abroad: A Challenge to Americans. Iran: One of Many." U.S. Department of Health, Education, and Welfare. Public Health Service Publication, No. 349, 1954.

Ibn Ishaq, *The Life of Muhammad* (Sirat Rasul Allah, with notes by Ibn Hisham). Translated by A. Guillaume. Oxford, U.K.: Oxford University Press, 1967.

Irvine, Richard. http://iran.theatlantic.com/blog/index.php?/archives/38-Our-Experience-in-Iran.html. He comments on Mark Bowden and his book, *Guests of the Ayatollah,* June 7, 2006.

Jung, Emma. *Animus and Anima.* New York: Spring Publications, 1969.

Kar, Mehrangiz. *Huquq siyasi yeh zanan-i iran.* Tehran: Roshangaran Publishers, 1376.

KNME-TV. "Voices." Albuquerque, N.M.: Colores, n.d.

Ladjevardi, Habib. Iranian Oral History Project, Center for Middle Eastern Studies, Harvard University, Cambridge, Mass.

Lawyers' Committee for Human Rights. *The Justice System of the Islamic Republic of Iran.* Washington, D.C.: Lawyers' Committee for Human Rights, May 1993.

Lyden, Jacki, and Davar Ardalan, speakers, June 1, 2000. The Women's Learning Partnership convened a pre-Beijing + 5 symposium at New York University titled "Cultural Boundaries and Cyber Spaces: Innovative Tools and Strategies for Strengthening Women's Leadership in Muslim Societies."

Mackey, Sandra. *The Iranians. Persia, Islam and the Soul of a Nation.* New York: Penguin Group, 1996.

Masse, Henri. *Persian Beliefs and Customs.* New Haven, Conn.: Human Relations Area Files, 1954.

Mimar 40: Architecture in Development. "A Fusion of Nature and Culture in Design." Akhtar Badshah, editor. London, UK: Concept Media, Ltd., 1991, pp. 36–38.

Mini, John. *The Aztec Virgin: The Secret Mystical Tradition of Our Lady of Guadalupe.* Sausalito, Calif.: Trans-Hyperbonean Institute, 2000.

Momen, Moojan. *An Introduction to Shi'i Islam: The History and Doctrines of Twelver Shi'ism.* New Haven, Conn.: Yale University Press, 1985.

Moosadegh, Mohammad. *SAVAK in Iran—A Country Study.* Library of Congress, Federal Research Division. http://rs6.loc.gov/frd/es/irtoc.html.

Mostofi, Abdollah. *The Administrative and Social History of the Qajar Period (The Story of My Life): From Mozaffar ad-Din Shah to Vosuq od-Dawleh's Anglo-Persian Agreement.* Translated by Nayer Mostofi Glenn. Costa Mesa, Calif.: Mazda Publishers, 1997.

Nasr, Seyyed Hossein. *A Young Muslim's Guide to the Modern World.* Chicago: Kazi Publications, 1993.

———. *Sufi Essays.* Albany: State University of New York Press, 1991. Third edition published by Kazi Publications, 1999.

Nasr, Vali. *The Shia Revival: How Conflicts within Islam Will Shape the Future.* New York: W. W. Norton and Company, 2006.

Nicholson, R. A. *Rumi: Poet and Mystic.* Oxford: One World, 1996.

———. *Selected Poems from the Divani Shamsi Tabriz.* Cambridge: Cambridge University Press, 1898.

NPR News, February 7, 1999. *All Things Considered* (weekend). Interview with Farah Pahlavi on the twentieth anniversary of the Iranian Revolution. Reporter Jacki Lyden, producer Davar Ardalan.

NPR News, May 21, 2000. *Profile: City of Yazd in Iran: The Spiritual Home of Zoroastrians.* Reporter Jacki Lyden, producer Davar Ardalan.

NPR News. April 2, 1995. *Weekend Edition Sunday,* "Iran at the Crossroads: Iranian Women Make Slow Careful Strides." Correspondent Jacki Lyden, series producer Davar Ardalan.

NPR News. February 2, 2004. *Morning Edition.* "My Name Is Iran." Reporter producer Davar Ardalan, coproducer Rasool Nafisi, editors Deborah George, Ted Clark, Jeffrey Katz, and Susan Feeney.

NPR News. March 26, 1995. *All Things Considered.* "Iran at the Crossroads: Political Freedom." Correspondent Jacki Lyden, series producer Davar Ardalan.

NPR News. May 19, 1996. *All Things Considered.* "Women's Writings Reveal Reality of Life in Iran." Reporter Jacki Lyden.

NPR News. May 21, 1997. *Morning Edition.* "Status of Women in Iran." Correspondent Jacki Lyden, producer Davar Ardalan, editor Loren Jenkins.

NPR News. April 15, 1995. *Weekend Edition Saturday.* "Profile of Iranian Literature Professor Azar Nafisi." Correspondent Jacki Lyden, producer Alice Winkler, series producer Davar Ardalan.

Parke, Adelia Routson. *Ramblings in Retrospect.* Fruitland, Idaho: Stranger Printing Service, 1968.

Pope, Arthur Upham, and Phyllis Ackerman. *A Survey of Persian Art.* London and Tokyo: Oxford University Press, n.d. 14 volumes.

Ransopher, James, and Janice von Schummer. "Ancestors of Davar Ardalan." Unpublished.

Renard, John. *Islam and the Heroic Image: Themes in Literature and the Visual Arts.* Columbia: University of South Carolina Press, 1993.

Rilke, Rainer Maria. "Letter Seven," *Letters to a Young Poet,* May 11, 1904.

Rumi, Jalal al-Din. *Discourses of Rumi.* Translated by A. J. Arberry. London: John Murray, 1961.

Rumi, Jalal al-Din. *The Mathnawi.* Translated by R. A. Nicholson. Tehran: Soad Publishers, 2002. 6 volumes.

Rumi, Jalaluddin. *The Mathnawi.* Translated by Reynold Nicholson. London: Luzac and Co., 1971. 8 volumes.

Shariati, Ali. *Hajj: Reflections on Its Rituals.* Translated by Laleh Bakhtiar. Chicago: ABJAD, 1992.

———. "The Islamic Modest Dress." Translated by Laleh Bakhtiar. In *Shariati on Shariati and the Muslim Woman.* Tehran: Hamdami Publishers, 1980.

Shuster, W. Morgan. *The Strangling of Persia.* Reprint. Washington, D.C.: Mage Publishers, 1987.

Smith, Margaret. *Al-Ghazzali, the Mystic.* London: Luzac and Co., 1944.

Stamberg, Susan, *Talk: NPR's Susan Stamberg Considers All Things.* New York: Random House, 1993.

Steele, Thomas J., and Rowena A. Rivera. *Penitente Self-Government: Brotherhoods and Councils 1797–1947.* Santa Fe, N.M.: Ancient City Press, 1985.

Stowasser, Barbara Freyer. *Women in the Quran, Traditions and Interpretation.* New York: Oxford University Press, 1994.

Sutton, Maya, and Nicholas R. Mann. *Druid Magic.* St. Paul, Minn.: Llewellyn Publications, 2000.

Trimingham, J. Spencer. *The Sufi Orders in Islam.* Oxford: The Clarendon Press, 1971.

Warne, William E. *Mission for Peace: Point 4 in Iran.* Indianapolis, Ind., and New York: Bobbs-Merrill Company, 1956.

Zuckerkandl, Victor. *Sound and Symbol: Music and the External World.* Princeton, N.J.: Princeton University Press, 1969.

· acknowledgments ·

To my editors, Vanessa Mobley and Supurna Banerjee, a deep sense of gratitude for your contributions to the book, your meticulous editing, and for the care, grace, and patience you showed while helping me distill my past and present. To Jennifer Barth and Elizabeth Shreve, thank you for believing in me.

To my father, Nader, thank you for your recollections of our lives and travels throughout Iran and most important, thank you for the legacy of your work in Islamic architecture and for teaching me to be a creative and alert representative of the age in which I live. To Shahla Ganji, thank you for all your love and encouragement.

To my sister, Mani Helene Ardalan Farhadi, who gave so generously of her time and expertise in editing and debating the various stages of this manuscript, I could not have done it without you. To my brother Karim, thank you for your unconditional love. Thank you also for your technical and design work of my Web site, my nameisiran.com. To my brother Ali Reza, thank you for your generous and loving support all these years.

To Kee Malesky, Vali Nasr, Issa Malek, Farah Ebrahimi, and Parinaz Bahadori for their valued review and comments on various stages of this manuscript.

To my agents, Jonathan Lazear, Christi Cardenas, and Julie Mayo, for their valued guidance. To Patrick Clark, thank you for all your care on the production of the book.

To Deborah George and Rasool Nafisi for their intellect and collaboration on our 2004 American RadioWorks and NPR series on Iran. For the American Radio-Works documentary my gratitude to Bill Buzenberg, Deborah Amos, Sasha

Aslanian, Ellen Guettler, Misha Quill, Andy Lyman, and Ochen Kaylan. For editorial and production help on the NPR series my thanks to Ellen McDonnell, Loren Jenkins, Ted Clark, Susan Feeney, Jeffrey Katz, Christine Arrasmith, and Jim Lesher. To Gary Sick and Gulf 2000 members for their valued entries and observations on Iran.

My gratitude also to Shervin Farhadi, Susan Khalili, Rodd Farhadi, Ryon Farhadi, Ryan Ardalan, and Layla Ardalan for all our fond family memories. To my aunt Pari Ardalan Malek for her constant love and support throughout the years and her recollections of life in Washington, D.C., and New Rochelle, New York. To my uncle Jamshid Bakhtiar, for his unconditional love and generosity throughout my life and for his review of this manuscript. To my aunt Lailee Bakhtiar for her support and love and her stories on the history of Iranian expats in Los Angeles. To my aunt Parvaneh Bakhtiar and uncle Mozafar Banihashemi for believing in me. To Liaquat Ali and Kazi Publications for your valued help with research and support. To Jay R. Crook for his exquisite photographs from Iran.

To Nayer Mostofi Glenn for your memories and remarkable body of work translating your father, Abdollah Mostofi's memoir of life during the Qajar Dynasty. To Faroukh and the Ardalan family, thank you, and may we continue to provide the children with the love and harmony that has blessed them these past few years.

To my cousins Janice von Schummer and James Ransopher, thank you for all the archival material on the Jeffreys, McRoberts, and Mackey families. To Kristin Palmquist, my gratitude for sharing her father Emil Palmquist's tremendous archives on Point Four. To my cousin Lailee Bakhtiar McNair for her loving support and her insights in *Mending Nations,* her powerful poetry book on the Bakhtiar tribes. To the late Soraya Serajeddini, my good friend and noted Kurdish activist, for her research on Kurdish history. Soraya, you will always be in my heart.

To my cousins Jahanshah Javid, Iran Javid, Soraya Ghahremani, Jam Ghajar, Roshanne Hemmat, Dina Tecimer, and Shireen Blair for your nurturing love and support when I needed it most. Jahanshah, thank you also for Iranian.com.

To my dearest friends, Mariam Abrahim, Leila Arsanjani, Parinaz Bahadori, Shirin Atabaki, Mahmoud Ladjevardi, Amy Atkins, Maya Sutton, Valencia De La Vega, Bill Messler, Will O'Leary, Karen Lillehei, Judy Garland Noormohammadi, Fred Wasser, Sally Robertson, Martina Castro, Nahid Naghshineh, Rachel Reef, Bill Summerville, and Karen Panhorst for their remarkable friendship throughout the years.

To professors Charles Coates, Fred Bales, and Miguel Gandert at the University of New Mexico for your guidance. To my KUNM colleagues Marcos Martinez and Franc Contreras, thank you for introducing me to public radio. To Nicole Zseltvay, Amanda Phaneuf, and Nikolina Valkdinova, thank you for loving my children.

Special thanks to photographer Mark Tucker and his crew for a most remarkable aesthetic journey down the Severn River. Thanks also to Gina Simpson Dark, Geri Theis, Theresa Ramsey, Scott and Connie Stevenson, Patti and Joe Child, and Vince Thomas.

To my NPR colleagues, Tracy Wahl, Jacki Lyden, Deborah George, Steve Inskeep, Renee Montagne, Liane Hansen, Robert Siegel, Daniel Zwerdling, Kee Malesky, Bob Malesky, Walter Watson, Carline Watson, Rebecca Davis, Kitty Eisele, Jennifer Ludden, Barbara Rehm, Ellen McDonnell, Bruce Auster, Jay Kernis, Loren Jenkins, Ted Clark, Susan Stamberg, Linda Wertheimer, Lynn Neary, Martha Wexler, Ned Wharton, Doreen McCallister, and, of course, Doug Mitchell, thank you. I have learned so much from you.

To my four beautiful children, my thanks and adoring love for enduring all my triumphs and failures. Saied, Samira, Aman, and Amir, your love and boundless energy for life is what keeps me going. In your own lives, I wish that you strive for moderation, harmony, and justice.

For all our love and happiness, I thank John Oliver Smith. As the poet Rumi says: "The minute I heard my first love story, I started looking for you, not knowing how blind that was. Lovers do not finally meet somewhere, they are in each other all along." It has been John's unconditional love that has helped me stay focused in this creative process. With an open heart and much empathy he has helped me approach the fuller possibilities life has dealt my way. He has read and reread this book all the while contributing to its logic and essence. And many thanks to John's sons, Zachary, Michael, Daniel, and Joseph, for their integrity and humanity. To Juanita Smith, the Smith family matriarch, your zest for life is inspiring.

To my late grandmother Mani joone who passed away one year before the completion of this book. Mani joone, it was the spirit of your father, Ali Akbar Davar, that inspired my quest and it was your stories that helped me uncover my own personhood. I love you. May you rest in peace.

· about the author ·

DAVAR ARDALAN is a senior producer at NPR News *Morning Edition,* the most widely heard radio news program in the United States. Ardalan helps make the creative decisions that shape a changing daily broadcast. Some of those decisions must be made during a live broadcast; others require elaborate coordination, like shaping broadcasts from Baghdad and New Orleans. Ardalan, whose full name is Iran Davar Ardalan, earned her B.A. in Communications and Journalism from the University of New Mexico. She was born in San Francisco and has also worked in Iran as a television newscaster. She is the mother of four—Saied, Samira, Aman, and Amir.